American Doctoral Dissertations
on the
araB world
Supplement 1981–1987

American Doctoral Dissertations
on the

ɑRɑʙ ωoRlɒ

Supplement
August 1981–December 1987

Compiled by

George Dimitri Selim
Near East Section
African and Middle Eastern Division

LIBRARY OF CONGRESS   WASHINGTON

1989

Library of Congress Cataloging-in-Publication Data
(Revised for vol. 2)

Selim, George Dimitri, 1931–
    American doctoral dissertations on the Arab world.
Supplement.
    Includes index.
    Supt. of Doc. no.: LC 41.2:Ar/1975–81/supp.
    Contents: [1] 1975–1981—[2] August 1981–
December 1987.
    1. Arab countries—Bibliography. 2. Dissertations,
Academic—United States—Bibliography.
I. Library of Congress. Near East Section.
II. Title. III. Title: Arab world.
Z3013.S43   1976 Suppl.   016.909′0974927   82-600200
[DS36.7]
ISBN 0-8444-0400-4 (v. 1)
ISBN 0-8444-0619-8 (v. 2)

For sale by the Superintendent of Documents, U.S. Government Printing Office
Washington, D.C. 20402

Contents

Preface

This bibliography is the second supplement to *American Doctoral Dissertations on the Arab World, 1883–1974* (Washington: Library of Congress, 1976). The first supplement, covering the years 1975–1981, was published by the Library of Congress in 1983. The present volume lists dissertations accepted by United States and Canadian universities and reported between August 1981 and December 1987, as well as a number of dissertations accepted before 1981 which were not reported in the previous two bibliographies. The dissertations cover the Arab World, the Middle East as a region, Islam, and the Organization of Petroleum Exporting Countries (OPEC), of which the Arab oil-producing countries are members.

The entries are arranged alphabetically by author and include the title of the dissertation, the National Union Catalog symbol for the university or academic institution (see Abbreviations for Names of Institutions), and the year the dissertation was accepted. Whenever they are available in the source, the number of pages is given and the Library of Congress call number (microform number) is entered at the right-hand margin of the entry. The microform number also serves as the order number when dissertation copies are ordered from University Microfilms International (P.O. Box 1764, Ann Arbor, MI 48106, U.S.A.). Each entry ends with the source of information given in abbreviated form.

Two primary sources were used in the compilation of this bibliography: *Dissertation Abstracts International*, vols. 42–48, August 1981-December 1987 (abbreviated DAI) and *Comprehensive Dissertation Index: Ten-Year Cumulation, 1973–1982* and subsequent annual supplements (abbreviated CDI). Some dissertations were also identified in secondary sources. The citations of these dissertations were sent to the librarians of the institutions granting the degrees to verify the names, titles and acceptance dates. The assistance of these librarians in this matter is greatly appreciated.

This publication includes an index based on the major subjects of the dissertations and key words in their titles.

March 1988   GEORGE DIMITRI SELIM

Abbreviations for Names of Institutions

AU	University of Alabama, University, AL 35486
ArU	University of Arkansas, Fayetteville, AR 72701
AzFU	Northern Arizona University, Flagstaff, AZ 86001
AzTeS	Arizona State University, Tempe, AZ 85281
AzU	University of Arizona, Tucson, AZ 85721
CBGTU	Graduate Theological Union, Berkeley, CA 94709
CCC	Claremont Graduate School, Claremont, CA 91711
CLavC	University of La Verne, La Verne, CA 91750
CLSU	University of Southern California, Los Angeles, CA 90007. Copies of dissertations accepted by this university are available exclusively from: Micrographics Department, Doheny Library, USC, Los Angeles, CA 90089-0182.
CLU	University of California, Los Angeles, CA 90024
CMalP	Pepperdine University, Malibu, CA 90265
CPFT	Fuller Theological Seminary, Pasadena, CA 91101
CPT	California Institute of Technology, Pasadena, CA 91109
CSdI	United States International University, San Diego, CA 92124
CSdU	University of San Diego, San Diego, CA 92110
CSfSI	Saybrook Institute, San Francisco, CA 94123
CSfU	University of San Francisco, San Francisco, CA 94117
CSt	Stanford University, Stanford, CA 94305
CStmoR	Rand Graduate Institute, Santa Monica, CA 90406
CU	University of California, Berkeley, CA 94720
CU-A	University of California, Davis, CA 95616
CU-I	University of California, Irvine, CA 92664
CU-Riv	University of California, Riverside, CA 92502

CU-S	University of California, San Diego, CA 92037
CU-Sf	University of California, San Francisco, CA 94143
CU-SB	University of California, Santa Barbara, CA 93106
CU-SC	University of California, Santa Cruz, CA 95060
CaAEU	University of Alberta, Edmonton, Alta., Canada
CaBVaU	University of British Columbia, Vancouver, B.C., Canada
CaMWU	University of Manitoba, Winnipeg, Man. Canada
CaOLU	University of Western Ontario, London, Ont., Canada
CaOOCC	Carleton University, Ottawa, Ont., Canada
CaOTU	University of Toronto, Toronto, Ont., Canada
CaOTY	York University, Toronto, Ont., Canada
CaQMM	McGill University, Montreal, Que., Canada
CoDU	University of Denver, Denver, CO 80210
CoFS	Colorado State University, Fort Collins, CO 80521
CoGrU	University of Northern Colorado, Greeley, CO 80631
CoU	University of Colorado, Boulder, CO 80302
CoU-H	University of Colorado Health Services Center, Denver, CO 80262
CtU	University of Connecticut, Storrs, CT 06268
CtY	Yale University, New Haven, CT 06520
DAU	American University, Washington, DC 20016
DCU	Catholic University of America, Washington, DC 20017
DGU	Georgetown University, Washington, DC 20007
DGW	George Washington University, Washington, DC 20006
DHU	Howard University, Washington, DC 20001
DeU	University of Delaware, Newark, DE 19711
FMU	University of Miami, Coral Gables, FL 33124
FTaSU	Florida State University, Tallahassee, FL 32306
FU	University of Florida, Gainesville, FL 32601
GASU	Georgia State University, Atlanta, GA 30303
GEU	Emory University, Atlanta, GA 30322
GU	University of Georgia, Athens, GA 30601
ICarbS	Southern Illinois University, Carbondale, IL 62901
ICIU	University of Illinois at Chicago Circle, Chicago, IL 60680
ICL	Loyola University, Chicago, IL 60611
ICU	University of Chicago, Chicago, IL 60637
IDeKN	Northern Illinois University, De Kalb, IL 60115
IEN	Northwestern University, Evanston, IL 60201
INS	Illinois State University, Normal, IL 61761
IU	University of Illinois, Urbana-Champaign, IL 61803
IU-M	University of Illinois Health Sciences Center, Chicago, IL 60680
IaAS	Iowa State University of Science & Technology, Ames, IA 50010
IaCfT	University of Northern Iowa, Cedar Falls, IA 50613
IaDmD	Drake University, Des Moines, IA 50311
IaU	University of Iowa, Iowa City, IA 52240
IdU	University of Idaho, Moscow, ID 83843
InLP	Purdue University, Lafayette, IN 47907
InMuB	Ball State University, Muncie, IN 47306

InNd	University of Notre Dame, Notre Dame, IN 46556
InTI	Indiana State University, Terre Haute, IN 47809
InU	Indiana University, Bloomington, IN 47401
KMK	Kansas State University, Manhattan, KS 66504
KU	University of Kansas, Lawrence, KS 66044
KyU	University of Kentucky, Lexington, Ky 40506
LNT	Tulane University, New Orleans, LA 70118
LU	Louisiana State University, Baton Rouge, LA 70803
MBU	Boston University, Boston, MA 02215
MBU-E	Boston University, School of Education, Boston, MA 02215
MChB	Boston College, Chestnut Hill, MA 02167
MCM	Massachusetts Institute of Technology, Cambridge, MA 02139
MH	Harvard University, Cambridge, MA 02138
MMeT	Tufts University, Medford, MA 02155
MU	University of Massachusetts, Amherst, MA 01002
MWalB	Brandeis University, Waltham, MA 02154
MWC	Clark University, Worcester, MA 01610
MdBJ	Johns Hopkins University, Baltimore, MD 21218
MdU	University of Maryland, College Park, MD 20740
MdU-BC	University of Maryland, Baltimore County Campus, Baltimore, MD 21228
MdU-P	University of Maryland Professional Schools, Adelphi, MD 20783
MiDW	Wayne State University, Detroit, MI 48202
MiEM	Michigan State University, East Lansing, MI 48823
MiKW	Western Michigan University, Kalamazoo, MI 49001
MiU	University of Michigan, Ann Arbor, MI 48104
MnCS	Saint John's University, Collegeville, MN 56321
MnU	University of Minnesota, Minneapolis, MN 55455
MoRM	University of Missouri, Rolla, MO 65401
MoSU	Saint Louis University, St. Louis, MO 63103
MoSW	Washington University, St. Louis, MO 63130
MoU	University of Missouri, Columbia, MO 65201
MsSM	Mississippi State University, State College, MS 39762
MsU	University of Mississippi, University, MS 38677
NAlU	State University of New York, Albany, NY 12201
NBiSU	State University of New York, Binghamton, NY 13901
NBuU	State University of New York, Buffalo, NY 14214
NIC	Cornell University, Ithaca, NY 14850
NNC	Columbia University, New York, NY 10027
NNC-T	Columbia University Teachers College, New York, NY 10032
NNCU-G	City University of New York, New York, NY 10021
NNF	Fordham University, New York, NY 10458
NNNS	New School for Social Research, New York, NY 10011
NNU	New York University, New York, NY 10003
NNU-B	New York University, Graduate School of Business Administration, New York, NY 10003
NNU-ES	New York University, School of Engineering and Science, New York, NY 10453

NRU	University of Rochester, Rochester, NY 14627
NSbSU	State University of New York, Stony Brook, NY 11790
NSyU	Syracuse University, Syracuse, NY 13210
NTR	Rensselaer Polytechnic Institute, Troy, NY 12181
NbU	University of Nebraska, Lincoln, NE 68508
NcD	Duke University, Durham, NC 27706
NcGU	University of North Carolina, Greensboro, NC 27412
NcRS	North Carolina State University, Raleigh, NC 27607
NcU	University of North Carolina, Chapel Hill, NC 27514
NhU	University of New Hampshire, Durham, NH 03824
NjMD	Drew University, Madison, NJ 07940
NjP	Princeton University, Princeton, NJ 08540
NjR	Rutgers University—The State University of New Jersey, New Brunswick, NJ 08903
NmLcU	New Mexico State University, Las Cruces, NM 88001
NmU	University of New Mexico, Albuquerque, NM 87106
OAkU	University of Akron, Akron, OH 44601
OAU	Ohio University, Athens, OH 45701
OBgU	Bowling Green State University, Bowling Green, OH 43402
OCU	University of Cincinnati, Cincinnati, OH 45221
OCUCE	Union for Experimenting Colleges and Universities, Cincinnati, OH 45201
OCUG	Union Graduate School, Cincinnati, OH 45201
OKentU	Kent State University, Kent, OH 44242
OTU	University of Telodo, Toledo, OH 43606
OU	Ohio State University, Columbus, OH 43210
OclW	Case Western Reserve University, Cleveland, OH 44106
OkS	Oklahoma State University, Stillwater, OK 74074
OkU	University of Oklahoma, Norman, OK 73069
OrCS	Oregon State University, Corvallis, OR 97331
OrPS	Portland State University, Portland, OR 97207
OrU	University of Oregon, Eugene, OR 97403
PBL	Lehigh University, Bethlehem, PA 18105
PBm	Bryn Mawr College, Bryn Mawr, PA 19010
PInU	Indiana University of Pennsylvania, Indiana, PA 15701
PPD	Drexel University, Philadelphia, PA 19104
PPDrop	Dropsie University, Philadelphia, PA 19132
PPiU	University of Pittsburgh, Pittsburgh, PA 15213
PPT	Temple University, Philadelphia, PA 19122
PSt	Pennsylvania State University, University Park, PA 16802
PU	University of Pennsylvania, Philadelphia, PA 19104
RPB	Brown University, Providence, RI 02912
RU	University of Rhode Island, Kingston, RI 02881
ScCleU	Clemson University, Clemson, SC 29631
ScU	University of South Carolina, Columbia, SC 29208
TMurS	Middle Tennessee State University, Murfreesboro, TN 37130
TNJ	Vanderbilt University, Nashville, TN 37240
TNJ-P	George Peabody College for Teachers, Nashville, TN 37203
TU	University of Tennessee, Knoxville, TN 37916
TxArU	University of Texas, Arlington, TX 76010

TxCM	Texas A&M University, College Station, TX 77843
TxDaM	Southern Methodist University, Dallas, TX 75222
TxDN	North Texas State University, Denton, TX 76203
TxDW	Texas Woman's University, Denton, TX 23715
TxEU	University of Texas, EL Paso, TX 79999
TxFS	Southwestern Baptist Theological Seminary, Fort Worth, TX 76122
TxFTC	Texas Christian University, Fort Worth, TX 76129
TxHR	Rice University, Houston, TX 77001
TxHU	University of Houston, Houston, TX 77004
TxLT	Texas Tech University, Lubbock, TX 79409
TxU	University of Texas, Austin, TX 78712
TxU-Da	University of Texas at Dallas, Richardson, TX 75230
TxU-H	University of Texas Health Science Center, Houston, TX 77025
ULA	Utah State University, Logan, UT 84321
UU	University of Utah, Salt Lake City, UT 84112
ViBlbV	Virginia Polytechnic Institute & State University, Blacksburg, VA 24061
ViU	University of Virginia, Charlottesville, VA 22903
WMM	Marquette University, Milwaukee, WI 53233
WMUW	University of Wisconsin—Milwaukee, Milwaukee, WI 53201
WU	University of Wisconsin, Madison, WI 53706
WaPS	Washington State University, Pullman, WA 99163
WaU	University of Washington, Seattle, WA 98105
WvU	West Virginia University, Morgantown, WV 26505
WyU	University of Wyoming, Laramie, WY 82070

American Doctoral Dissertations
on the
ARAB WORLD
Supplement 1981–1987

1

Abahsain, Muhammad Mansour. Aḥmad b. Abī Numaī and his dīwān: the perceptible intertwining of politics and poetry in Mecca during the eleventh century A.H. [with] the collected poems of the Meccan Sharif Aḥmad b. Abī Numaī. UU, 1983. 267 p.   Micro 83–12,299
DAI, v. 44A, Aug. 1983: 498.

2

Abanami, Abdulmohsin Abdulaziz. Readability analysis of the 11th grade earth science textbooks used in public schools in Saudi Arabia. TxHU, 1982. 155 p.
                                                                                   Micro 82–29,339
DAI, v. 43A, Jan. 1983: 2212.

3

Abbadi, Karrar Ahmed. Analysis of world market demand, supply and price of Sudan's ELS cotton, 1956–1977. WU, 1981. 198 p.   Micro 81-25,700
DAI, v. 42A, Feb. 1982: 3680.

4

Abbadi, Suleiman Mahmoud. Monetary policy in LDCs with special reference to the Middle East. TxU, 1981. 271 p.   Micro 81–19,246
DAI, v. 42A, Sept. 1981: 1243.

5

Abbas, Hisham Abdullah. A plan for public library system development in Saudi Arabia. PPiU, 1982. 147 p.   Micro 82–19,916
DAI, v. 43A, Oct. 1982: 960.

6

Abbas, Shafika Ebrahim. The roles of administrators and faculty in university governance: a comparative study of a state university in the U.S. and the University of the United Arab Emirates. CCC, 186. 187 p.   Micro 86–7817
DAI, v. 47A, Aug. 1986: 352.

7

al-Abd al-Hay, Abdalkhalek A. Contemporary women's participation in public activities: differences between ideal Islam and Muslim interpretation with emphasis on Saudi Arabia. CoDU, 1983. 362 p.   Micro 83–15,891
   DAI, v. 44A, Sept. 1983: 853.

8

Abdalla, Eitedal M. Basouni. The SCAMIN [Self-Concept and Motivation Inventory], "what face would you wear" and the Piers-Harris evaluation as measures of self-concept in immigrant Arabic children: a comparative study of construct validity and reliability. MiDW, 1983. 210 p.   Micro 84–5949
   DAI, v. 44A, June 1984: 3663.

9

Abdalla, Elhadi Abdal-Samad. Development administration and regionalism: towards a communalist approach to decisional process in the Sudan. PPiU, 1981. 507 p.   Micro 82–2313
   DAI, v. 42A, Feb. 1982: 3746.

10

Abdalla, Ismail Hussein. Islamic medicine and its influence on traditional Hausa practitioners in northern Nigeria. WU, 1981. 250 p.   Micro 81–25,701
   DAI, v. 42A, Apr. 1982: 4547.

11

Abdalla, Osman Albadri. An Islamic alternative for management and development: an analysis of the Gezira Scheme [Sudan]. CLSU, 1982.
   DAI, v. 43A, Oct. 1982: 1285.

12

Al-Abdalwahed, Ahmad Murtada. Human resource development and manpower planning in Saudi Arabia. CCC, 1981. 130 p.   Micro 81–14,033
   DAI, v. 42A, Oct. 1981: 1783.

13

Abdan, Abdulrahman A. The effect of sentence-combining practice on the written syntactic maturity, overall writing quality, and reading comprehension of EFL Saudi students. KU, 1983. 188p.   Micro 84–3603
   DAI, v. 44A, May 1984: 3307.

14

Abdel Hameed, Salwa M. Dietary overlaps of tiang, buffalo, reedbuck, waterbuck and sheep in Dinder National Park, Sudan. CoFS, 1985. 163 p.
                                                                    Micro 86–7624
   DAI, v. 47B, Aug. 1986: 461.

15

Abdel-Jawad, Hassan Rashid E. Lexical and phonological variation in spoken Arabic in Amman. PU, 1981. 411 p.   Micro 82–7924
   DAI, v. 42A, May 1982: 4814.

16

Abdel-Maksoud, Ahmed Abdel-Azim. Egypt's open door policy: the impact of financial repression on economic development. DGW, 1985. 284 p.

Micro 86–13,062

DAI, v. 47A, Oct. 1986: 1388–1389.

17

Abdelgadir, Hamad Abdalla. An evaluation of secondary school library media collections in Khartoum Province, Sudan. PPT, 1983. 181 p.

Micro 83–21,239

DAI, v. 44A, Jan. 1984: 2108.

18

Abdelhak, Fatma Aly. An analytic study of the language proficiency skill of Egyptian college students learning English as a foreign language. CtU, 1986. 109 p.   Micro 87–9017

DAI, v. 48A, July 1987: 68.

19

Abdelhamid Nimer, Kamal Kamel. The role of women's organizations in eradicating illiteracy in Jordan. MiU, 1983. 235 p.   Micro 84–2231

DAI, v. 44A, Apr. 1984: 2951.

20

Abdeljaber, Naji Abdeljabbar. Evaluation of Ibn Maḍā''s criticism of the Arab grammarians. MiU, 1985. 304 p.   Micro 85–20, 850

DAI, v. 46A, Jan. 1986: 1918.

21

Abdeljaouad, Hedi. Tendences surréalistes dans la littérature maghrebine d'expression française. PPT, 1983. 316 p.   Micro 83–11,575

DAI, v. 44A, July 1983: 182–183.

22

Abdelkheir, Ahmed Yousif. A study of some aspects of food pricing policy in the Sudan and their economic consequences. ViU, 1984. 192 p. Micro 85–15,543

DAI, v. 46A, Jan. 1986: 1998.

23

Abdelmagid, Mohamed Hassan. Sudan's outflow of human capital: the external labor migration, magnitude, causes and effects. CCC, 1983. 200 p.

Micro 83–21,039

DAI, v. 44A, Nov. 1983: 1568.

24

Abdelmuti, Abdelaziz Mustafa. Training needs for teachers of the mentally retarded in Jordan. MiEM, 1985. 114 p.   Micro 85–13,877

DAI, v. 46A, Nov. 1985: 1246.

25

Abdelrahiem, Zahir Hamad. The long-term growth of government expenditure and economic development of the Sudan, 1956–1980. NSyU, 1982. 277 p.

Micro 83–1622

DAI, v. 43A, Mar. 1983: 3068.

26

Abdelrhman, Mohamed Bushara. Bureaucracy and development: a study of the civil service in Sudan. FTaSU, 1983. 383 p.   Micro 84–6997
DAI, v. 44A, June 1984: 3804–3805.

27

Abdelsalam, Elfatih Abdullahi. Pan-Arabism and charismatic leadership: a study of Iraq's foreign policy behavior towards the Arab region, 1968–1982. IEN, 1984. 301 p.   Micro 84–23,196
DAI, v. 45A, Jan. 1985: 2238.

28

Abdelsalam, Sharafeldin Elamin. A study of contemporary Sudanese Muslim saints' legends in sociocultural contexts. InU, 1983. 344 p.   Micro 84–6776
DAI, v. 44A, June 1984: 3767.

29

Abdo, Mekhag B. The academic library in the electronic age: the case of six Arabian Peninsula countries. NBuU, 1987. 345 p.   Micro 87–10,682
DAI, v. 48A, Aug. 1987: 239.

30

Abdo-Khalil, Zeinab M. Public sector administration in Egypt. CCC, 1983. 118 p.   Micro 83–23,109
DAI, v. 44A, Dec. 1983: 1917.

31

Abdrabou, Abdelrahman Abdalla. Relationship between reading-comprehension skills and achievement in other selected language skills of college-bound Yemeni EFL learners. KU, 1983. 122 p.   Micro 83–17,932
DAI, v. 44A, Oct. 1983: 1040.

32

Abdu, Anwar Sheikh Eldin. Patterns of rural household energy use: a study in the White Nile Province, the Sudan. MWC, 1984. 346 p.   Micro 85–7345
DAI, v. 46A, Aug. 1985: 495–496.

33

Abdul-Ghany, Muhammad Kamal Eldeen. Government binding in classical Arabic. TxU, 1981. 185 p.   Micro 81–28,600
DAI, v. 42A, Jan. 1982: 3134.

34

Abdul-Raheem, Nabeel Jaffar. Identification of high risk drivers in the Third World nations [Kuwait included]. WvU, 1983. 304 p.   Micro 83–26,641
DAI, v. 44B, Jan. 1984: 2202.

6

35

Abdulali, Abdulkarim Jwili. Changing the role of inspector in the Libyan educational system. PPiU, 1986. 184 p.   Micro 86–20,289
    DAI, v. 47A, Dec. 1986: 1997.

36

Abdulghani, Abdulhamid Mohamed. Culture and interest in Arab foreign aid: Kuwait and the United Arab Emirates as case studies. CU-SB, 1986. 520 p.
                                                          Micro 87–9093
    DAI, v. 48A, July 1987: 214.

37

Abdulghani, Jasim Mohammad. Ba'thist Iraq's relations with Iran, 1968–1978. DGW, 1983. 390 p.
    Thesis and dissertation card catalog, Gelman Library, George Washington University.

38

Abdulghani, Khaled M. R. Driver characteristics and their relation to traffic conflict occurrence [in Saudi Arabia]. MiEM, 1982. 171 p. Micro 82–24,390
    DAI, v. 43B, Nov. 1982: 1560.

39

Abduljabbar, Mohammed Shihab. An econometric model of the Iraqi economy, 1960–78. OkS, 1982. 170 p.   Micro 83–130
    DAI, v. 43A, Feb. 1983: 2728.

40

Abdulla, Abdulkhaleq. Political dependency: the case of the United Arab Emirates. DGU, 1985. 370 p.   Micro 86–6898
    DAI, v. 47A, July 1986: 296.

41

Abdullah, Ahmad Abbas. Developmental differences in WISC subsets among children with learning problems in Kuwait. CLSU, 1982.
    DAI, v. 43A, Oct. 1982: 1109–1110.

42

Abdulmatlub, Abdulmatlub Abdulhamid. The contemporary Libyan short story: its emergence, development, and dominant themes. UU, 1983. 257 p.
                                                          Micro 84–5918
    DAI, v. 44A, June 1984: 3704.

43

Abdulrahman-O-Elsheikh, Sheikh Musa. Factors contributing to a community health education model for the prevention and control of schistosomiasis (bilharziasis) in the Sudan. CU, 1984. 175 p.   Micro 84–26,887
    DAI, v. 45A, June 1985: 3553.

44

al-Abdulwahhab, Hamad Ibrahim. Evaluation of emulsified asphalt for use in

Saudi Arabia. OrCS, 1985. 344 p. Micro 85-14,816
DAI, v. 46B, Nov. 1985: 1635.

45

Abdussalam, Abdelrahim Saleh. External forces, economic development and
regional inequality in Libya. OkU, 1983. 179 p. Micro 84-3968
DAI, v. 44A, May 1984: 3492.

46

Abed, Shoukri Boutros. Logic and language in al-Fārābī. MH, 1984. 281 p.
Micro 85-3507
DAI, v. 45A, June 1985: 3629.

47

al-Abed al-Haq, Fawwaz Mohammad. A case study of language planning in
Jordan. WU, 1985. 326 p. Micro 86-1084
DAI, v. 47A, Sept. 1986: 884.

48

Abed-Rabbo, Samir A. Might does not make right: international law and the
Question of Palestine. FMU, 1981. 238 p. Micro 81-21,121
DAI, v. 42A, Oct. 1981: 1778.

49

Abednejad, Farough. A comparison of eye movement tendencies as used by
Oriental, Semitic, and Western cultures. InU, 1982. 80 p. Micro 83-3953
DAI, v. 43A, Mar. 1983: 2860.

50

Abegaz, Berhanu. Modeling manpower in development planning: methodologi-
cal and empirical problems with Sudanese illustrations. PU, 1982. 242 p.
Micro 82-17,073
DAI, v. 43A, Sept. 1982: 883.

51

Abida, Amira Shehadeh. High school students' perceptions of sport sanction in
Jordan. PPiU, 1985. 114 p. Micro 86-1406
DAI, v. 46A, June 1986: 3648.

52

Abinader, Elmaz. Letters from home: stories of fathers and sons. NbU, 1985.
192 p. Micro 85-26,582
DAI, v. 46A, Apr. 1986: 3028.
Diaries by Rachid and Jean Abinader.

53

Abo-Amasha, el-Esawey. Imperialism, peripheral capitalism and trade integration among peripheries: the case of the Arab countries, 1962-1981. OrU, 1985.
235 p. Micro 85-14,791
DAI, v. 46A, Nov. 1985: 1416.

54

Abohobiel, Abdulfattah Abdulsalam. An econometric model for the Libyan economy, 1962–1977. InU, 1983. 292 p.   Micro 84–1541
   DAI, v. 44A, Apr. 1984: 3116.

55

Abolkhair, Yahya Mohammed Sheikh. Sand encroachment by wind in al-Hasa of Saudi Arabia. InU, 1981. 214 p.   Micro 81–19,015
   DAI, v. 42B, Sept. 1981: 950.

56

Abosedra, Salaheddin Saieh. A simulation study of the impact of world oil prices on the development of the Libyan economy. CoU, 1984. 140 p.
                                          Micro 84–22,582
   DAI, v. 45A, Jan. 1985: 2205–2206.

57

Abou-Helwa, Ahmad Essam. Macro-planning of postsecondary education: a strategic plan for Egypt's human resource development in a period of transition. KMK, 1984. 170 p.   Micro 84–15,639
   DAI, v. 45A, Oct. 1984: 1047.

58

Abou-Khamseen, Manssour Ahmad. The first French-Algerian War, 1830–1848: a reappraisal of the French colonial venture and the Algerian resistance. CU, 1983. 317 p.   Micro 83–28,775
   DAI, v. 44A, Feb. 1984: 2547.

59

Abou-Mhaya, Salwa H. Type of counseling confidants preferred by Lebanese/ Syrian churchgoers. MChB, 1983. 168 p.   Micro 83–14,847
   DAI, v. 44A, Aug. 1983: 424.

60

Abou-Settit, Mohammad Fouad. Foreign capital and economic performance: the case of Egypt. TxU-Da, 1986. 214 p.   Micro 86–27,549
   DAI, v. 47A, Feb. 1987: 3117.

61

Abou Shariefeh, Abdel-Qader Sharif. The prison in the contemporary Arabic novel. MiU, 1983. 247 p.   Micro 83–24,129
   DAI, v. 44A, Dec. 1983: 1807.

62

al-Aboudi, Fahmi Basil Shukri. The syntax of *iḍāfah*: annexation in Arabic. InU, 1985. 388 p.   Micro 85–25,350
   DAI, v. 46A, Mar. 1986: 2677.

63

Abrishami, Hamid. Oil products distribution in Iran: a planning approach. DAU,

1986. 350 p.   Micro 86–26,316
   DAI, v. 47A, Feb. 1987: 3117.

64

Abu-Dawood, Abdulrazak Suliam. Political boundaries of Saudi Arabia: their
   evolution and functions. KyU, 1984. 198 p.   Micro 84–16,117
   DAI, v. 45A, Dec. 1984: 1868.

65

Abu Dayeh, Fahmi. Rates of return to investment in education in Jordan: a case
   study. OrU, 1982. 197 p.   Micro 82–15,294
   DAI, v. 43A, Aug. 1982: 317.

66

Abu-Duhou, Ibtisam Y. An analytical model for cost-effectiveness analysis in
   higher education with application to university education in the West Bank.
   PPiU, 1987. 232 p.   Micro 87–19,276
   DAI, v. 48A, Dec. 1987: 1359.

67

Abu el-Haija, Lutfi Ahmad. The acquisition of the negation system in Arabic as
   spoken in Jordan. PSt, 1981. 145 p.   Micro 81–29,130
   DAI, v. 42A, Jan. 1982: 3134–3135.

68

Abu-Ghararah, Ali Hamzah. An analysis of the status of the English language
   curriculum and instruction in the public secondary schools of Medina, Saudi
   Arabia. CLSU, 1986.
   DAI, v. 47A, Mar. 1987: 3291.

69

Abu-Ghazaleh, Ilham Nayef. Theme and the function of the verb in Palestinian
   Arabic narrative discourse. FU, 1983. 255 p.   Micro 84–20,304
   DAI, v. 45A, Dec. 1984: 1738.

70

Abu-Ghazaleh, Munir Zaki. Economics of tourism in Jordan. TNJ, 1985. 170 p.
                                                               Micro 85–22,385
   DAI, v. 46A, Feb. 1986: 2371.

71

Abu Ghazzeh, Tawfig M. Industrialization of building systems in Jordan: the
   investigation and analysis of housing problems in Jordan and the potential role
   of systems in alleviating the housing shortage. DCU, 1985. 516 p.
                                                               Micro 85–15,056
   DAI, v. 46A, Jan. 1986: 1759.

72

Abu-Hilal, Maher M. Foreign students' interaction, satisfaction, and attitudes
   toward certain aspects of the American culture: a case of Arab students in

Southern California. CU-Riv, 1986. 225 p.   Micro 87–6974
   DAI, v. 47A, June 1987: 4307.

73

Abu-Hommos, Naim M. West Bank university students' attitudes toward handicapped people. CSfU, 1985. 88 p.   Micro 85–16,318
   DAI, v. 46A, Dec. 1985: 1591.

74

Abu-Jaber, Majed A. A study of factors affecting the use of media in instruction at
   Jordanian community colleges. InU, 1985. 202 p.   Micro 86–7401
   DAI, v. 47A, Aug. 1986: 510.

75

Abu-Jarad, Hassan Ali. English interlanguage of Palestinian university students
   in Gaza Strip: an analysis of relative clauses and verb tense. InMuB, 1986.
   149 p.   Micro 86–9657
   DAI, v. 47A, Aug. 1986: 518.

76

Abu Khalaf, Nader Abdul Mughni. The development of higher education in the
   West Bank, 1971–1983. PPiU, 1985. 166 p.   Micro 85–19,468
   DAI, v. 46A, Jan. 1986: 1842.

77

Abu-Lughod, Lila. Honor, modesty, and poetry in a Bedouin society: ideology
   and experience among Awlād ʿAlī of Egypt. MH, 1984. 364 p.
                                          Micro 84–19,435
   DAI, v. 45A, Dec. 1984: 1804.

78

Abu-Mansour, Anas Hasan. A functional analysis of sentence structure in standard Arabic: a three-level approach. FU, 1986. 412 p.   Micro 87–15,963
   DAI, v. 48A, Oct. 1987: 913.

79

Abu Nahleh, Lamis Yacoub. A syntactic-semantic analysis of object clitics and
   pronouns in Ramallah Palestinian Arabic. MiU, 1985. 214 p.   Micro 86–394
   DAI, v. 47A, July 1986: 164.

80

Abu-Rizaiza, Omar Seraj. Municipal, irrigational and industrial future water
   requirements in Saudi Arabia. OkU, 1982. 222 p.   Micro 83–6735
   DAI, v. 44B, Aug. 1983: 560.

81

Abu Saleh, Ali Mohammad. Physiological responses to heat stress of Arabs and
   Americans. OrU, 1983. 133 p.   Micro 84–3709
   DAI, v. 44A, May 1984: 3317.

82

Abu-Salim, Issam M. A reanalysis of some aspects of Arabic phonology: a metrical approach. IU, 1982. 239 p.   Micro 83–2785
DAI, v. 43A, Mar. 1983: 2981.

83

Abu-Ulbah, Walid Mahmoud. A study of factors influencing readers' comprehension of cultural content embedded in Arabic literature. IU, 1983. 198 p.
Micro 83–24,495
DAI, v. 44A, Dec. 1983: 1748.

84

Abu-Zaid, Mohammed Saddaga. Potential evapotranspiration in arid environments: case studies in Phoenix, Arizona, and Taif, Saudi Arabia. AzTeS, 1986. 135 p.   Micro 86–13,998
DAI, v. 47B, Nov. 1986: 1908.

85

Abubakar, Dauda. Oil, the state and power politics: the political economy of Nigeria's foreign policy, 1960–80. WU, 1986. 364 p.   Micro 86–18,256
DAI, v. 47A, Feb. 1987: 3179.

86

Abueita, Siham Darwish. An analysis of assessment of the secondary school counseling programs in Kuwait as perceived by counselors, administrators and teachers. DGW, 1982. 237 p.   Micro 83–7875
DAI, v. 43A, June 1983: 3811.

87

Abuelayan, Iqbal Fakhri. The social structural aspects of women's role in early Islam in the sixth and seventh centuries [A.D.]. CSdI, 1987. 159 p.
Micro 87–15,375
DAI, v. 48A, Oct. 1987: 1015.

88

Abuelkeshk, Abdelkarim Ahmad. A portrayal of the Arab-Israeli conflict in three U.S. journals of opinion [*The Nation, The New Republic* and *National Review*], 1948–1982. WU, 1985. 291 p.   Micro 86–1816
DAI, v. 47A, Sept. 1986: 694.

89

Abugeilah, Bashir Abdulgasem. Family patterns and newly emerging attitudes toward marriage and the status of women in the south of Libya: the case of Marzuk. PPiU, 1984. 228 p.   Micro 84–29,984
DAI, v. 45A, Apr. 1985: 3219.

90

Abuhalimeh, Faiq Husni. The effect of two 10-week training programs on self-concept and student attitude toward physical activity of male and female

Jordanian college physical education majors. FTaSU, 1986. 105 p.

Micro 86–26,786

DAI, v. 47A, Apr. 1987: 3693.

91

Abulfaraj, Waleed Hussain. Development and application of a decision methodology for the planning of nuclear research and development in Saudi Arabia. IaAS, 1983. 262 p. Micro 83–16,134

DAI, v. 44B, Sept. 1983: 888.

92

Abulgasem, Mustafa Abdalla. The voting behavior of the Afro-Arab states in the General Assembly of the United Nations in the period 1956–1974 and 1978–1981. LNT, 1985. 743 p. Micro 86–24,409

DAI, v. 47A, Mar. 1987: 3551.

93

Abumdas, Abdul Hamid Ali. Libyan Arabic phonology. MiU, 1985. 312 p.

Micro 85–20,852

DAI, v. 46A, Jan. 1986: 1918–1919.

94

Abunabaa, Abdelaziz Mustafa. An analysis of marketing in Saudi Arabia and American marketing executives' knowledge about the Saudi Arabian market. TxDN, 1981. 252 p. Micro 82–8082

DAI, v. 42A, May 1982: 4915.

95

Abuoaf, Ibrahim. Public corporations in the Sudan: relationship between successful performance and the structure and quality of the board of directors. CCC, 1985. 167 p. Micro 85–12,013

DAI, v. 46A, Oct. 1985: 1081.

96

Abu 'Osba-Saqr, Saleh Khalil. A centrist theory of Afro-Arab communication: a model for development. DHU, 1982. 248 p. Micro 83–11,216

DAI, v. 44A, July 1983: 13.

97

Aburayieth, Abdulhamid. The phonology of the verb in Libyan Arabic. WaU, 1982. 184 p. Micro 83–4373

DAI, v. 43A, Apr. 1983: 3305.

98

Abusneina, Mohamed Abduljalil. Development alternatives in a surplus economy with skilled labor constraints: the case of Libya. InU, 1981. 326 p.

Micro 81–28,054

DAI, v. 42A, Jan. 1982: 3228.

99

Abuswa, Mahmud Ahmed. The Arabization and Islamization of the Maghrib: a

social and economic reconstruction of the history of the Maghrib during the first two centuries of Islam. CLU, 1984. 345 p.   Micro 84–11,841
   DAI, v. 45A, Aug. 1984: 602.

100

Abuzied, Hassan T. H. Geology of the Wadi Hamrawin area, Red Sea hills, Eastern Desert, Egypt. ScU, 1984. 234 p.   Micro 85–631
   DAI, v. 45B, Apr. 1985: 3185.

101

Adam, Adam Ibrahim. Mineralogy and micronutrient status of the major soils in the Gezira Scheme (Sudan, Africa). TxCM, 1982. 110 p.   Micro 82–26,056
   DAI, v. 43B, Dec. 1982: 1689.

102

Adar, Korwa Gombe. The significance of the legal principle of 'territorial integrity' as the modal determinant policy towards Somalia, 1963–1983. ScU, 1986. 309 p.   Micro 86–26,253
   DAI, v. 47A, Mar. 1987: 3552.

103

Addeweesh, Rashid Abdulrahman. A syntactic and semantic study of *ḥāl* 'circumstantial' structures in modern literary Arabic prose literature. MiU, 1985. 213 p.   Micro 85–20,853
   DAI, v. 46A, Jan. 1986: 1959–1960.

104

Adeinat, Mohammed K. The price of oil and OPEC behavior: a utility maximization model. CLSU, 1985.
   DAI, v. 46A, May 1986: 3403–3404.

105

Aden, Suad Barkhed. A proposed model for community schools in Somalia. OkS, 1984. 113 p.   Micro 84–27,640
   DAI, v. 45A, Mar. 1985: 2725.

106

Adra, Najwa. *Qabyala*: the tribal concept in the central highlands of the Yemen Arab Republic. PPT, 1982. 323 p.   Micro 83–11,576
   DAI, v. 44A, July 1983: 210.

107

Adulhadi, Abdulaziz Saad. Evaluation of the mathematics curriculum for the intermediate schools in the Eastern Province of Saudi Arabia. NIC, 1984. 277 p.   Micro 84–7393
   DAI, v. 44A, June 1984: 3585.

108

al-Adwan, Sami Yousef. The League of Arab States and regional collective security. CCC, 1987. 234 p.   Micro 87–13,499
   DAI, v. 48A, Dec. 1987: 1537.

109

Adwani, Saad Hamad. The relationship between teacher and supervisor as perceived by teachers, supervisors, and principals in secondary schools in Saudi Arabia. OrU, 1981. 321 p. Micro 82–9648
DAI, v. 42A, May 1982: 4699.

110

Afifi, Larry Anna. An exploratory study to investigate the determinants of health behavior towards smoking in Bahreini secondary school males. IaU, 1983. 194 p. Micro 83–25,128
DAI, v. 44A, Jan. 1984: 2048–2049.

111

Afifi, Zeinab Emam Mohamed. The determinants of growth of infants in an Egyptian village. MH, 1984.
CDI, 1985, v. 5: 5.

112

Aftat, Mokhtar. The acquisition of negation and *wh*-questions in a Moroccan Arabic speaking four-year-old child. TxU, 1982. 371 p. Micro 82–17,819
DAI, v. 43A, Sept. 1982: 783.

113

Ageel, Hamza Abdullah. Job satisfaction of staff members of Umm al-Qura University in Makkah, Saudi Arabia. MiEM, 1982. 162 p. Micro 83–3744
DAI, v. 43A, Mar. 1983: 2836.

114

Ageil, Mukhtar Abugaila. Naval policy and the rise of the Fleet of Ifriqiyya from the 1st to 3d centuries A.H. (7th to 9th centuries A.D.). MiU, 1985. 392 p.
Micro 85–20,854
DAI, v. 46A, Jan. 1986: 2042.

115

Agel, Elias George. The Arab theater: a quest for unity and identity. CLSU, 1982.
DAI, v. 43A, Apr. 1983: 3311.

116

el Agha, Ehsan Khalil. Effects of instruction on teaching skills of prospective science teachers in Kuwait. KU, 1984. 161 p. Micro 84-24,326
DAI, v. 45A, Feb. 1985: 2373.

117

al-Agha, Nahda Kamal H. An analysis of the growth and development of the Palestinian higher educational system in the West Bank and Gaza Strip. KU, 1983. 187 p. Micro 84–3605
DAI, v. 44A, May 1984: 2113.

118

Agius, Dionisius A. Arabic literary works as a source of documentation for

technical terms of the material culture. CaOTU, 1984.
DAI, v. 45A, Mar. 1985: 2855.

119

al-Agla, Abdulaziz Ali. The strengths and weaknesses of the elementary new mathematics curriculum in Saudi Arabia: the views of four groups of educators. InU, 1985. 366 p.   Micro 86-2402
DAI, v. 46A, June 1986: 3578.

120

Ahady, Anwar-ul-Haq. The politics of abundance: resources allocation in the public sector in the developed and oil-rich countries. IEN, 1986. 258 p.
Micro 86-27,319
DAI, v. 47A, Feb. 1987: 3173.

121

Aharoni, Abraham. Israeli Arab university students' perceptions of their educational and social experience in Israel. MiU, 1982. 181 p.   Micro 82-24,903
DAI, v. 43A, Dec. 1982: 1880.

122

al-Ahaydib, Mohammed E. A. Teaching English as a foreign language in the intermediate and secondary schools of Saudi Arabia: a diagnostic study. KU, 1986. 197 p.   Micro 86-19,876
DAI, v. 47A, Dec. 1986: 1997-1998.

123

Ahmad, Abdul-Majeed Rashid. The phonemic system of modern standard Kurdish. MiU, 1986. 169 p.   Micro 86-12,458
DAI, v. 47A, Sept. 1986: 924.

124

Ahmad, Anis. Two approaches to Islamic history: a critique of [Muḥammad] Shiblī Nu'mānī's and Syed Ameer 'Alī's interpretations of history. PPT, 1980. 242 p.   Micro 81-15,848
DAI, v. 42A, Aug. 1981: 742.

125

Ahmad, Mubarak Idris. Factors influencing university students' choice of teaching as a career in the Sudan. PSt, 1982. 206 p.   Micro 82-28,850
DAI, v. 43A, Jan. 1983: 2213.

126

Ahmadian, Majid. Cooperative and non-cooperative discrete differential models of oil pricing and the OPEC cartel. NBuU, 1984. 147 p.   Micro 84-10,516
DAI, v. 45A, Sept. 1984: 884-885.

127

Ahmed, Elamin Abdalla. The Sudan's experience in local government: an evaluation study. CCC, 1983. 237 p.   Micro 83-2623
DAI, v. 43A, Mar. 1983: 3108.

128

Ahmed, Ferial Abd el-Kader. Fertility transition in Egypt. PU, 1987. 226 p.
Micro 87–13, 996
DAI, v. 48A, Sept. 1987: 753.

129

Ahmed, Galal el Din M. Planning for basic needs in the Sudan: performance, policies and prospects. PSt, 1983. 172 p.　　　　Micro 83–12,599
DAI, v. 44A, Oct. 1983: 1220.

130

Ahmed, Hashim Moinuddin. The al-Ain (United Arab Emirates) adult literacy program: a study of student, teacher and program goals. CaOTU, 1983.
DAI, v. 45A, Aug. 1984: 422.

131

Ahmed, Medani Mohamed Mohamed. The political economy of development and underdevelopment in the Sudan. CU-Riv, 1985. 259 p.
Micro 85–20,620
DAI, v. 46A, Jan. 1986: 2013.

132

Ahmed, Saad Noah. Desert quest: French and British writers in Arabia and North Africa, 1850–1950. IU, 1983. 161 p.　　　　Micro 83–24,498
DAI, v. 44A, Dec. 1983: 1782.

133

Ahsan, Abdullahil. Muslim society in crisis: a case study of the Organization of the Islamic Conference. MiU, 1985. 216 p.　　　　Micro 86–395
DAI, v. 46A, May 1986: 3467.

134

Ajami, Joseph Georges. The Arabic press in the United States since 1892: a socio-historical study. OAU, 1987. 216 p.　　　　Micro 87–19,358
DAI, v. 48A, Dec. 1987: 1345.

135

Ajlan, Ajlan Mohammad. The effectiveness of two academic libraries in Saudi Arabia: an enquiry into the main factors affecting their services. OclW, 1985. 120 p.　　　　Micro 85–10,119
DAI, v. 46A, Sept. 1985: 543.

136

Akacem, Mohammed. Supply and demand for money in a capital surplus economy: the case of Kuwait. CoU, 1981. 174 p.　　　　Micro 81–22,265
DAI, v. 42A, Oct. 1981: 1733–1734.

137

Akkad, Adnan Abdulhamid. The development of indigenous manpower in Saudi Arabia. CoFS, 1983. 298 p.　　　　Micro 83–27,948
DAI, v. 44A, Feb. 1984: 2599.

138

Akol, Joshua O. Refugee migration and repatriation: case-studies of some affected rural communities in southern Sudan. CaMWU, 1986.
DAI, v. 47A, Oct. 1986: 1442.

139

Al Saud, Mashaal Abdullah Turki. Permanence and change: an analysis of the Islamic political culture of Saudi Arabia with special reference to the Royal Family. CCC, 1982. 206 p.   Micro 82–28,739
DAI, v. 43A, Jan. 1983: 2435.

140

Alabbadi, Abdallah Hasan. Nomadic settlements in Saudi Arabia: a socio-historical and analytical case study. MiEM, 1981. 269 p.   Micro 81–26,462
DAI, v. 42A, Dec. 1981: 2890.

141

Alagheely, Abdulaziz M. Factors affecting teachers' utilization of language laboratories in secondary schools in Saudi Arabia. TMurS, 1983. 187 p.
Micro 84–11,704
DAI, v. 45A, Aug. 1984: 439–440.

142

Alakayleh, Abdallah Ali. Public administrative theory in the context of an Islamic state. CLSU, 1982.
DAI, v. 43A, July 1982: 259–260.

143

Alam, Ibrahim Ahmad M. Using non-print instructional media in the teaching of English in Saudi Arabia: a feasibility study. OU, 1983. 244 p.
Micro 84–3480
DAI, v. 44A, May 1984: 3251.

144

Alam, Mohammed Assad. The effects of three experimental interventions on the spoken English proficiency of eighth grade Saudi Arabian students. CoDU, 1986. 238 p.   Micro 86–19, 133
DAI, v. 47A, Dec. 1986: 2060.

145

Albadah, Omar Ali. A plan for teaching American culture to Saudi high school students. KU, 1985. 285 p.   Micro 86–8368
DAI, v. 47A, Aug. 1986: 396.

146

Albar, Hamed Omer. Analysis of the applicability of a network simulation model to traffic performance in the city of Jeddah, Saudi Arabia. MiEM, 1985. 131 p.
Micro 85–13,878
DAI, v. 46B, Nov. 1985: 1635.

147

Albis, Abdul Hameid Ahmed. An energy efficient urban center in the Egyptian desert. DCU, 1985. 398 p.   Micro 85–15,057
  DAI, v. 46A, Jan. 1986: 1759.

148

Alderman, Harold H. Allocation of goods through non-price mechanisms: implications of rationing and waiting times in Egypt. MH, 1984. 165 p.
                                Micro 84–19,295
    DAI, v. 45A, Jan. 1985: 2187.

149

Aldoghan, Abdulla Ahmad. The predictive validity of selection measures used by the University of Petroleum and Minerals in Saudi Arabia. MiEM, 1985. 218 p.
                                Micro 86–7045
    DAI, v. 47A, Aug. 1986: 466.

150

Aldosary, Fahad Saad. Impact of the oil sector on the development of the non-oil economy of Saudi Arabia. DAU, 1983. 413 p.   Micro 83–13,938
    DAI, v. 44A, Aug. 1983: 533.

151

Alehaideb, Ibrahim Soliaman. Precipitation distribution in the southwest of Saudi Arabia. AzTeS, 1985. 232 p.   Micro 86–2833
    DAI, v. 47B, Aug. 1986: 551.

152

Alesifeer, Ali Salem. Spatial transferability of trip generation models [in six Saudi cities]. CoU, 1987. 162 p.   Micro 87–16,234
    DAI, v. 48B, Nov. 1987: 1446–1447.

153

Alexander, David G. *Dhu l-faḳār*. NNU, 1984. 320 p.   Micro 85–5465
    DAI, v. 46A, July 1985: 3.

154

Alexander, Paula K. Foreign policy decision-making: an analysis of three United States policy decisions towards Saudi Arabia. MMeT, 1985. 224 p.
                                Micro 85–26,845
    DAI, v. 46A, Apr. 1986: 3148–3149.

155

Alfalahi, Hussain Ali. The relationship between discourse universals and discourse structure of English and Arabic. ScU, 1981. 562 p.   Micro 81–29,487
    DAI, v. 42A, Jan. 1982: 3135.

156

Alfayz, Abdelkarim Metab. Determinants and differentials of fertility in Jordan. MsSM, 1986. 220 p.   Micro 86–28,613
    DAI, v. 47A, Feb. 1987: 3196.

157

Alghamdi, Ali Ahmad S. Bosaili. Selected factors associated with intermediate and high school dropouts in rural southwestern Saudi Arabia. TNJ-P, 1982. 284 p.   Micro 82–27,115

   DAI, v. 43A, Dec. 1982: 1753.

158

Alghamedy, Ahmed A. G. Investigation of conditions affecting art teacher preparation and art education curriculum implementation in Saudi Arabia. OU, 1986. 200 p.   Micro 87–3506

   DAI, v. 47A, Apr. 1987: 3639.

159

AlHaider, Khalid Abdulrahman. A study of quality, importance, provisions, and effectiveness of student personnel services at King Faisal University, Saudi Arabia. MiEM, 1986. 292 p.   Micro 86–25,002

   DAI, v. 47A, Jan. 1987: 2472.

160

Alhajri, Abdullah Jassem. Effect of seat position on school performance of Kuwaiti students. MoU, 1981. 190 p.   Micro 82–5361

   DAI, v. 42A, Mar. 1982: 3850.

161

Alhassan, Hassan A. Physical education and sport programs in Jordanian public schools: perceptions of physical educators. IaU, 1985. 182 p.

Micro 85–27,952

   DAI, v. 46A, June 1986: 3648.

162

Alhumaid, Abdulrhman I. An empirical study of the characteristics of the governmental budgetary process in rich and uncertain environments: the case of Saudi Arabia. LU, 1981. 182 p.   Micro 81–26,945

   DAI, v. 42A, Dec. 1981: 2733.

163

Ali, Abbas J. An empirical investigation of managerial value systems for working in Iraq. WvU, 1982. 329 p.   Micro 82–26,914

   DAI, v. 43A, Jan. 1983: 2429–2430.

164

Ali, Abdel-Fatah Diab. Toward an Islamic managerial alternative: an analysis of Faisal Islamic Bank of Egypt. CCC, 1986. 248 p.   Micro 86–16,527

   DAI, v. 47A, Dec. 1986: 2226.

165

Ali, Amal Eltigani. Sudan General Petroleum Corporation: a study of the evolution of its organization. DGW, 1984. 353 p.   Micro 84–28,943

   DAI, v. 45A, Apr. 1985: 3163.

166

Ali, Kamal Hassan. Muslim school planning in the United States: an analysis of issues, problems and possible approaches. MU, 1981. 286 p.

Micro 81–17,971

DAI, v. 42A, Sept. 1981: 917.

167

Ali, Khair Shafe. Leadership behavior of secondary school principals as perceived by teachers and principals in the state of Kuwait. CLSU, 1984.

DAI, v. 45A, July 1984: 25.

168

Ali, Mohammad Husain. Kuwait: religion and politics. MiEM, 1986. 585 p.

Micro 87–7087

DAI, v. 48A, July 1987: 228.

169

Ali, Mohammed Abdeljawad Mohammed. Health systems in western Saudi Arabia: location analysis and spatial planning, monitoring and evaluation. WMUW, 1984. 362 p.   Micro 85–16,884

DAI, v. 46A, Dec. 1985: 1708.

170

Ali, Muhammad Jabir. The impact of cultural and personal adjustment on progress towards completion of graduate degrees as perceived by Iraqi scholars in the United States. MdU, 1982. 132 p.   Micro 83–18,865

DAI, v. 44A, Oct. 1983: 919.

171

el-Ali, Nasser Moh'd. Jordanian students' performance under lecture-discussion and four pacing contingencies in the personalized system of instruction. WU, 1983. 141 p.   Micro 83–14,997

DAI, v. 44A, Oct. 1983: 1027–1028.

172

Ali, Taisier Mohamed Ahmed. The cultivation of hunger: towards the political economy of agricultural development in the Sudan, 1956–1964. CaOTU, 1982.

DAI, v. 44A, Sept. 1983: 859.

173

Ali, Zahra Ahmed Hussein. Between Shahrazad and Marcel Proust: narrative techniques in *The Alexandria Quartet*. RPB, 1985. 200 p.   Micro 85–19,799

DAI, v. 46A, Jan. 1986: 1945.

174

Alianak, Sonia Lutfi. Hierarchical dissonance in values and the Iranian Revolution. TxU, 1987. 318 p.   Micro 87–17,355

DAI, v. 48A, Nov. 1987: 1303.

175

Alibhai, Mohamed Abualy. Abū Yaʿqūb al-Sijistānī and *Kitāb sullam al-najāt*: a

study in Islamic Neoplatonism. MH, 1983. 306 p.   Micro 84–3063
DAI, v. 44A, June 1984: 3704.

176
Aljeaid, Mansour Owaid. Perceptions of American college students about Arabs: the role of mass media and personal contact in the formation of stereotypes. MiKW, 1986. 123 p.   Micro 86–25,606
DAI, v. 47A, Feb. 1987: 2990.

177
Aljiffry, Mohammed Sadik Abdullah. Manpower projection model for economic planning in Saudi Arabia using the input-output technique. OkS, 1983. 255 p.
Micro 84–14,137
DAI, v. 45B, Sept. 1984: 966.

178
Alkana, Linda A. K. Suzanne Voilquin: feminist and Saint-Simonian [in 1830's Egypt]. CU-I, 1985. 259 p.   Micro 85–16,535
DAI, v. 46A, Dec. 1985: 1715.

179
Alkatheery, Rashid Hamad. Important characteristics of student teaching using the Delphi Method. MoU, 1982. 231 p.   Micro 83–10,363
DAI, v. 43A, June 1983: 3877–3878.

180
Alkayed, Nail A. Hafez. The relationship between foreign aid and development: the Jordanian experience. CLSU, 1981.
DAI, v. 42A, Dec. 1981: 2849–2850.

181
Alkhunaizi, Mohamed Mahdi. Needs related to a school food service system in Saudi Arabia. CoGrU, 1984. 268 p.   Micro 85–1950
DAI, v. 45A, May 1985: 3244.

182
Alkurdy, Misbah Mohammad Makky. Educational and occupational aspirations among the Saudi female college students in Riyadh, Saudi Arabia. FTaSU, 1986. 208 p.   Micro 87–2228
DAI, v. 47A, Apr. 1987: 3728.

183
Allaghi, Farida Abdulkasam. Rural women and decision making: a case study in the Kufra Settlement Project, Libya. CoFS, 1981. 258 p.   Micro 81–26,416
DAI, v. 42A, Dec. 1981: 2881–2882.

184
Allam, Etimad Muhammad Ali. Organizational and professional correlates of knowledge obsolescence among Egyptian engineers. PSt, 1981. 187 p.
Micro 82–6955
DAI, v. 42A, June 1982: 5266–5267.

185

Allawi, Jabbar Audah. Television and film in Iraq: socio-political and cultural study, 1946–1980. MiU, 1983. 343 p. Micro 83–24,133 DAI, v. 44A, Dec. 1983: 1614.

186

Alldredge, Elham-Eid. Child-rearing practices in the homes of Arab immigrants: a study of ethnic persistence. MiEM, 1984. 262 p. Micro 85–3179 DAI, v. 45A, June 1985: 3753–3754.

187

Allemano, Eric P. An ancillary educational sector in a developing country: a case study from Mauritania. NNC, 1984. 307 p. Micro 84–27,342 DAI, v. 45A, Apr. 1985: 3108.

188

Allen, Malcolm D. The medievalism of T. E. Lawrence ("of Arabia"). PSt, 1983. 220 p. Micro 83–27,467 DAI, v. 44A, Feb. 1984: 2466.

189

al-Alloush, Khaled Mahmoud. Labor migration and income distribution: the case of the Arab region. MdBJ, 1981. 296 p. Micro 82–5075 DAI, v. 42A, Mar. 1982: 4161.

190

Almahboob, Abdulrahman Ebrahim. An investigation of the degree of job satisfaction among university faculty in Saudi Arabian universities. PPiU, 1987. 152 p. Micro 87–19,281 DAI, v. 48A, Dec. 1987: 1402.

191

Almana, Aisha Mohamed. Economic development and its impact on the status of women in Saudi Arabia. CoU, 1981. 297 p. Micro 82–782 DAI, v. 42A, Feb. 1982: 3776.

192

Almangour, Abdulkarim M. Feasibility of establishing a guidance and counseling center at King Faisal University in Saudi Arabia. CoGrU, 1985. 188 p. Micro 85–19,429 DAI, v. 46A, June 1986: 3598.

193

Almangour, Lamya. The relationship between conversation skills of Lebanese Moslem children and child rearing attitudes. CoGrU, 1985. 182 p. Micro 85–19,430 DAI, v. 46A, Jan. 1986: 1832.

194

Almas, Hassan Mahmoud. Investigation of opinions and performance regarding

physics instructional procedures in Saudi secondary schools. CoGrU, 1983. 279 p. Micro 83–13,971
DAI, v. 44A, Aug. 1983: 450.

195
Almasriuf, Luay Mohammed Yahya. Personal motives and sociological factors related to participation in specific sports by teenagers in Baghdad, Iraq. PPiU, 1984. 208 p. Micro 84–21,326
DAI, v. 45A, Dec. 1984: 1682.

196
Almefleh, Khalid Yousuf. A comparative study of university-level media centers in Jordan and in the United States. OkS, 1985. 259 p. Micro 85–28,077
DAI, v. 46A, Apr. 1986: 3004.

197
Almofadda, Omar A. Age and sex differences in spontaneous self-concept in Saudi Arabia: preadolescents, adolescents and youth adults. OU, 1985. 119 p.
Micro 86–2968
DAI, v. 46A, June 1986: 3652.

198
Almohawis, Soliman Abdullah. Motivation of construction workers in Saudi Arabia: an expectancy theory approach. TxU, 1986. 371 p. Micro 87–162
DAI, v. 47B, Mar. 1987: 3880.

199
Almolhem, Mohammad Ali. A classification of adult offenders in Dammam Central Prison, Saudi Arabia. MsSM, 1986. 112 p. Micro 86–28,614
DAI, v. 47A, Feb. 1987: 3195.

200
Almomani, Riad Abdullah. External borrowing and economic development: the case of Jordan. ULA, 1985. 214 p. Micro 85–23,680
DAI, v. 46A, Feb. 1986: 2371–2372.

201
Almoneef, Majid Abdullah. The impact of OPEC's pricing and investment decisions on the U.S. balance of payments and the exchange value of the dollar. OrU, 1981. 216 p. Micro 81–23,481
DAI, v. 42A, Nov. 1981: 2212.

202
Alnajim, Saad Abdul Rahman. Administrators' participation in the decision-making process: a case study of King Faisal University in Saudi Arabia. KMK, 1985. 87 p. Micro 85–15,915
DAI, v. 46A, Dec. 1985: 1448–1449.

203
Alnassar, Saleh Nassar. Professional job knowledge and skills needed by extension

24

personnel in the central region of Saudi Arabia. OU, 1981. 214 p.

Micro 81–28,952

DAI, v. 42A, Jan. 1982: 2975.

204

Alnimir, Saud Mohammed. Present and future bureaucrats in Saudi Arabia: a survey research. FTaSU, 1981. 197 p.　　　　　　　　　　Micro 81–27,537

DAI, v. 42A, Dec. 1981: 2850.

205

Alnowaiser, Mohamed Abdullah. The role of traditional and modern residential rural settlements on the quality of environmental experience: a case study of Unyzeh and New Alkabra in Saudi Arabia. CLSU, 1983.

DAI, v. 44A, Mar. 1984: 2906.

206

Alon, Hanan. Countering Palestinian terrorism in Israel: toward a policy analysis of countermeasures. CStmoR, 1980. 296 p.　　　　　　　　Micro 81–20,587

DAI, v. 42A, Oct. 1981: 1792.

207

Alosh, Muhammad Mahdi. The perception and acquisition of pharyngealized fricatives by American learners of Arabic and implications for teaching Arabic phonology. OU, 1987. 191 p.　　　　　　　　　　　　Micro 87–17,599

DAI, v. 48A, Nov. 1987: 1135.

208

Alouda, Rashed Hamed. Self-planned learning projects by adult male college-educated Saudis working with Arabian American Oil Company (ARAMCO), 1980–1985. PPiU, 1986. 123 p.　　　　　　　　　　Micro 86–20,269

DAI, v. 47A, Dec. 1986: 1978.

209

Alowaish, Rashed A. Compliance with, and effectiveness of, specialized care of hypertension in Kuwait, 1983/84. NcU, 1985. 184 p.　　　　Micro 85–27,254

DAI, v. 46B, May 1986: 3802.

210

Alsabah, Mohammed Sabah S. General equilibrium analysis of government expenditures in an oil exporting country: the case of Kuwait. MH, 1985. 205 p.　　　　　　　　　　　　　　　　　　　　　Micro 85–20,162

DAI, v. 46A, Jan. 1986: 2013.

211

Alsadek, Jihad Abdalla. Simulating lifetime incomes and the impacts of government distributive policies: the case of Kuwait. DGW, 1983. 179 p.

Micro 83–11,186

DAI, v. 44A, July 1983: 216–217.

212

Alsaffy, Mohamed Tawhid M. el Anwer. Demand for wheat and rice in selected

Arab countries: the current situation and projections to year 2000. WaPS, 1985. 187 p. Micro 86–10,349
DAI, v. 47A, Sept. 1986: 997.

213
Alsahlani, Salih Kadhum. Secondary teacher competence and teacher preparation programs in Iraq. PPiU, 1983. 86 p. Micro 84–11,795
DAI, v. 45A, Aug. 1984: 496.

214
Alsaigh, Mohammed Noor Hussan. A proposed model for evaluating teacher performance in the Saudi Arabian high schools. InU, 1981. 230 p.
Micro 82–839
DAI, v. 42A, Feb. 1982: 3353–3354.

215
Alsamarraie, Fouad Jassim. The impact of the U.S. environment on the Iraqi student. PPiU, 1983. 141 p. Micro 83–27,730
DAI, v. 44A, Feb. 1984: 2409.

216
Alsaud, Mansour Mutib. Productivity improvement in the public sector of Saudi Arabia. DGW, 1986. 490 p. Micro 87–546
DAI, v. 47A, Mar. 1987: 3554.

217
Alsehabany, Abdulaziz Ali. An investigation of students' attitudes toward high school in Riyadh, Saudi Arabia. OU, 1985. 114 p. Micro 86–2969
DAI, v. 47A, Aug. 1986: 396.

218
Alshamali, Abdullatif Mohummad Ali. A study of the impact of culture on organizational communication of a Kuwaiti government's organization. CoDU, 1983. 178 p. Micro 83–21,063
DAI, v. 44A, Nov. 1983: 1241.

219
Alsharhan, Abdulrahman Sultan. Petrography, sedimentology, diagenesis and reservoir characteristics of the Shuaiba and Kharaib formations (Barremian-mid Aptian) carbonate sediments of Abu Dhabi, United Arab Emirates. ScU, 1985. 189 p. Micro 86–4252
DAI, v. 46B, June 1986: 4161.

220
Alsuwaigh, Siham Abdulrahman. The impact of social and economic change on child socialization in Saudi Arabia. OrU, 1984. 346 p. Micro 85–1970
DAI, v. 45A, June 1985: 3540.

221
Alsuwayeh, Wadad. The impact of culture and environment on architectural

training: a needs assessment approach to designing an architecture program for Kuwait. DCU, 1985. 348 p.   Micro 85–15,058
DAI, v. 46A, Jan. 1986: 1759.

222

Altaha, Fawaz Mohamed. Knowledge of English/Applied Linguistics and student perceptions of secondary school teachers of English as a foreign language in Jordan. NAlU, 1982. 301 p.   Micro 83–751
DAI, v. 43A, Apr. 1983: 3200.

223

Althbia, Rashid Ali. Statistical analysis of an evaluation technique for predicting success of training programs at Kuwait Institute for Scientific Research (KISR), Kuwait. CoGrU, 1984. 146 p.   Micro 85–1951
DAI, v. 45B, May 1985: 3552.

224

Altrairy, Abdulrahman. Test anxiety and academic performance of Saudi Arabian university students. WaPS, 1984. 129 p.   Micro 85–4199
DAI, v. 45A, June 1985: 3621.

225

Altwaijri, Abdulaziz Othman. The adequacy of students' preparation in English as a foreign language in the Saudi schools. OrU, 1982. 196 p.
Micro 82–24,818
DAI, v. 43A, Dec. 1982: 1809.

226

Altwaijri, Ahmed Othman. Academic freedom in Islam and the West: a study of the philosophical foundations of academic freedom in Islam and the Western liberal philosophy. OrU, 1983. 143 p.   Micro 83–25,254
DAI, v. 44A, Jan. 1984: 2054.

227

Alumran, Dhafer A. A predictive model of the oil crisis in Bahrain and the search for a new development strategy. CLSU, 1986.
DAI, v. 47A, Oct. 1986: 1478.

228

Alumran, Jihan I. Abu Rashed. Major factors influencing school discipline of Bahraini youths in secondary general education. CLSU, 1986.
DAI, v. 47A, Mar. 1987: 3360.

229

Alvani, Seyed Mehdi. Islamic organization theory. CLSU, 1981.
DAI, v. 43A, Oct. 1982: 1271.

230

Alwelaie, Abdullah Nasser Ali. The role of natural and human factors in the degradation of the environment in central, eastern, and northern Saudi Arabia.

CU-Riv, 1985. 475 p.   Micro 86–4121
DAI, v. 47A, July 1986: 272.

231
Aly, Abdel Monem Said. The United States and the October 1973 Middle East
crisis. IDeKN, 1982. 811 p.   Micro 83–11,288
DAI, v. 44A, July 1983: 277.

232
Aly, Hassan Youssef. Infant and child mortality in Egypt: an economic, proximate
determinants approach. ICarbS, 1987. 182 p.   Micro 87–12,820
DAI, v. 48A, Sept. 1987: 701–702.

233
Aly, Mohamed Abd-el-Sabour Mohamed. An "open-door" policy and foreign
direct investment: the recent Egyptian experience. CoFS, 1982. 252 p.
                                                       Micro 82–27,906
DAI, v. 43A, Jan. 1983: 2392.

234
Alyahya, Khaled Ahmad M. Constructing a comprehensive orientation program
for Saudi Arabian students in the United States. PPiU, 1981. 284 p.
                                                       Micro 82–8289
DAI, v. 43A, July 1982: 75.

235
Alyamani, Abdulrahman Abdullah. Women's higher education, and women's
employment in Saudi Arabia. IU, 1985. 211 p.   Micro 86–113
DAI, v. 46A, May 1986: 3407.

236
Alzand, Walid K. Using student and teacher perceptions to predict curricular
program efficacy: an Iraqi school system study. CU-Riv, 1985. 249 p.
                                                       Micro 85–11,457
DAI, v. 46A, Oct. 1985: 881.

237
el Amach, Hussein Merhej. The public sector and regional development: investigation of the integration projects approach in the Arab region. PSt, 1985.
220 p.   Micro 86–6324
DAI, v. 47A, July 1986: 262.

238
Amayreh, Mohammad Ahmad. A linguistic analysis and evaluation of Arabic
textbook materials and methodology. InU, 1984. 255 p.   Micro 84–17,150
DAI, v. 45A, Nov. 1984: 1415.

239
Amer, Abdul-Karim Ahmed. Economic planning in Yemen Arab Republic: the

dependency problem. CoFS, 1985. 210 p.   Micro 85–27,806
DAI, v. 46A, Apr. 1986: 3096.

240
Ameri, Anan. Socioeconomic development in Jordan, 1950–1980: an application
of dependency theory. MiDW, 1981. 370 p.   Micro 82–9263
DAI, v. 42A, May 1982: 4950–4951.

241
Ameziane, Ahmed. A study of the implementation of educational objectives in
Morocco since 1956 with implications for administrators. WMM, 1983. 214 p.
                                                         Micro 84–10,832
DAI, v. 45A, Aug. 1984: 355.

242
el-Amin, Ahmed el-Sheikh. A comparative study on human resources, basic needs
performance, and economic development with special emphasis on the Sudan.
CLSU, 1981.
DAI, v. 42A, Dec. 1981: 2523.   ꞌ

243
Amin, Hussein Yousry. An Egypt-based model for the use of television in national
development. OU, 1986. 311 p.   Micro 87–3508
DAI, v. 47A, Apr. 1987: 3601.

244
Ammar, Khalifa Sharef Salam. Proposed guidelines for the improvement of the
art and art teacher education programs at al-Fateh University in Libya. AzU,
1986. 141 p.   Micro 86–23,840
DAI, v. 47A, Jan. 1987: 2546.

245
Ammarin, Faris Adib. An assessment of water pollution issues under conditions of
development: the Jordan Zerka River case. CLSU, 1984.
DAI, v. 45A, July 1984: 319.

246
Amr, Kayed Mohamed. The interaction of cultural and natural factors in the
drawings of Jordanian children. PSt, 1982. 432 p.   Micro 82–13,286
DAI, v. 43A, July 1982: 52.

247
Anagnostakis, Christopher. The Arabic version of Ptolemy's *Planisphaerium*. CtY,
1984. 323 p.   Micro 85–14,852
DAI, v. 46A, Nov. 1985: 1387.

248
Anderson, Gary. Differential urban growth in the Eastern Province of Saudi
Arabia: a study of the historical interaction of economic development and socio-
political change. MdBJ, 1985. 356 p.   Micro 85–18,473
DAI, v. 46A, Dec. 1985: 1708.

249
Anderson, Lisa S. States, peasants and tribes: colonialism and rural politics in Tunisia and Libya. NNC, 1981. 371 p. Micro 81–25,236
DAI, v. 42A, Dec. 1981: 2844–2845.

250
Andretta, Elizabeth H. A reconsideration of the basis of group cohesion among the Murle of the Southern Sudan. PU, 1985. 247 p. Micro 85–23,392
DAI, v. 46A, Feb. 1986: 2350.

251
Angeles, Vivienne S. M. Islam and politics: Philippine government policies and Muslim responses, 1946–1976. PPT, 1987. 444 p. Micro 87–11,291
DAI, v. 48A, Aug. 1987: 414.

252
al-Ankary, Khalid Mohammed. A comparative factorial ecology: Kuwait City, Kuwait, and Jacksonville, Florida. FU, 1981. 205 p. Micro 81–27,407
DAI, v. 42A, Dec. 1981: 2857.

253
Anwar, Muhammad. A macroeconomic model for interest-free economies: an integrative study of Western and Islamic economic systems. NhU, 1985. 159 p.
Micro 86–7453
DAI, v. 47A, Aug. 1986: 619.

254
al-Anzi, Abdulla Meshail A. The Gulf Cooperation Council: reasons and challenges, critical and analytic study. CCC, 1986. 296 p. Micro 86–19,072
DAI, v. 47A, Nov. 1986: 1863.

255
Aqil, Mahmoud Abdulla. The Palestinian family in the West Bank and Gaza Strip after 1967. CSdI, 1986. 138 p. Micro 86–6164
DAI, v. 47A, July 1986: 322.

256
Arab, Asem Taher. The theory of economic development in capital-rich, labor-poor economies: the case of Gulf Cooperative Council states. TxDaM, 1983. 120 p. Micro 83–20,668
DAI, v. 44A, Nov. 1983: 1533.

257
Arafa, Mohamed Mahmoud Ali. Communication structure and social structure in an Egyptian village. ViU, 1986. 282 p. Micro 87–5674
DAI, v. 48A, Aug. 1987: 241.

258
Arafat, Fadel Hasan. Development with unlimited supplies of imported labor: a

case study of the Kingdom of Saudi Arabia. DAU, 1985. 416 p.
Micro 85–22,917
DAI, v. 46A, Feb. 1986: 2372.

259
Aref, Mohamed Kheder. The current linguistic and curricular approaches in teaching Arabic as a foreign language: problems and suggested solutions. CLSU, 1986.
DAI, v. 47A, May 1987: 4005.

260
Arfaj, Nasser Abdulaziz. Saudi Arabia's maritime policy, 1948–1978: a study in the law of the sea as applied by developing countries. CCC, 1980. 217 p.
Micro 81–14,035
DAI, v. 42A, Aug. 1981: 841.

261
al-Arif, Shoala Ismail. An historical analysis of events and issues which have led to the growth and development of the University of Baghdad. DGW, 1986. 133 p.
Micro 86–27,891
DAI, v. 47A, Feb. 1987: 2809.

262
Arishi, Ali Yahya. A study of EFL teachers' behavior in EFL classes in Saudi Arabia. InU, 1984. 213 p.   Micro 85–6082
DAI, v. 46A, July 1985: 90.

263
Artz, Neal E. The development implications of heterogeneity in a traditional Moroccan pastoral system: the social/technical interface. ULA, 1986. 241 p.
Micro 86–19,422
DAI, v. 47B, Jan. 1987: 2716.

264
Asaad, Mohamed Mohsen. Saudi Arabia's national security: a perspective derived from political, economic, and defense policies. CCC, 1981. 494 p.
Micro 81–14,036
DAI, v. 42A, Dec. 1981: 2850.

265
Asaad, Salahiddeen Bilal. The construction and validation of a multiple-choice and a performance test of communicative writing ability for the EFL classroom [at United Arab Emirates University]. PInU, 1984. 184 p.
Micro 84–26,550
DAI, v. 45A, Mar. 1985: 2880.

266
As'ad, Ibrahim Ahmad. Government budgeting and its control in Saudi Arabia. CCC, 1982. 150 p.   Micro 82–15,200
DAI, v. 43A, Aug. 1982: 509.

267

Asad, Mohammed Ahmed. The possibility of change in Bedouin society: a study of current developments in Saudi Arabia. CCC, 1981. 150 p.

Micro 81–26,399

DAI, v. 42A, Dec. 1981: 2850–2851.

268

Asani, Ali Sultaan Ali. The *Bujh Niranjan*: a critical edition of a mystical poem in medieval Hindustani with its Khojki and Gujarati recensions. MH, 1984. 513 p. Micro 84–19,437

DAI, v. 45A, Dec. 1984: 1755.

269

Aseeri, Mohammad Saeed. Evaluation of social studies student teaching programs in the junior colleges of Taif and Abha—goals, procedures, resources, and program management. CoU, 1986. 302 p. Micro 86–18,921

DAI, v. 47A, Dec. 1986: 2109.

270

Asfoor, John Mikhail. An anthology of modern Arabic poetry, 1945–1984, with a critical introduction. CaQMM, 1985.

DAI, v. 46A, May 1986: 3367.

271

Asfoor, Majid Ahmad. Difficulties English speakers encounter in Arabic phonology. CSfU, 1982. 118 p. Micro 82–20,758

DAI, v. 43A, Oct. 1982: 1129.

272

Asher, Catherine E. B. The patronage of the Sher Shah Sur: a study of form and meaning in 16th-century Indo-Islamic century architecture. MnU, 1984. 474 p. Micro 84–18,439

DAI, v. 45A, Nov. 1984: 1226.

273

Ashkanani, Mohammad G. A. A cross-cultural perspective on work-related values [among Americans, Arabs and Iranians]. CSdI, 1984. 176 p.

Micro 84–25,919

DAI, v. 45A, Feb. 1985: 2583.

274

Ashshowwaf, Saied Ali. Administrative linkages between planning and organizational implementation in Saudi Arabia. NAlU, 1985. 444 p.

Micro 85–14,078

DAI, v. 46A, Nov. 1985: 1395.

275

Ashuraey, Nadeem Muhamed. Adolescents and culture in Yemen. MBU, 1986. 354 p. Micro 86–15,314

DAI, v. 47B, Oct. 1986: 1752.

276

Asi, Morad Osman. Arabs, Israelis and U.S. television networks: a content analysis of how ABC, CBS and NBC reported the news between 1970–1979. OU, 1981. 188 p.   Micro 81–15,761
DAI, v. 42A, Aug. 1981: 436–437.

277

al-Askar, Abdullah Ibrahim. Regional politics, a case-study: al-Yamama in the 6th and 7th centuries. CLU, 1985. 259 p.   Micro 85–22,319
DAI, v. 46A, Feb. 1986: 2394.

278

Askar, Ali G. A study of teacher job satisfaction in Kuwait. MiU, 1981. 252 p.
Micro 81–16,195
DAI, v. 42A, Aug. 1981: 466.

279

Askari, Yassar. An analysis of the government of Canada's foreign policy with respect to the Middle East and North Africa, 1948 to 1982: an Arab perspective. DAU, 1984. 376 p.   Micro 84–25,722
DAI, v. 45A, Feb. 1985: 2640.

280

Assad, Soraya Wali el-Deen. Women and work in Saudi Arabia: a study of job satisfaction in higher education. CoFS, 1983. 298 p.   Micro 83–27,951
DAI, v. 44A, Feb. 1984: 2600.

281

Assaf, Ibraheem Abdalaziz. The economic impact of guestworkers in Saudi Arabia. CoFS, 1982. 151 p.   Micro 82–18,369
DAI, v. 43A, Sept. 1982: 867.

282

Assaf, Saleh Hamad. Factors influencing secondary school male teachers in Saudi Arabia to leave teaching. MiEM, 1982. 231 p.   Micro 83–8900
DAI, v. 43A, June 1983: 3760.

283

Assefa, Hizkias. Preconditions for the success of mediation as a means of conflict resolution: the Sudan Civil War, 1955–72; a case study. PPiU, 1983. 382 p.
Micro 84–17,703
DAI, v. 45A, Nov. 1984: 1514–1515.

284

Assefi Soleimany, Shaida. The survival of OPEC, as viewed by a selected sample of OPEC's leaders. CSdI, 1985. 100 p.   Micro 85–27,093
DAI, v. 46A, May 1986: 3423.

285

Assiri, Abdul-Reda Ali. The impact of arms and politics on United States relations

33

with the Arabian Gulf States, 1968–78. CU-Riv, 1981. 324 p.

Micro 81–22,892

DAI, v. 42A, Dec. 1981: 2845.

286

Assous, Omar. Arabization and cultural conflicts in Algeria. IEN, 1985. 289 p.

Micro 85–17,964

DAI, v. 46A, Dec. 1985: 1723–1724.

287

al-Aswad, Mohamed Kaleefa. Contrastive analysis of Arabic and English verbs in tense, aspect, and structure. MiU, 1983. 265 p.   Micro 84–2233

DAI, v. 44A, Apr. 1984: 3046.

288

Atari, Omar Fayez. A contrastive analysis of Arab and American university students' strategies in accomplishing written English discourse functions: implications for EFL. DGU, 1983. 256 p.   Micro 84–1491

DAI, v. 44A, Apr. 1984: 3047.

289

Athubaity, Mulaihan Mueidh. An exploratory study of the leadership behavior of deans and presidents in higher education institutions in Saudi Arabia. MiEM, 1981.

DAI, v. 42A, June 1982: 5033–5034.

290

Atiyah, Asaad Mohammed. The American population abroad: a case study of their residential patterns and the selection of residential housing in Jeddah City, Saudi Arabia. MiEM, 1984. 246 p.   Micro 84–15,203

DAI, v. 45A, Oct. 1984: 1206.

291

Atram, Mohammed A. Availability of periodicals in major Saudi Arabian libraries: a descriptive study of factors contributing to availability within the framework of national librarianship. CLU, 1984. 258 p.   Micro 84–20,142

DAI, v. 45A, Dec. 1984: 1561.

292

Attar, Abdullah Ishaq. A survey of the teacher training junior college program upon the influence of elementary school teachers' use of instructional technology in Medina, Saudi Arabia. PPiU, 1986. 194 p.   Micro 87–1953

DAI, v. 47A, Apr. 1987: 3737.

293

Attar, Eqbal Ahmed. Major personal and social problems faced by divorced Saudi Arabian women. CSfU, 1987. 169 p.   Micro 87–18,314

DAI, v. 48A, Nov. 1987: 1148.

294

al-Attibi, Abdulrahman Abdullah M. Interpersonal communication competence

34

and media consumption and needs among young adults in Saudi Arabia. OU, 1986. 264 p. Micro 87–3505
DAI, v. 47A, Apr. 1987: 3601.

295

Atwan, Ahmad Mohammad. Selected factors influencing industrial education and training program selection by Jordanian students and their characteristics and aspirations. OkS, 1984. 229 p. Micro 85–4335
DAI, v. 45A, June 1985: 3566.

296

Aube, Raymond F. Worlds apart: the roots of America's diplomatic failures in other cultures—the Barbary Coast in the early nineteenth century. NNU, 1986. 340 p. Micro 87–6717
DAI, v. 47A, June 1987: 4491.

297

Auda, Gehad A. M. An inquiry into the dynamics of Sadat's political order. NBuU, 1984. 244 p. Micro 84–26,017
DAI, v. 45A, May 1985: 3438.

298

Augla, Ali Jassim. Positive justice development in Iraqi children, and its relationship to age, sex, urbanization, religious knowledge, academic achievement, and family income level. InU, 1984. 137 p. Micro 85–1423
DAI, v. 45A, May 1985: 3303.

299

Aurbakken, Kristine. L'étoile d'araignée: une approche à *Nedjma* de Kateb Yacine. TNJ, 1984. 296 p. Micro 84–11,391
DAI, v. 45A, Aug. 1984: 535–536.

300

Avin, Rose-Marie. Money windfalls and oil-exporting developing countries: a comparative study of Algeria, Ecuador, Trinidad and Tobago, and Indonesia. MdU, 1986. 248 p. Micro 86–28,958
DAI, v. 47A, Apr. 1987: 3839.

301

Awad, Nadir M. Food habits of giraffe, roan antelope, oribi and camel in Dinder National Park, Sudan. CoFS, 1985. 139 p. Micro 86–7628
DAI, v. 47B, Aug. 1986: 461–462.

302

Ayish, Muhammad Ibrahim. The Voice of America between diplomacy and journalism: a case study of the VOA Arabic Service. MnU, 1986. 243 p.
Micro 86–20,181
DAI, v. 47A, Dec. 1986: 1912.

303

El Ayoubi, Mohamad Abdelrahim. The United States, the Jews, and the Pales-

tinian Refugee Problem, 1939–1956. KU, 1985. 462 p.   Micro 85–29,083
DAI, v. 46A, Apr. 1986: 3134.

304
Ayubi, Shaheen. Foreign policy making in the Arab Republic of Egypt: the role of
leadership in decision-making, 1970–1972. PU, 1982. 416 p.
Micro 82–17,078
DAI, v. 43A, Sept. 1982: 915–916.

305
Azarruk, Salim A. Teachers' perceptions of the Libyan junior high school. CLSU,
1982.
DAI, v. 43A, Sept. 1982: 644.

306
Azeredo, Sandra M. Representations of sexual identity and domestic labor:
women's writings from the United States, Morocco and Brazil. CU-SC, 1986.
273 p.   Micro 86–19,243
DAI, v. 47A, Dec. 1986: 2342.

307
Ba-Hashwan, Turki Saeed Basha. Perceptions of broadcast training in two Saudi
Arabian universities: a survey of graduates, professionals, and students. WU,
1986. 211 p.   Micro 87–3817
DAI, v. 48A, July 1987: 4.

308
al-Baadi, Hamad Muhammad. Social change, education, and the roles of women
in Arabia. CSt, 1982. 309 p.   Micro 82–20,420
DAI, v. 43A, Oct. 1982: 1303.

309
Babeair, Abdul-Wahab Saleh. Ottoman penetration of the eastern region of the
Arabian Peninsula, 1814–1841. InU, 1985. 161 p.   Micro 85–26,981
DAI, v. 46A, Apr. 1986: 3128.

310
Babiker, Babiker Idris. Regional efficiency in the organization of agricultural
processing facilities: an application to oilseeds industry in the Sudan. OU, 1982.
154 p.   Micro 82–14,070
DAI, v. 43A, July 1982: 219–220.

311
Babiker, Faysal Abdullahi. The Sudanese bureaucratic elite under Numayri: an
inquiry into a ruling class. CLSU, 1986.
DAI, v. 47A, May 1987: 4184.

312
el-Babour, Mansour Muhammad. Urban networks in eastern ʿAbbāsid lands: an
historical geography of settlement in Mesopotamia and Persia, ninth- and

tenth-century A.D. AzU, 1981. 212 p.   Micro 81–28,331
DAI, v. 42A, Jan. 1982: 3301.

313
al-Babtain, Abdul-Aziz Abdul-Wahab. An investigation in the relationship between teacher effectiveness and indirect and direct teaching of intermediate
social science teachers in Riyadh, Saudi Arabia. CoGrU, 1982. 155 p.
         Micro 82–13,263
DAI, v. 43A, July 1982: 134.

314
Backer, Abdulkader Saleh. Analysis and recommendations for restructuring the
administrative configuration of King Abdul Aziz University, Saudi Arabia.
OkS, 1982. 104 p.   Micro 83–134
DAI, v. 43A, Feb. 1983: 2565.

315
el-Badarin, Mohammed Nasser. Transfer, strategies, and structural complexity in
the acquisition of English syntax by Arabic speakers. TxU, 1982. 201 p.
         Micro 82–17,854
DAI, v. 43A, Sept. 1982: 705–706.

316
Badawi, Abobakr Abdeen. An analysis of job tasks in selected occupations as
related to vocational school curriculum in Egypt. InU, 1982. 225 p.
         Micro 82–9872
DAI, v. 42A, May 1982: 4805.

317
Badeeb, Saeed Mohammed. The Saudi-Egyptian conflict over North Yemen,
1962–1970. DGW, 1985. 347 p.   Micro 85–29,607
DAI, v. 47A, July 1986: 302.

318
Bader, Hussain. Principals' and teachers' perceptions of the organizational cli-
mate of Bahraini elementary schools. TNJ, 1985. 152 p.   Micro 85–22,389
DAI, v. 46A, Feb. 1986: 2137–2138.

319
Bader, Yousef Farhan. Kabyle Berber phonology and morphology: outstanding
issues. IU, 1984. 330 p.   Micro 84–22,011
DAI, v. 45A, Jan. 1985: 2082.

320
Badi, Yousef Mohamed. Regional growth impact of Libyan development budget
expenditures. NbU, 1982. 191 p.   Micro 83–6469
DAI, v. 43A, May 1983: 3649.

321
Badran, Abdel-Kreem Ahmed. An analysis of the administrative competencies

needed by vocational administrators: an Egyptian case study. PPiU, 1985. 249 p. Micro 86–2799
DAI, v. 46A, June 1986: 3541–3542.

322
Badran, Badran Abdel-Rizzaq. Editorial treatment of the Arab-Israeli conflict in U.S. and European newspapers, 1980–1982. MU, 1984. 350 p.
Micro 85–55
DAI, v. 45A, Apr. 1985: 3021.

323
Badran, Sanna Mohamed. An investigation of the Egyptian auditor's perceptions of the independence of the auditor. ArU, 1983. 163 p. Micro 83–22,952
DAI, v. 44A, Dec. 1983: 1838.

324
Badran, Wadouda Abd-el-Rahman. The role of third parties in conflict between small states: a case study of the United States and the Egyptian-Israeli conflict, January 1967-December 1978. CaOOCC, 1981.
DAI, v. 44A, Jan. 1984: 2236.

325
Badri, Abdelmoniem Abdelkarim. Youth and nonformal education in the Sudan: an assessment and planning model. CU-SB, 1982. 240 p. Micro 82–24,633
DAI, v. 43A, Jan. 1983: 2326.

326
al-Badri, Tarik Abdulhamid. Relationships between and among leadership styles and leadership characteristics of youth leaders in the General Federation of Iraqi Youth Organizations, al-Fatwah and al-Taliah. KU, 1984. 151 p.
Micro 84–24,292
DAI, v. 45A, Feb. 1985: 2490.

327
Badry, Fatima. Acquisition of lexical derivational rules in Moroccan Arabic: implications for the development of standard Arabic as a second language through literacy. CU, 1983. 219 p. Micro 83–28,783
DAI, v. 44A, Feb. 1984: 2392.

328
Baeshen, Lamia Mohamed Saleh. *Robinson Crusoe* and *Ḥayy ibn Yaqẓān*: a comparative study. AzU, 1986. 241 p. Micro 87–4754
DAI, v. 47A, May 1987: 4087.

329
Baeshen, Nadia Mohammed Saleh. The effect of organizational communication on the middle- and lower-level managers' participation in the decision-making process in Saudi Arabia. AzU, 1987. 237 p. Micro 87–11,624
DAI, v. 48A, Aug. 1987: 248.

330

Bafakih, Abbas H. Ṭāhā Ḥusayn and the classical Arabic literary heritage. UU, 1987. 272 p.   Micro 87–14,244
DAI, v. 48A, Sept. 1987: 661.

331

Bagby, Ihsan Abdul-Wajid. Utility in classical Islamic law: the concept of *maṣlaḥah* in uṣūl al-fiqh. MiU, 1986. 252 p.   Micro 86–12,469
DAI, v. 47A, Sept. 1986: 1038.

332

Bagour, Omar Salem. Limits on Saudi Arabia's oil pricing policy: a short-run econometric-simulation model. MiEM, 1985. 296 p.   Micro 86–3375
DAI, v. 46A, June 1986: 3811–3812.

333

el-Bah, Khalifah Shehata. Fascist colonial schooling of Libyan Muslim Arab children, 1922–1942: a political system analysis. CLU, 1985. 214 p.
Micro 85–13,109
DAI, v. 46A, Oct. 1985: 881.

334

Bahammi, el-Sghayer Abdulgader. An analysis of teachers perceptions of current geographic education programs in Libyan general secondary schools. LU, 1984. 240 p.   Micro 85–15,128
DAI, v. 46A, Nov. 1985: 1242.

335

Bahanshal, Osama Mohamed. Saudi Arabia's domestic crude oil production requirements: a physical and monetary approach. CoFS, 1984. 207 p.
Micro 85–6446
DAI, v. 46A, July 1985: 207.

336

Bahgat, Hisham Amir. Housing generation in the *informal* sector in Egypt. CU, 1984. 337 p.   Micro 84–26,899
DAI, v. 45A, Mar. 1985: 2677.

337

Bahous, Sima Sami. Communication policy and planning for development: the Jordan Television Corporation—a case study. InU, 1986. 417 p.
Micro 86–27,975
DAI, v. 47A, Feb. 1987: 2782.

338

Bait-Almal, Hamza Ahmad. A descriptive analytical study of regional television cooperation among Arabian Gulf countries. MiDW, 1986. 254 p.
Micro 87–6148
DAI, v. 47A, June 1987: 4220–4221.

339
Baker, Cathy. Selected studies in Permian ammonoids [from Tunisia]. IaU, 1986.
235 p. Micro 86–22,744
DAI, v. 47B, Jan. 1987: 2814.

340
Bakhsh, Amira Taha. Characteristics of a medical and educational center for Down's Syndrome children in Jeddah, Saudi Arabia. CSfU, 1987. 178 p.
Micro 87–10,634
DAI, v. 48A, Oct. 1987: 906.

341
Bakhtiari, Bahman. Religion and politics: the Middle East and Latin America.
ViU, 1984. 245 p. Micro 84–24,888
DAI, v. 45A, Feb. 1985: 2635.

342
Bakkar, Nadia Ahmed. Qualitative aspects of Egyptian social studies textbooks.
IU, 1985. 138 p. Micro 85–21,712
DAI, v. 46A, Jan. 1986: 1897.

343
al-Bakr, Mohammed Salim. An exploratory study of the efficacy of health care in Saudi Arabia: objective and subjective assessment. CLSU, 1983.
DAI, v. 44B, Nov. 1983: 1419.

344
Bakri, Nadhim J. A study of the feasibility of developing a training model to incorporate management by objectives in higher education in Iraq. MiKW, 1985. 206 p. Micro 85–16,527
DAI, v. 46A, Dec. 1985: 1449.

345
Bakri, Talal Hassan. Factors influencing the use of instructional media by middle school teachers in two school districts in Saudi Arabia. OkU, 1983. 208 p.
Micro 83–14,757
DAI, v. 44A, Aug. 1983: 361–362.

346
Baldovin, John F. The urban character of Christian worship in Jerusalem, Rome, and Constantinople from the fourth to the tenth centuries: the origins, development, and meaning of stational liturgy. CtY, 1982. 574 p. Micro 83–10,483
DAI, v. 43A, June 1983: 3944.

347
Ballerini, Julia. Photography conscripted: Horace Vernet, Gérard de Nerval and Maxime du Camp in Egypt. NNCU-G, 1987. 435 p. Micro 87–8273
DAI, v. 47A, June 1987: 4214.

348
Ballool, Mukhtar Mohammad. Economic analysis of the long-term planning

investment strategies for the oil surplus funds in Saudi Arabia: an optimal control approach. TxHU, 1981. 384 p. Micro 81–19,865
DAI, v. 42A, Sept. 1981: 1243–1244.

349

Baltow, Abdullatif Mohammad. A historical analysis of the Saudi Arabian Ministry of Education's policies regarding fathers' involvement in the schooling of their children. MiEM, 1983. 165 p. Micro 83–15,431
DAI, v. 44A, Sept. 1983: 700.

350

Bamakhramah, Ahmed Saied. Policies for transfer of technology to developing countries: the case of Middle Eastern oil-exporting countries. FMU, 1981. 267 p. Micro 82–11,799
DAI, v. 42A, June 1982: 5184.

351

Banjar, Fowzi Saleh. Attitudes of supervisors and teachers toward the social studies curriculum in Saudi Arabian secondary schools. CoDU, 1984. 261 p.
Micro 85–3359
DAI, v. 45A, June 1985: 3603.

352

al-Banna, Linah Habbab. The educational attitudes of early childhood teachers in Lebanon. NNC-T, 1984. 210 p. Micro 84–24,195
DAI, v. 45A, Feb. 1985: 2384.

353

el Bannany, Sherif Abdel Raouf. Energy-conscious design guidelines for Egyptian housing. DCU, 1984. 246 p. Micro 84–4522
DAI, v. 44A, May 1984: 3187.

354

Banning, Edward B. Pastoral and agricultural land use in the Wadi Ziqlab, Jordan: an archaeological and ecological survey. CaOTU, 1985.
DAI, v. 47A, Sept. 1986: 952.

355

Baqqain, Akram Saleh. The role of the agricultural extension service as perceived by officials in allied institutions in Jordan. MsSM, 1982. 154 p.
Micro 83–7444
DAI, v. 43A, May 1983: 3487–3488.

356

Barakat, Ghias Abdulwahab. A model for teaching English as a foreign language in Syria with particular reference to listening comprehension. TxU, 1985. 366 p. Micro 86–9453
DAI, v. 47A, Aug. 1986: 505.

357

Barbar, Aghil Mohamed. The Tarabulus (Libyan) resistance to the Italian inva-

sion, 1911–1920. WU, 1980. 430 p. Micro 81–6489
DAI, v. 42A, Sept. 1981: 1274.

358
Barcelona, Delia R. A sociology of negative beliefs about the contraceptive pill in Egypt. ICU, 1983.
DAI, v. 44A, Jan. 1984: 2258.

359
Bard, Mitchell G. The water's edge and beyond: defining the limits to domestic influence on U.S. Middle East policy. CLU, 1987. 762 p. Micro 87–19,929
DAI, v. 48A, Dec. 1987: 1534.

360
Barhoum, Khalil Issa. A study of the English oral proficiency of secondary school students in Jordan. DGU, 1985. 237 p. Micro 86–2359
DAI, v. 46A, June 1986: 3703.

361
el-Barouki, Foazi Youssef. A culturally based analysis of selected idiomatic expressions in Syrian Arabic. CSfU, 1985. 156 p. Micro 86–5314
DAI, v. 47A, July 1986: 108–109.

362
Barr, James H. Education for the handicapped in the Arabian Peninsula: issues and trends. NNC-T, 1983. 170 p. Micro 83–22,174
DAI, v. 44A, Nov. 1983: 1415–1416.

363
Barsalou, Judith-Marie. Foreign labor in Sa'udi Arabia: the creation of a plural society. NNC, 1985. 316 p. Micro 85–23,115
DAI, v. 46A, Feb. 1986: 2424.

364
Bartlett, Jean E. Baha'i world faith: a case study in adult socialization. CU-Riv, 1984. 183 p. Micro 84–22,734
DAI, v. 45A, Jan. 1985: 2159.

365
Bartson, Lester J. Cyrenaica in antiquity. MH, 1982. 800 p. Micro 82–22,567
DAI, v. 43A, Nov. 1982: 1637.

366
Basabrain, Abdulla Abdulrahman Ahmad A. Modernization of agriculture: an analysis of incentives, disincentives, and the economical, educational factors influencing the adopting of agricultural innovations in Saudi Arabia. MU, 1983. 404 p. Micro 83–10,265
DAI, v. 44A, July 1983: 231.

367
Basanti, Rifaat Karam. The monetary approach to structural adjustment prob-

lems in less developed countries: a case study of Sudan. IEN, 1985. 245 p.

Micro 85–11,798

DAI, v. 46A, Oct. 1985: 1020.

368

Bashaireh, Ahmed Suleiman. Centralization and decentralization in educational administration: implications for Jordan. InTI, 1982. 207 p.

Micro 83–22,809

DAI, v. 44A, Jan. 1984: 1980.

369

Bashir, Samih Mahmoud. A functional approach to Arabic relative clauses with implications for language teaching. NNC-T, 1982. 199 p.   Micro 82–23,101

DAI, v. 43A, Nov. 1982: 1526.

370

Bassam, Abdulhamid A. An examination of absorptive capacity in Saudi Arabia. MiEM, 1981. 192 p.   Micro 82–2395

DAI, v. 42A, Feb. 1982: 3669–3670.

371

al-Batal, Mahmoud Mohammad Adel. The cohesive role of connectives in a modern expository Arabic text. MiU, 1985. 185 p.   Micro 85–20,857

DAI, v. 46A, Jan. 1986: 1960.

372

Batsh, Moh'd Walid Musa. Adapting McCarthy Scales of Children Abilities (MSCA) for the Jordanian children: a cross-cultural study. InU, 1986. 234 p.

Micro 87–4026

DAI, v. 47A, May 1987: 4069–4070.

373

Battah, Ahmad Mohamad. The occupational ethos of superintendents: comparison between Jordan and the United States. CLSU, 1986.

DAI, v. 47A, Jan. 1987: 2381.

374

Battal, Hamad Saif. Water resources allocation in Saudi Arabia: the case study of al Kharj District. NbU, 1986. 226 p.   Micro 87–4541

DAI, v. 47A, May 1987: 4145.

375

Bauzon, Kenneth E. Islamic nationalism in the Philippines: reflections in socio-political analysis. NcD, 1981. 409 p.   Micro 82–371

DAI, v. 42A, Feb. 1982: 3735.

376

Baylson, Joshua C. Territorial allocation by imperial rivalry: the human legacy in the Near East. ICU, 1985. 138 p.

CDI, 1986, v. 5: 39.

377
Baynard, Sally A. Sudanese foreign policy under Nimeiri, 1969–1982. DGW, 1983. 420 p.   Micro 84–1316
DAI, v. 44A, Apr. 1984: 3149–3150.

378
Bayuk, Mary E. A study of change in the four secular Saudi Arabian universities with an examination of influences of American-educated Saudis. PPiU, 1987. 179 p.   Micro 87–19,286
DAI, v. 48A, Dec. 1987: 1403.

379
Baz, Ahmed Abdullah Saad. Political elite and political development in Kuwait. DGW, 1981. 323 p.   Micro 81–19,893
DAI, v. 42A, Sept. 1981: 1294–1295.

380
al-Bazei, Saad Abdulrahman. Literary Orientalism in nineteenth-century Anglo-American literature: its fomation and continuity. InLP, 1983. 258 p.
                                    Micro 84–7500
DAI, v. 44A, June 1984: 3690.

381
al-Bazi, Mohammed Abdullah. Scopal properties of the Arabic relative clause. WaU, 1983. 232 p.   Micro 84–4877
DAI, v. 44A, May 1984: 3373.

382
el-Bdour, Radi Ibrahim. The Islamic economic system: a theoretical and empirical analysis of money and banking in the Islamic economic framework. ULA, 1984. 437 p.   Micro 85–23,692
DAI, v. 46A, Feb. 1986: 2356.

383
Beattie, Kirk J. Egypt: the struggle for hegemony, 1952–1981. MiU, 1985. 628 p.
                                    Micro 85–12,359
DAI, v. 46A, Oct. 1985: 1072.

384
Beeson, Caroline J. The origins of conflict in the Safawi religious institution. NjP, 1982. 147 p.   Micro 82–21,565
DAI, v. 43A, Oct. 1982: 1251.

385
Beighley, Donn H. Short-branch and cluster habit inheritance in crosses of upland and Egyptian cotton. NmLcU, 1986. 74 p.   Micro 86–29,861
DAI, v. 47B, Mar. 1987: 3864.

386
Beileh, Abdirahman Dualeh. Development financing: the Somali experience and

Arab development finance institutions. WU, 1984. 268 p.   Micro 85–665
DAI, v. 46A, Oct. 1985: 1049.

387
Beinin, Joel. Class conflict and national struggle: labor and politics in Egypt, 1936–1954. MiU, 1982. 548 p.   Micro 83–4441
DAI, v. 43A, Apr. 1983: 3393.

388
Bel-Hag, Ramadan Senussi. Factors related to migration plans among male high school students in a rural area of Libya. MiEM, 1982. 209 p.
                                                                        Micro 82–16,522
DAI, v. 43A, Nov. 1982: 1700.

389
Belaid, Abderrezak. Farmers' risk attitudes in the eastern high plateau region of Algeria: an application of the experimental approach. OrCS, 1985. 247 p.
                                                                        Micro 86–5872.
DAI, v. 47A, July 1986: 254.

390
Belateche, Messaoud. Voix et visages de femmes dans le roman algérien de la langue française. DGW, 1982. 434 p.   Micro 82–17,570
DAI, v. 43A, Dec. 1982: 1988.

391
Belkhamza, Nour-Eddine. Development and improvement of the telephone network in Algeria as a communication and environmental problem: analysis and modeling. NTR, 1982. 217 p.   Micro 83–8227
DAI, v. 43A, May 1983: 3729.

392
Bello, Iysa Ade. *Ijmāʿ* and *taʾwīl* in the conflict between al-Ghazālī and Ibn Rushd. CaOTU, 1985.
DAI, v. 46A, Mar. 1986: 2793.

393
Ben-Marzouk, Karim Ahmed. Comparative investment strategies of the Arab petro-dollars in the United States and Europe. CSdI, 1982. 74 p.
                                                                        Micro 82–20,371
DAI, v. 43A, Oct. 1982: 1238.

394
Ben-Senia, Mohamed. Supply response of cereals in Tunisia. IaAS, 1981. 139 p.
                                                                        Micro 82–9096
DAI, v. 42A, May 1982: 4880.

395
Benabdeljalil, Khalid. Internal migration in Morocco: examination of structural

determinants. PU, 1984. 291 p.   Micro 84–17,262
DAI, v. 45A, Nov. 1984: 1548.

396
Bencherifa, Abdellatif. Agropastoral systems in Morocco: cultural ecology of
tradition and change. MWC, 1986. 415 p.   Micro 86–27,753
DAI, v. 47A, Feb. 1987: 3153–3154.

397
Benco, Nancy L. Organization and technology of pottery production in early
medieval Morocco. NBiSU, 1986. 286 p.   Micro 86–17,889
DAI, v. 47A, Nov. 1986: 1786.

398
Benkato, Omar Mukhtar. Forecasting models for commercial bank asset manage-
ment: the case of Libya. OCU, 1981. 244 p.   Micro 81–23,740
DAI, v. 42A, Nov. 1981: 2204.

399
Benkhial, Abdulhamed Saleh. The socio-economic impacts of wadi irrigation
projects: the case of Wadi Darnah/al-Fatayah Scheme, Libya. MWC, 1985.
451 p.   Micro 85–19,160
DAI, v. 46A, Feb. 1986: 2403.

400
Bennett, Alexander J. Arms transfer as an instrument of Soviet policy in the
Middle East: toward a more complete understanding. DGW, 1986. 376 p.
                                                        Micro 86–15,745
DAI, v. 47A, Oct. 1986: 1475.

401
Benomran, Mohamed Mehdi. al-Ghazzālī's epistemology and cognitive educa-
tional objectives. InU, 1983. 143 p.   Micro 84–29,339
DAI, v. 45A, Mar. 1985: 2795.

402
Berihe, Kassem Mohammed. Assessment of citizens' attitudes toward alternative
approaches to financing public education: the case of the Yemen Arab Republic. FTaSU, 1985. 220 p.   Micro 85–28,696
DAI, v. 46A, Apr. 1986: 2920–2921.

403
Bernal, Victoria. Household agricultural production and off-farm work in a Blue
Nile village, Sudan. IEN, 1985. 457 p.   Micro 86–850
DAI, v. 46A, May 1986: 3394.

404
Bezboruah, Monoranjan. The United States strategy in the Indian Ocean, 1968–
1976. MsU, 1977. 475 p.   Micro 77–28,951
DAI, v. 38A, Jan. 1978: 4357.

405
Bhairi, Abdulmonem Mohamed. Foreign labor in Libya. OkS, 1981. 209 p.
Micro 82–13,009
DAI, v. 43A, July 1982: 229.

406
Biandudi, Joncker K. Ibn. A review of selected materials on the development strategies of Zhou Enlai, Fidel Castro and Gamal Abdel Nasser. OU, 1984. 560 p. Micro 84–18,916
DAI, v. 45A, Dec. 1984: 1856.

407
Biazar, Esfandiar. Rating political risk in Middle Eastern countries and its relationship with foreign direct investment. CSdI, 1982. 143 p.
Micro 82–16,478
DAI, v. 43A, Aug. 1982: 496.

408
Bibas, David. The ethnicization of immigrants: Moroccan Jews in the United States. CLU, 1984. 362 p. Micro 84–28,482
DAI, v. 45A, Mar. 1985: 2910.

409
Bierman, Irene A. Art and politics: the impact of Fatimid uses of *ṭirāz* fabrics. ICU, 1980.
CDI, 1973–1982, v. 33: 390.

410
Bikhazi, Ilyas G. The "news" in the Lebanese foreign exchange market. CLSU, 1986.
DAI, v. 47A, May 1987: 4140.

411
Bikhazi, Ramzi Jibran. The Hamdanid dynasty of Mesopotamia and north Syria, 254–404/868–1014. MiU, 1981. 1055 p. Micro 81–25,070
DAI, v. 42A, Dec. 1981: 2800.

412
al-Bin Ali, Hamad Khalifah. Project analysis procedures for an OPEC country: case study of Qatar's Northwest Gas Dome Project. CoFS, 1986. 221 p.
Micro 87–5437
DAI, v. 47B, May 1987: 4624.

413
Bin Haji Othman, Haji Faisal. Women and nation building: systematic and historical analysis of the problem of women in Islam with special reference to the situation in Malaysia. PPT, 1984. 432 p. Micro 85–9395
DAI, v. 46A, Feb. 1986: 2333.

414
Bin Hamid, Ismail. The emergence of Islamic Malay literature: a case study of

ḥikāyāt. PPT, 1981. 465 p.   Micro 82–10,491
DAI, v. 42A, June 1982: 5155–5156.

415
Bin Manie, Sid Ali. Quality of marriage: role importance, competence, and satisfaction in Saudi Arabia as represented by a sample of Saudi students and their wives in the United States. CLU, 1985. 313 p.   Micro 85–25,835
DAI, v. 46A, Mar. 1986: 2622.

416
Bin Mohd. Yaacob, Abdul Aziz. Islamic banking and economic development.
MdU, 1986. 318 p.   Micro 86–25,759
DAI, v. 47A, Feb. 1987: 3140.

417
Bina, Cyrus. The economics of oil crisis: the cause of the world oil crisis of 1973–74.
DAU, 1983. 224 p.   Micro 83–24, 083
DAI, v. 44A, Dec. 1983: 1879–1880.

418
Binagi, Lloyd A. The genesis of the modern Sudan: an interpretive study of the rise of Afro-Arab hegemony in the Nile Valley, A.D. 1260–1826. PPT, 1981. 495 p.
                                                               Micro 81–24,554
DAI, v. 42A, Nov. 1981: 2249–2250.

419
Binsaleh, Abdullah Mohammed. The civil service and its regulation in the Kingdom of Saudi Arabia. CCC, 1982. 195 p.   Micro 82–20,599
DAI, v. 43A, Oct. 1982: 1285.

420
Birmani, Turki Khabbaz. The impact of the adult educational program on socio-economic development in rural areas of Iraq as perceived by citizens who participated in the program. CoGrU, 1981. 141 p.   Micro 82–6162
DAI, v. 42A, Apr. 1982: 4248.

421
Bishku, Michael B. The British Empire and the question of Egypt's future, 1919–1922. NNU, 1981. 190 p.   Micro 82–10,958
DAI, v. 42A, June 1982: 5213.

422
Blaustein, Michael A. Averroës on the imagination and intellect. MH, 1984.
315 p.   Micro 85–3512
DAI, v. 45A, June 1985: 3659.

423
Blay-Abramski, Irit I. From Damascus to Baghdad: the ʿAbbāsid administrative system as a product of the Umayyad heritage, 41/661–320/932. NjP, 1982.
336 p.   Micro 82–16,291
DAI, v. 43A, Aug. 1982: 516.

424
Blejer, Hatte A. R. Discourse markers in early Semitic, and their reanalysis in subsequent dialects. TxU, 1986. 644 p. Micro 86–18,423
DAI, v. 47A, Nov. 1986: 1712–1713.

425
Blessing, James A. The suspension of foreign aid by the United States, 1948–1972. NAIU, 1975. 261 p. Micro 75–28,878
DAI, v. 36A, Dec. 1975: 4001.

426
Bligh, Alexander B. Succession to the throne in Saudi Arabia: court politics in the twentieth century. NNC, 1981. 295 p. Micro 83–27,183
DAI, v. 44A, Apr. 1984: 3154–3155.

427
Boddy, Janice P. Parallel worlds: humans, spirits, and *zār* possession in rural Northern Sudan. CaBVaU, 1982.
DAI, v. 43A, June 1983: 3956–3957.

428
Bokhorji-Ghawanni, Abdul-Fattah. Utilization of field trips in teaching science in the boys' intermediate schools in Saudi Arabia: a study of educational policy implementation. MiEM, 1985. 308 p. Micro 86–3380
DAI, v. 46A, June 1986: 3671.

429
Boneh, Dan. Facing uncertainty: the social consequences of forced sedentarization among the Jaraween Bedouin, Negev, Israel. MWalB, 1983. 373 p.
Micro 83–18,220
DAI, v. 44A, Oct. 1983: 1139.

430
Bonsnes, Marjorie P. The pilgrimage to Jerusalem: a typological metaphor for women in early medieval religious orders. NNU, 1982. 264 p.
Micro 82–14,786
DAI, v. 43A, Aug. 1982: 516.

431
Bony, Ahmed Mohammed. An evaluation of the guidance and counseling service needs in Libya as perceived by students, teachers, and administrators. CoGrU, 1981. 168 p. Micro 81–19,791
DAI, v. 42A, Sept. 1981: 1004.

432
el-Boraiy, Esam Badrawe. The Egyptian open door policy towards foreign investment: an economic view. ScU, 1982. 175 p. Micro 82–20,196
DAI, v. 43A, Oct. 1982: 1226.

433
Bornstein, Michael S. From revolution to crisis: Egypt-Israel relations, 1952–

1956. NjP, 1986. 562 p.   Micro 86–21,183
DAI, v. 47A, Dec. 1986: 2285.

434
Botman, Selma. Oppositional politics in Egypt: the Communist Movement,
1936–1954. MH, 1984. 594 p.   Micro 84–19,302
DAI, v. 45A, Jan. 1985: 2223.

435
Bou-Rabee, Firyal Ahmed. The geology and geophysics of Kuwait. ScU, 1986.
246 p.   Micro 87–4615
DAI, v. 47B, May 1987: 4452.

436
Bouguerra, Belgacem. The question of the Asiatic mode of production and pre-
colonial Algeria. DAU, 1986. 287 p.   Micro 86–7159
DAI, v. 47A, July 1986: 266.

437
Bourenane, Karima Radja Roudesli. English learning in Algeria: an analysis of
errors and attitudes. TxU, 1984. 269 p.   Micro 84–21,665
DAI, v. 45A, Jan. 1985: 2016.

438
Bourouh, Chaoura. Industrialization and class structure in Algeria. DAU, 1985.
217 p.   Micro 86–7967
DAI, v. 47A, Aug. 1986: 672.

439
Boutata, Mohammed. Education and socio-economic development: the casestudy
of Morocco in the post-colonial period, 1956–1980. CoU, 1983. 206 p.
                                                           Micro 83–17,645
DAI, v. 44A, Oct. 1983: 1164.

440
Bowen, Donna L. Muslim religious attitudes toward family planning in Morocco.
ICU, 1981.
CDI, 1973–1982, v. 33: 484.

441
Bowen, Richard L. Allocative efficiency and equity in charging for irrigation
water: a case study in Egypt. CoFS, 1982. 258 p.   Micro 82–27,911
DAI, v. 43A, Jan. 1983: 2403.

442
Brafman, David A. The Arabic *De Mundo*: an edition with translation and
commentary. NcD, 1985. 462 p.   Micro 86–14,427
DAI, v. 47A, Nov. 1986: 1740.

443
al-Braik, Mubarak Salem. Investigation of the successful attributes of English as a

second language of Saudi Arabian students studying in the United States of America. PSt, 1986. 144 p. Micro 87–5318
DAI, v. 47A, May 1987: 4005.

444
al-Braik, Nasser Ahmad M. Islam and world order: foundations and values. DAU, 1986. 302 p. Micro 86–25,124
DAI, v. 47A, Jan. 1987: 2726.

445
Brand, Laurie A. Building the bridge of return: Palestinian corporate mobilization in Egypt, Kuwait and Jordan. NNC, 1985. 461 p. Micro 86–4599
DAI, v. 47A, July 1986: 302.

446
Brandriss, Marc G. Internal politics and foreign policy in Israel: the search for peace, 1967–1973. NNC, 1983. 355 p. Micro 83–11,823
DAI, v. 44A, July 1983: 272.

447
Brann, Ross I. Structure and meaning in the secular poetry of Moshe ibn Ezra [c. 1055–1138]. NNU, 1981. 277 p. Micro 82–10,961
DAI, v. 42A, June 1982: 5138.

448
Breima, Ali Zayed. Regional government in the Sudan: a conflict resolution formula. CCC, 1984. 292 p. Micro 85–1411
DAI, v. 45A, June 1985: 3742.

449
Bremer, Jennifer A. Alternative for mechanization: public cooperatives and the private sector in Egypt's agriculture. MH, 1982. 451 p. Micro 82–22,594
DAI, v. 43A, Nov. 1982: 1620.

450
Brewer, Douglas J. Cultural and environmental change in the Fayum, Egypt: an investigation based on faunal remains. TU, 1986. 222 p. Micro 86–24,230
DAI, v. 47A, Apr. 1987: 3794.

451
Brink, Judy H. The effect of education and employment on the status of rural Egyptian women. PPiU, 1985. 217 p. Micro 85–19,455
DAI, v. 46A, Jan. 1986: 1988–1989.

452
Browder, Michael H. al-Bīrūnī as a source for Mani and Manichaeism. NcD, 1982. 305 p. Micro 82–21,140
DAI, v. 43A, Oct. 1982: 1193.

453
Brown, Nathan J. Peasants against the state: the political activity of the Egyptian

51

peasantry, 1882–1952. NjP, 1987. 405 p.   Micro 87–14,901
DAI, v. 48A, Oct. 1987: 1006.

454
Brunger, Charles S. The development of the internal market in Algeria, Nigeria, and the Ivory Coast. NNNS, 1983. 283 p.   Micro 85–17,172
DAI, v. 46A, Dec. 1985: 1691–1692.

455
Bu-Salih, Ridha Mohammed. The attitude toward physical recreation of male Saudi students studying in the United States. OrU, 1984. 157 p.
Micro 84–22,836
DAI, v. 45A, Jan. 1985: 2027–2028.

456
Bukhary-Haddad, Mohammed Abdulkarim. Administrative training for development: a survey study of the in-service administrative training programs in Saudi Arabia. PPiU, 1986. 380 p.   Micro 87–8480
DAI, v. 48A, Sept. 1987: 743.

457
Buras, Khalifa Mehdi. The effect of free composition and controlled composition on the performance of twelfth-grade students in the Libyan secondary schools. KU, 1986. 174 p.   Micro 86–19,887
DAI, v. 47A, Mar. 1987: 3339–3340.

458
Burchfield, Shirley A. Improving energy data collection and analysis in developing countries: a comparative study in Uganda, Liberia and Sudan. TxArU, 1986. 356 p.   Micro 87–1096
DAI, v. 47A, Mar. 1987: 3588.

459
Burgess, Fawzi Assaad. Dr. Dahesh's Arabic work, *Memoirs of Jesus, the Nazareth*, an edited translation and an introduction. TMurS, 1982. 231 p.
Micro 83–5558
DAI, v. 43A, Apr. 1983: 3330.

460
Burke, Joseph G. Determinants of U.S. Mideast arms sales policy: a comparative case study. CoDU, 1986. 297 p.   Micro 87–8826
DAI, v. 48A, July 1987: 214.

461
Burkush, Antoine J. Lebanon: ethnicity and change; the politics of administrative reforms. NAlU, 1985. 349 p.   Micro 85–23,303
DAI, v. 46A, Feb. 1986: 2433.

462
Burroughs, Diana. China's foreign policy toward the Arab world. NjP, 1983.

52

150 p. Micro 83–18,716
DAI, v. 44A, Oct. 1983: 1200.

463
Burtoff, Michele J. The logical organization of written expository discourse in English: a comparative study of Japanese, Arabic, and native speaker strategies. DGU, 1983. 211 p. Micro 84–28,443
DAI, v. 45A, Mar. 1985: 2857.

464
Busack, Stephen D. A biogeographical analysis of a vicariant event: the herpeto-fauna of the Gibraltar Strait. CU, 1985. 251 p. Micro 85–24,899
DAI, v. 46B, Mar. 1986: 2973.

465
Canjar, Riec E. I. A structural comparison of spatial organization in conventional and unconventional military systems: the case of the 1954 Algerian Revolution. MiU, 1983. 272 p. Micro 84–2254
DAI, v. 44A, Apr. 1984: 3166.

466
Cantor, Milton. The life of Joel Barlow. NNC, 1954. 496 p. Micro 55–717
DAI, v. 15, Apr. 1955: 562.

467
Carapico, Sheila H. The political economy of self-help: development cooperatives in the Yemen Arab Republic. NBiSU, 1984. 381 p. Micro 84–8393
DAI, v. 45A, July 1984: 289–290.

468
Card, Caroline E. Tuareg music and soclial identity. InU, 1982. 258 p.
Micro 83–1055
DAI, v. 43A, Feb. 1983: 2753.

469
Card, Elizabeth A. A phonetic and phonological study of Arabic emphasis. NIC, 1983. 198 p. Micro 83–9429
DAI, v. 43A, June 1983: 3895.

470
Casillas, Rex J. Oil and diplomacy: the evolution of American foreign policy in Saudi Arabia, 1933–1945. UU, 1983. 244 p. Micro 83–11,119
DAI, v. 44A, July 1983: 264.

471
Caton, Steven C. Tribal poetry as political rhetoric from Khawlan at-Tiyal, Yemen Arab Republic. ICU, 1984. 547 p.
Letter from University of Chicago Library.

472
Chanis, Jonathan A. Soviet policy toward Syria and the lessons of Egypt. NNCU-

G, 1987. 485 p. Micro 87–13,749
DAI, v. 48A, Sept. 1987: 740–741.

473

Chapelle, Carol A. The relationship between ambiguity tolerance and success in acquiring English as a second language in adult [Arab] learners. IU, 1983. 144 p. Micro 84–9888
DAI, v. 45A, July 1984: 102.

474

Charrad, Mounira. Women and the state: a comparative study of politics, law and the family in Tunisia, Algeria and Morocco. MH, 1981.
CDI, 1973–1982, v. 33: 768.

475

Chatah, Mohamad Baha. A monetary framework for the Saudi Arabian economy. TxU, 1983. 280 p. Micro 83–19,575
DAI, v. 44A, Oct. 1983: 1153.

476

Chaudry, Sayeeda Ahmad. Female labor force participation and its relationship to fertility rate: some policy implications for developing countries [Egypt and Morocco]. DGW, 1984. 410 p. Micro 84–14,999
DAI, v. 44A, Oct. 1984: 1204.

477

Chehabi, Houchang Esfandiar. Modernist Shi'ism and politics: the Liberation Movement of Iran. CtY, 1986. 598 p. Micro 86–27,240
DAI, v. 47A, Feb. 1987: 3175.

478

Chergui, Boumediene. On optimization methods for gas liquefaction production in Algeria and for a firewater safety system for the Holy Area of Mina, in Saudi Arabia. TxU, 1986. 215 p. Micro 87–176
DAI, v. 47B, Apr. 1987: 4285.

479

Chevedden, Paul E. The Citadel of Damascus. CLU, 1986. 767 p.
Micro 87–2605
DAI, v. 47A, Apr. 1987: 3854.

480

Chiao, Yen-Shong. Frontier production function approaches for measuring efficiency of Egyptian farmers. CU-A, 1985. 122 p. Micro 86–7575
DAI, v. 47B, Aug. 1986: 705.

481

Chiarelli, Leonard C. Sicily during the Fatimid age. UU, 1986. 285 p.
Micro 86–19,552
DAI, v. 47A, Dec. 1986: 2286.

482
Childs, Timothy W. Mediterranean imbroglio: the diplomatic origins of modern Libya (the diplomacy of the belligerents during the Italo-Turkish War, 1911–1912). DGU, 1982. 358 p. Micro 83–2764
DAI, v. 43A, Mar. 1983: 3080.

483
Cicekdag, Mehmet Ali. The dependence of Middle Eastern countries on foreign food. CU-SB, 1980. 338 p. Micro 81–20,744
DAI, v. 42A, Oct. 1981: 1778–1779.

484
Clark, Arthur L. Ecology of the Eleonora's falcon in Morocco. NIC, 1981. 415 p.
Micro 81–29,712
DAI, v. 42B, Feb. 1982: 3099.

485
Clark, Grace C. Pakistan's *zakāt* and *'ushr* system: an Islamic public welfare system in a developing country. MdU-P, 1985. 460 p. Micro 86–3199
DAI, v. 47A, Aug. 1986: 658.

486
Cloud, Kathleen O. Gender equity and efficiency in AID's agricultural projects: a study of policy implementation. MH, 1986. 244 p. Micro 86–20,692
DAI, v. 47A, Dec. 1986: 2249.

487
Coddington, Iqbal Jwaideh. A study in Arab polygyny. InU, 1980. 365 p.
Micro 81–12,482
DAI, v. 42A, Aug. 1981: 756–757.

488
Coffin, Millard F. Evolution of the conjugate East African-Madagascan margins and the Western Somali Basin. NNC, 1985. 338 p. Micro 85–23,139
DAI, v. 46B, May 1986: 3762.

489
Cohen, Ben-Zion. Jewish and Arab male offenders in Israel: a study of ethnicity, class and minority experience. PBm, 1981. 178 p. Micro 82–9722
DAI, v. 42A, May 1982: 4939.

490
Cole, Juan R. I. Imāmī Shi'ism from Iran to North India, 1722–1856: state, society and clerical ideology in Awadh [Oudh]. CLU, 1984. 495 p.
Micro 84–28,498
DAI, v. 45A, Mar. 1985: 2966–2967.

491
Cole, Penny J. The preaching of the crusades to the Holy Land, 1095–1270. CaOTU, 1985.
DAI, v. 46A, Mar. 1986: 2720.

492
Coles, Catherine M. Muslim women in town: social change among the Hausa of
Northern Nigeria. WU, 1983. 556 p.   Micro 83–23,369
DAI, v. 44A, Mar. 1984: 2813.

493
Collins, Jeffrey G. The Egyptian elite under Cromer, 1882–1907. CLU, 1981.
396 p.   Micro 81–20,934
DAI, v. 42A, Oct. 1981: 1749.

494
Combs-Schilling, Margaret E. Traders on the move: a Moroccan case study in
change. CU, 1981. 253 p.   Micro 82–60
DAI, v. 42A, Jan. 1982: 3213.

495
Commins, David D. The *salafi* Islamic reform movement in Damascus, 1885–
1914: religious intellectuals, politics, and social change in late Ottoman Syria.
MiU, 1985. 432 p.   Micro 86–426
DAI, v. 46A, May 1986: 3467.

496
Connelly, Nancy D. Temporary middlemen: Hindu and Moslem Asians in
Bulawayo. TxDaM, 1983. 284 p.   Micro 84–8240
DAI, v. 45A, July 1984: 229.

497
Conner, Thomas H. Parliament and the making of foreign policy [related to
Tunisia (1881), Egypt (1882) and Morocco (1911–1912)]: France under the
Third Republic, 1875–1914. NcU, 1983. 480 p.   Micro 83–26,205
DAI, v. 44A, Jan. 1984: 2220.

498
Conrad, Lawrence I. The plague in the early medieval Near East. NjP, 1981.
543 p.   Micro 81–19,113
DAI, v. 42A, Sept. 1981: 1269.

499
Cornell, Marguerite L. The University of Kuwait: an historical-comparative
study of purposes in a new university in a developing nation. CaQMM, 1982.
DAI, v. 43A, Mar. 1983: 2901.

500
Coronis, Susan D. The impact of trade unions on policy making in Egypt,
1952–1984. IEN, 1985. 319 p.   Micro 85–11,810
DAI, v. 46A, Oct. 1985: 1073.

501
Coury, Ralph M. Abd al-Rahman Azzam and the development of Egyptian Arab

nationalism. NjP, 1984. 706 p. Micro 84–17,411
DAI, v. 45A, Jan. 1985: 2225–2226.

502
Craig, Richard S. Expectations and adjustment in energy markets. MBU, 1986.
254 p. Micro 86–2337
DAI, v. 46A, June 1986: 3800.

503
Crawford, LouEllen. An examination of the relationship between women's formal
education and national income [Egypt]. CoDU, 1982. 177 p.
Micro 83–15,895
DAI, v. 44A, Sept. 1983: 885.

504
Crosby, Elise W. *Akhbār al-Yaman wa-ashʿāruhā wa-ansābuhā*: the history, poetry, and
genealogy of the Yemen of ʿAbīd [ʿUbayd] b. Sharya al-Jurhumī. CtY, 1985.
387 p. Micro 86–1079
DAI, v. 46A, May 1986: 3367.

505
Crystal, Jill. Patterns of state-building in the Arabian gulf: Kuwait and Qatar.
MH, 1986. 401 p. Micro 86–20,450
DAI, v. 47A, Dec. 1986: 2297.

506
Cuno, Kenneth M. Landholding, society and economy in rural Egypt, 1740–
1850: a case study of al-Daqahliyya Province. CLU, 1985. 604 p.
Micro 85–25,844
DAI, v. 46A, Mar. 1986: 2787.

507
Dabaan, Ibrahim S. Implications of error analysis for the teaching of English
phonology to Saudi students. KU, 1983. 111 p. Micro 84–3608
DAI, v. 44A, May 1984: 3309.

508
Dabashi, Hamid. Prophetic authority and its aftermath: variations in the process
of institutionalization of Muhammad's charismatic authority. PU, 1984. 308 p.
Micro 84–17,282
DAI, v. 45A, Nov. 1984: 1532–1533.

509
Dablan, Farouk A. The rise and fall of a U.N. Peace-Keeping Force. NjP, 1979,
240 p. Micro 80–3776
DAI, v. 40A, Feb. 1980: 4735.

510
Dabous, Adel Ahmed A. Mineralogy, geochemistry and radioactivity of some

57

Egyptian phosphorite deposits. FTaSU, 1981. 217 p.   Micro 82–5690
DAI, v. 42B, Apr. 1982: 3987–3988.

511
Daffa, Mohamad Saied. An experimental EFL unit on the sound structure of
English for seventh grade students of Saudi junior high schools. KU, 1983.
198 p.   Micro 84–3609
DAI, v. 44A, May 1984: 3387.

512
Dagel, Gena E. Paul Bowles: manufactured savage. TxU, 1984. 300 p.
                                                         Micro 86–21,749
DAI, v. 47A, Dec. 1986: 2205.

513
Daham, Abdullah Abdulrahman. The growth of the *ḥajj*: a decade of increasing
pilgrims to Mecca, 1970–1979. CCC, 1981. 231 p.   Micro 81–26,405
DAI, v. 42A, Dec. 1981: 2724.

514
Dahbi, Mohammed. The development of English writing skills by Moroccan
university students. DGU, 1984. 307 p.   Micro 85–15,682
DAI, v. 46A, Nov. 1985: 1264.

515
Dahdah, Mary Sue. Guidelines for a model American school for Jordanians. ArU,
1982. 228 p.   Micro 83–5090
DAI, v. 43A, Apr. 1983: 3164.

516
Daher, Salim A. From crisis to crisis: Saudi-American relations, 1973–1979. MH,
1983. 362 p.   Micro 83–11,923
DAI, v. 44A, July 1983: 278.

517
al-Daihan, Mohammed Abdul-Rahman. Perception of Saudi male academic
public secondary school administrators and teachers in Riyadh concerning
shortages of Saudi male teachers in secondary public schools in Saudi Arabia.
CoGrU, 1982. 262 p.   Micro 83–1130
DAI, v. 43A, Mar. 1983: 2869.

518
Dajani, Munther S. Conflict and conflict resolution: political initiatives and
formulas for peace in the Middle East. TxU, 1982. 373 p.   Micro 82–17,845
DAI, v. 43A, Sept. 1982: 911–912.

519
el-Dajani, Nour Kamel. Popular participation: a Jordanian attempt. NSyU,
1984. 253 p.   Micro 85–3326
DAI, v. 45A, June 1985: 3761–3762.

520
Dajani, Souad R. Health care and development: case study of the Israeli occupied West Bank. CaOTU, 1984.
DAI, v. 45A, Mar. 1985: 3006.

521
al-Dakheel, Fawaz Mohammed. The potential of videotex in the Kingdom of Saudi Arabia: a descriptive study. MiDW, 1984. 390 p.   Micro 85–4843
DAI, v. 45A, June 1985: 3472.

522
el-Dalee, Mohamed Saleh. The feature of retraction in Arabic. InU, 1984. 190 p.
Micro 84–17,197
DAI, v. 45A, Nov. 1984: 1383.

523
Damous, Hassan Mohammed Hassan. Economic analysis of government policies with respect to supply and demand for wheat and wheat products in Sudan. WaPS, 1986. 255 p.   Micro 87–2536
DAI, v. 47A, Apr. 1987: 3826.

524
al-Daood, Nasir Abdulaziz. The effectiveness of the curriculum as perceived by faculty and students in the Department of Education, Social Science College, Imam Mohammed Ibn Saud Islamic University. CoGrU, 1983. 136 p.
Micro 83–24,318
DAI, v. 44A, Mar. 1984: 2662.

525
Daoudi, Mohammed S. Political dynamics of economic sanctions: a case study of Arab oil embargoes. ScU, 1981. 534 p.   Micro 81–29,493
DAI, v. 42A, Jan. 1982: 3291–3292.

526
Daoudi, Mohammed S. The politactics of iternational cartels: economic illusions, political realities, and OPEC. TxU, 1984. 474 p.   Micro 84–21,685
DAI, v. 45A, Jan. 1985: 2248.

527
al-Darazi, Farida Abdulwahab. Assessment of Bahraini women's health and illness cognitions and practices. IU-M, 1987. 241 p.   Micro 87–12,355
DAI, v. 48B, Sept. 1987: 701.

528
Darrat, Ali Frag. A monetarist approach to inflation for Saudi Arabia. InU, 1982. 221 p.   Micro 83–1058
DAI, v. 43A, Feb. 1983: 2748–2749.

529
D'Aste Surcouf, Alexandra A. The impact of socio-economic and nationalistic

factors on the international uses of English: a case study of Birzeit University. MiU, 1983. 206 p.　　　　　　　　　　　　　　　　Micro 84–2227
DAI, v. 44A, Apr. 1984: 3053–3054.

530
David, Amal Khalil. The Arab stereotype as portrayed in Detroit public high schools: impact of social environment. OU, 1982. 151 p.　　　Micro 83–5314
DAI, v. 43A, Apr. 1983: 3151.

531
David, Steven R. The realignment of Third World regimes from one superpower to the other: Ethiopia's Mengistu, Somalia's Siad and Egypt's Sadat. MH, 1981.
CDI, 1973–1982, v. 34: 188.

532
Davies, Humphrey T. Seventeenth-century Egyptian Arabic: a profile of the colloquial material in Yūsuf al-Shirbīnī's *Hazz al-quhūf fī sharh qaṣīd Abī Shādūf.* CU, 1981. 519 p.　　　　　　　　　　　　　　　　Micro 82–73
DAI, v. 42A, Jan. 1982: 3135–3136.

533
Davis, Ruth F. Modern trends in the *Maʻlūf* of Tunisia, 1934–1984. NjP, 1986. 296 p.　　　　　　　　　　　　　　　　Micro 86–29,428
DAI, v. 47A, Mar. 1987: 3229.

534
Dawood, Ibrahim Abdallah S. *The Panchatantra, Kalīlah wa Dimnah,* and *The Morall Philosophie of Doni*: a comparative study. InU, 1983. 165 p.
Micro 83–21,371
DAI, v. 44A, Nov. 1983: 1443.

535
Dawoud, Tahia Abdel-Hameed. How Egypt and the United States portray each other: changes in world history textbooks, 1960–1980. PPiU, 1982. 113 p.
Micro 83–3609
DAI, v. 43A, Mar. 1983: 2953.

536
Daza, Mahmoud Hassan. Understanding the traditional built environment: crisis, change, and the issue of human needs in the context of habitations and settlements in Libya. PU, 1982. 389 p.　　　　　　　　Micro 83–7302
DAI, v. 43A, May 1983: 3443.

537
de Jong, Olga A. Perception of the female role in Saudi Arabian society. AzU, 1986. 227 p.　　　　　　　　　　　　　　　　Micro 87–8558
DAI, v. 47A, June 1987: 4351.

538

De Mabior, John G. Identifying, selecting, and implementing rural development strategies for socio-economic development in the Jonglei Projects Area, Southern Region, Sudan. IaAS, 1981. 288 p.   Micro 82–9113
DAI, v. 42A, May 1982: 4873.

539

De Munck, Victor C. Cross-currents of conflict and cooperation in Kotabowa [Sri Lanka]. CU-Riv, 1985. 516 p.   Micro 86–4125
DAI, v. 46A, June 1986: 3767.

540

De Waard, Hendrik. The spiritual experience of al-Ghazzālī: a Christian response. CPFT, 1981. 243 p.   Micro 81–18,656
DAI, v. 42A, Sept. 1981: 1189.

541

De Young, Gregg R. The arithmetic books of Euclid's *Elements* in the Arabic tradition: an edition, translation, and commentary. MH, 1981.
CDI, 1973–1982, v. 34: 275.

542

al-Debassi, Saleh Mobarak. The impact of training programs, availability of educational media and school facilities on teachers' use of educational media in Saudi intermediate and high schools. PPiU, 1983. 158 p.   Micro 83–27,720
DAI, v. 44A, Feb. 1984: 2331.

543

Deguilhem-Schoem, Randi C. History of *waqf* and case studies from Damascus in late Ottoman and French Mandatory times. NNU, 1986. 445 p.
Micro 86–26,861
DAI, v. 47A, Feb. 1987: 3164–3165.

544

Deiry, Ali Mahid. An evaluation of the physical education programs in selected secondary school districts in Jordan. NmU, 1983. 302 p.   Micro 84–10,687
DAI, v. 45A, Nov. 1984: 1333.

545

Delin, Ayla S. Identity characteristics of seventh through twelfth grade third culture dependents at Cairo American College, Egypt. MiEM, 1986. 307 p.
Micro 86–25,013
DAI, v. 47A, Jan. 1987: 2500.

546

Deng, Lual Acuek Lual. The Abyei Development Project: a case study of cattle herders in the Sudan. WU, 1984. 276 p.   Micro 84–24,502
DAI, v. 46A, July 1985: 209.

547

Derbas, Ahmed Said Sulayman. To establish the degree of interest for new technical instructional programs at Taif Junior College, Saudi Arabia. MiKW, 1985. 130 p.   Micro 85–26,122
DAI, v. 46A, Mar. 1986: 2536.

548

al-Derhim, Abdul Rahman Hasan. A study of organizational climate perceptions in elemantary and intermediate schools in Qatar. NBuU, 1984. 209 p.
Micro 85–3678
DAI, v. 46A, Aug. 1985: 305.

549

Dethier, Jean-Jacques. The political economy of food prices in Egypt. CU, 1985. 309 p.   Micro 85–24,930
DAI, v. 46A, Mar. 1986: 2762.

550

Deuson, Robert R. The Lower Moulouya Irrigation Project: an assessment of its socio-economic impact on the northeast of Morocco. MnU, 1983. 441 p.
Micro 83–29,510
DAI, v. 44A, Mar. 1984: 2832.

551

DeWeese, Devin A. The *Kashf al-hudá* of Kamāl al-Dīn Ḥsayn Khorezmi: a fifteenth-century sufi commentary on the *Qaṣīdat al-burdah* in Khorezmian Turkic (Text edition, translation, and historical introduction). InU, 1985. 607 p.   Micro 85–26,998
DAI, v. 46A, Apr. 1986: 3131.

552

al-Dhafiri, Abdul Wahab Mohammed. Women, labor force participation, and equality: a study of educated women in Kuwait. OU, 1987. 214 p.
Micro 87–9968
DAI, v. 48A, July 1987: 219.

553

al-Dharrab, Ibrahim Abdul-Aziz. Economic analysis of interest-free economies. CSt, 1987. 301 p.   Micro 87–7620
DAI, v. 48A, Aug. 1987: 450.

554

Dhohayan, Abdulrahman Ibrahim. Islamic resource sharing network: a feasibility study for its establishment among university libraries of Saudi Arabia and the Republic of Turkey as representative Islamic nations. CLSU, 1981.
DAI, v. 42A, Apr. 1982: 4189.

555

Dhufar, Talal Obaid. A survey of the English language supervisors and teachers'

perceptions of the English language curriculum in the secondary schools in Saudi Arabia. MiEM, 1986. 183 p. Micro 86–25,015
DAI, v. 47A, Jan. 1987: 2548.

556
Diab, Ismail Mohamed. The development of a mathematical planning model for the estimation of school enrollment and teaching staff demand in Egypt. PSt, 1981. 242 p. Micro 81–20,418
DAI, v. 42A, Oct. 1981: 1395–1396.

557
Dileym, Fahd Abdullah Ali. Determinant factors in the utilization process of social services in Saudi Arabia. MiKW, 1985. 225 p. Micro 85–14,485
DAI, v. 46A, Nov. 1985: 1415.

558
Djabelkhir, Aissa. Africa and the Third United Nations Conference on the Law of the Sea: case study of Algeria. FMU, 1984. 261 p. Micro 84–25,901
DAI, v. 45A, Feb. 1985: 2641–2642.

559
Dodoo, Nii Martey Samuel. On the micro-level decisions to limit fertility: a theoretical framework and econometric estimation using Taiwan, Korea and urban Sudan data. PU, 1985. 165 p. Micro 85–23,406
DAI, v. 46A, Feb. 1986: 2374–2375.

560
al-Dokheal, Ibrahim Ali. The relationship between mathematics problem solving ability and Piagetian level of cognitive development in sixth grade male, Saudi Arabian pupils. CoGrU, 1983. 155 p. Micro 83–24,319
DAI, v. 44A, Mar. 1984: 2675.

561
Doost-Mohammadi, Ahmad. The line of the Imam [Khomeini]. CCC, 1984. 213 p. Micro 84–7452
DAI, v. 44A, June 1984: 3794.

562
Dora, Mohamed Kamal Mohamed. Wittgenstein's conception of philosophy and its implications for the teaching of philosophy in secondary schools [in Egypt]. PPiU, 1984. 290 p. Micro 85–270
DAI, v. 45A, May 1985: 3317–3318.

563
Dorani, Mohamed B. Benefits and constraints in establishing and maintaining a multi-country computer and information network system for the Gulf Co-operation Council's (GCC) community. DGW, 1986. 428 p.
Micro 87–13,513
DAI, v. 48A, Sept. 1987: 693–694.

564
Dossa, Parin Aziz. Ritual and daily life: transmission and interpretation of the Ismaili tradition in Vancouver. CaBVaU, 1985.
DAI, v. 47A, Oct. 1986: 1383.

565
Dossary, Saleh Jassim. Guidance needs of secondary school students in Saudi Arabia. CoDU, 1981. 378 p.   Micro 82–9743
DAI, v. 42A, June 1982: 5024.

566
al-Dousary, Ibrahim Salih. Shopping destination choice: a case study of Riyadh, Saudi Arabia. OCU, 1987. 173 p.   Micro 87–12,705
DAI, v. 48A, Sept. 1987: 719–720.

567
Dowdy, William L. International politics of the Persian Gulf states from a sub-systemic core perspective. LNT, 1982. 571 p.   Micro 82–26,691
DAI, v. 43A, Dec. 1982: 2087.

568
Dredi, Ibrahim B. OPEC as a non-state actor: formation and dynamics. MoU, 1982. 255 p.   Micro 83–10,384
DAI, v. 44A, Aug. 1983: 565.

569
al-Drees, Ibrahim Andulrahman. Leadership as a variable in institution building: toward qualified leadership for junior colleges in Saudi Arabia. InU, 1982. 251 p.   Micro 83–1091
DAI, v. 43A, Feb. 1983: 2565.

570
Drejer, Francis J. From *negaʿ* [camp] to *ʿizba* [village]: continuity and change among the Awlād ʿAlī of Egypt's Western Desert. IEN, 1985. 238 p.
Micro 85–11,812
DAI, v. 46A, Oct. 1985: 1014.

571
Dressler, James B. Anglo-American rivalry at the Cairo and Teheran Conferences, 1943. TMurS, 1983. 214 p.   Micro 84–4782
DAI, v. 44A, May 1984: 3409.

572
Driss, Sadok. Evaluation research and agricultural development: a Tunisian case study. IU, 1986. 250 p.   Micro 86–23,286
DAI, v. 47A, Jan. 1987: 2672.

573
al-Duaij, Abdulaziz D-M. A study of the impact of supervisory style on teachers'

job satisfaction in the secondary schools in Kuwait. MiKW, 1986. 138 p.
Micro 87–3915
DAI, v. 48A, July 1987: 12.

574
al-Dubaiban, Saleh Mossa. Analysis of teaching behaviors of science teachers trained at the SMC [Science and Mathematics Center] and determination of faculty policies toward these bahaviors in Dammam, Saudi Arabia. CoGrU, 1983. 134 p.   Micro 84–8141
DAI, v. 45A, July 1984: 142.

575
Dubuisson, Patricia R. A history of ʿUmān and Masqat, c. 1750–1800. CaQMM, 1982.
DAI, v. 43A, Oct. 1982: 1251.

576
Duella, Abdunasser Ibrahim. An econometric model of Iraq, 1960–1976. OCU, 1983. 165 p.   Micro 83–23,205
DAI, v. 44A, Mar. 1984: 2819.

577
Dulyakasem, Uthai. Education and ethnic nationalism: a study of the Muslim-Malays in southern Siam. CSt, 1981. 279 p.   Micro 81–24,055
DAI, v. 42A, Nov. 1981: 2063–2064.

578
Dumiati, Fouziah Ibraheem. A study of influences on student attrition in girls' secondary schools in Saudi Arabia. MiEM, 1986. 309 p.   Micro 86–25,017
DAI, v. 47A, Jan. 1987: 2435.

579
Dumiati, Sultanah Ibraaheem. An exploratory study of the educational behaviors, aspirations, and attitudes of Saudi wives who reside abroad with their husbands who are studying in the United States. MiEM, 1986. 344 p.
Micro 87–462
DAI, v. 47A, Mar. 1987: 3293–3294.

580
Dundas, Mary L. Socio-economic influence on the use of sorghum products and nutritional status of children in Sudan. MsSM, 1984. 143 p.
Micro 84–28,141
DAI, v. 45B, Mar. 1985: 2874.

581
al-Duri, Dhia Hassan. Developing a youth leadership curriculum: perceptions of the Iraqi family. CoGrU, 1983. 126 p.   Micro 83–24,320
DAI, v. 44A, Dec. 1983: 1675.

582

al-Duwaihees, Mohammad E. Long-range planning and Kuwaiti commercial banks' executives: assessment and evaluation. CSdI, 1987. 247 p.

Micro 87−14,637

DAI, v. 48A, Oct. 1987: 978.

583

Dyer, Mark F. The foreign trade of western Libya, 1750−1830. MBU, 1987. 410 p.   Micro 87−9636

DAI, v. 48A, July 1987: 200.

584

Ead, Ragaa Ahmed. Attitudes of Egyptian teachers toward selected inquiry/ discovery techniques and curricular content in secondary social studies. MsSM, 1983. 127 p.   Micro 84−13,940

DAI, v. 45A, Sept. 1984: 700.

585

Early, Evelyn A. *Baladī* women of Cairo, Egypt: sociability and therapeutic action. ICU, 1980.

CDI, 1973−1982, v. 34: 396.

586

al-Ebraheem, Yousef Hamad. The optimal rate of oil production and economic development: the case of Kuwait. CCC, 1984. 267 p.   Micro 84−11,900

DAI, v. 45A, Aug. 1984: 578.

587

Ebrahim, Abdul Fadl Mohsin. Islamic ethics and the implications of modern biomedical technology: an analysis of some issues pertaining to reproductive control, biotechnical parenting and abortion. PPT, 1986. 216 p.

Micro 86−27,445

DAI, v. 47A, Feb. 1987: 3066.

588

Eddebbarh, Abdesselam. Study and modeling of dairy cattle production systems in four areas of Morocco. MnU, 1986. 191 p.   Micro 86−25,885

DAI, v. 47B, Feb. 1987: 3178.

589

Egger, Vernon O. A Fabian in Egypt: Salāmah Mūsá's ideology for the new class, 1909−1939. MiU, 1983. 390 p.   Micro 83−14,271

DAI, v. 44A, Aug. 1983: 551−552.

590

al-Eidarous, al-Sayed Omar Hussein. An objective policy for selection and assignment of Saudi Arabian foreign ministry personnel. CoGrU, 1982. 94 p.

Micro 82−13,264

DAI, v. 43B, July 1982: 176.

591
al-Eisa, Abdulaziz Ahmed. An ecological study of Bedouin elementary school education in Hail Province, Saudi Arabia. AzU, 1985. 237 p.
Micro 85–29,393
DAI, v. 46A, May 1986: 3246.

592
al-Eisa, Bader Hamad. A qualitative study: the low and middle-income housing problem in the State of Kuwait. MnU, 1985. 248 p.　　　Micro 86–2885
DAI, v. 46A, June 1986: 3860.

593
Eisa, Mustafa M. A. A cross-cultural study of work motivation: a comparison of motivational issues with salespersons in the U.S.A. and Iraq. InLP, 1982. 153 p.
Micro 83–901
DAI, v. 43A, Feb. 1983: 2602.

594
Eissa, Garoot Suleiman. International migration as a channel for the transfer of productive capacity between rich and poor countries: the case of the Sudan. PPiU, 1986. 262 p.　　　Micro 86–20,198
DAI, v. 47A, Feb. 1987: 3119.

595
Ekhtiar, Rochelle S. Fictions of Enlightenment: the [Middle East] Oriental tale in eighteenth-century England. MWalB, 1985. 358 p.　　　Micro 85–9822
DAI, v. 46A, Sept. 1985: 705.

596
Elarabi, Ali Mohamed. The political attitudes, ideologies, and activities of trade unionism in the Sudan public sector. CCC, 1983. 219 p.　　　Micro 83–9656
DAI, v. 43A, June 1983: 4034–4035.

597
Elarabi, Ali Mohamed Ali. Education and bureaucratic modernization in Sudan. CCC, 1985. 168 p.　　　Micro 85–17,261
DAI, v. 46A, Dec. 1985: 1456.

598
Elbadri, Sadat Abdurrazagh. Education in Syria: an historical review and report on the status of curriculum and curriculum planning. NBuU, 1984. 186 p.
Micro 84–17,921
DAI, v. 45A, Nov. 1984: 1283–1284.

599
Elbashir, Hassabel Rasoul Abbas. Monetary approach to the balance of payments under fixed exchange rates: the case of Sudan. InU, 1984. 222 p.
Micro 85–1444
DAI, v. 45A, May 1985: 3397.

600

Elbhloul, Taeib Abdallah. Italian colonialism, the Young Turks and the Libyan resistance, 1908–1918. CU-SB, 1986. 547 p.   Micro 87–3650
DAI, v. 48A, July 1987: 204.

601

Elbiad, Mohamed. A sociolinguistic study of the Arabization process and its conditioning factors in Morocco. NBuU, 1985. 468 p.   Micro 85–28,252
DAI, v. 46A, May 1986: 3334–3335.

602

Elcott, David M. The political resocialization of German Jews in Palestine, 1933–1939. NNC, 1981. 413 p.   Micro 81–25,279
DAI, v. 42A, Dec. 1981: 2935.

603

Eldahry, Ahmed Kamal. Budgeting and policy analysis: the Egyptian case. NBiSU, 1981. 167 p.   Micro 81–21,166
DAI, v. 42A, Dec. 1981: 2852.

604

Eldahry, Ragaa Osman. Comparative labor policy in Egypt. NBiSU, 1987. 185 p.
Micro 87–8612
DAI, v. 48A, Aug. 1987: 478.

605

Eldamatty, Abdul Ghaffar Abdul Hakim. A descriptive and demographic analysis of educable mentally retarded graduates of the Mataria Center in Egypt and perceptions of competencies, knowledge, and skills required for independent living: a need-assessment study. MiEM, 1984. 294 p.   Micro 85–3203
DAI, v. 46A, Aug. 1985: 398.

606

Elebiary, Sohier Hussein Ahmed. Population education instructional objectives for Egyptian secondary schools. MBU-E, 1983. 230 p.   Micro 83–19,887
DAI, v. 44A, Nov. 1983: 1342.

607

Elfiki, Fakhry A. Foreign economic assistance and the Egyptian economy. MWC, 1984. 146 p.   Micro 84–22,512
DAI, v. 45A, Jan. 1985: 2169.

608

Elgadi, Abdalla Salem. Tripolitanean Arabic phonology and morphology: a generative approach. DGU, 1986. 252 p.   Micro 87–7342
DAI, v. 47A, June 1987: 4375.

609

Elgari, Mohamed Ali. The pattern of economic development in Saudi Arabia as

a product of its social structure. CU-Riv, 1983. 243 p.   Micro 84–5520
DAI, v. 44A, June 1984: 3746.

610
Elgibali, Alaa Abdelmoneim. Towards a sociolinguistic analysis of language variation in Arabic: Cairene and Kuwaiti dialects. PPiU, 1985. 158 p.
Micro 86–17,152
DAI, v. 47A, Nov. 1986: 1713–1714.

611
Elgindi, Ibtessam A. Rural radio in Egypt: its promise and performance. FTaSU, 1986. 322 p.   Micro 86–12,199
DAI, v. 47A, Sept. 1986: 700.

612
Elhillali, Ahmed Mohammad. Legal and economic aspects of agriculture investments in the Democratic Republic of the Sudan. DGW, 1984. 224 p.
Micro 87–3110
DAI, v. 47A, June 1987: 4498–4499.

613
Eliraqi, Iraqi A. The impact of Egyptian investment incentives on the investment decisions of multinational enterprises. ArU, 1982. 146 p.   Micro 83–22,898
DAI, v. 44A, Dec. 1983: 1839–1840.

614
Eljazz, Awad Ahmed Mohammed. Managerial motivation for organization effectiveness in the Sudan. CLSU, 1982.
DAI, v. 43A, July 1982: 261.

615
Elkaddi, Ibrahim Mohamed. Typological production in architecture: the underlying principles in modern mass housing [Gourna, Egypt]. PU, 1983. 290 p.
Micro 84–6663
DAI, v. 44A, June 1984: 3521.

616
Elkadi, Jihad Atef. Money supply determination and policies of the Central Bank in Kuwait. GU, 1985. 136 p.   Micro 85–19,602
DAI, v. 46A, Jan. 1986: 2016.

617
Elkhanjari, Alkoni Ahmed. Effects of different teaching strategies and preinstructional backgrounds of the learners upon the instructional effectiveness of Libyan high school teachers. AzU, 1981. 139 p.   Micro 81–16,821
DAI, v. 42A, Aug. 1981: 610.

618
Elkhatib, Ahmed Shafik Abdelwahab. Case studies of four Egyptian college

freshman writers majoring in English. NNC-T, 1984. 285 p.   Micro 85–5361
DAI, v. 46A, Oct. 1985: 969.

619
Ellis, Marsha A. A re-examination of the contributions of Nelson Glueck to the archeological study of Transjordan in light of recent evidence. TxFS, 1985.
DAI, v. 46A, Feb. 1986: 2347–2348.

620
Elmassian, Sarkis A. The relationship of the Lebanese conflict to the educational achievement of Lebanese Armenian students. MiU, 1983. 137 p.
Micro 83–14,272
DAI, v. 44A, Aug. 1983: 458.

621
Elmekki, Abdelgalil Mahdi. Peasants and capital: the politial economy of oilseeds marketing in the Sudan. CaOTU, 1986.
DAI, v. 47A, Dec. 1986: 2298.

622
Elmoghirah, Abdullah Othman. A survey of the availability and use of instructional aids in mathematics in the public elementary schools in the District of Riyadh in Saudi Arabia. MoU, 1983. 173 p.   Micro 84–6184
DAI, v. 44A, June 1984: 3620.

623
Elmuti, Salah Dean. The effect of participatory programs similar to quality control circles on organizational productivity in selected multinational organizations in Saudi Arabia. TxDN, 1985. 191 p.   Micro 85–15,716
DAI, v. 46A, Nov. 1985: 1344.

624
Elnashar, Adel Mohamed. An evaluative study of the Egyptian Sport Council. PPiU, 1984. 132 p.   Micro 85–12,547
DAI, v. 46A, Oct. 1985: 923.

625
Elnashar, Narymane Abdulhameed. Islamic education: a resource unit for secondary schools in Egypt. OU, 1982. 256 p.   Micro 83–5323
DAI, v. 43A, Apr. 1983: 3279.

626
Elobeid, Hashim Ahmed. Economics of charging for irrigation water in the Gezira Scheme, Sudan. CoFS, 1986. 211 p.   Micro 87–5450
DAI, v. 47A, May 1987: 4145–4146.

627
Eloul, Rohn. Culture change in a bedouin tribe: an ethnographic history of the

'Arab al-Hjerat, lower Galilee, Israel ca. A.D. 1790–1977. MiU, 1982. 603 p.
Micro 82–24,941
DAI, v. 43A, Dec. 1982: 2017.

628
Elrousan, Faroug Farie. Developing a Jordanian adaptation of the American Association on Mental Deficiency Adaptive Behavior Scale, Public School Version, Part 1. MiEM, 1981. 183 p. Micro 81–26,498
DAI, v. 42A, Dec. 1981: 2609–2610.

629
Elsayed, Mahmoud Kamel. A selective historical study of Egyptian, United States and European domestic woodworking styles: its application to art education. OrU, 1981. 341 p. Micro 81–23,486
DAI, v. 42A, Nov. 1981: 1911.

630
Elsayed, Yousria Ahmed. The successive-unsettled transitions of migration and their impact on postpartum concerns of Arab immigrant women. CU-Sf, 1986. 186 p. Micro 86–19,571
DAI, v. 47B, Dec. 1986: 2370–2371.

631
Elshaygi, Gaafar Hassan. A road investment model for the Sudan. TU, 1983. 252 p. Micro 83–19,320
DAI, v. 44A, Oct. 1983: 1203–1204.

632
Eltrug, Nuri Sadegh. Analysis of the Arab learners' errors in pronunciation of English utterances in isolation and context. KU, 1984. 217 p.
Micro 85–13,798
DAI, v. 46A, Oct. 1985: 963–964.

633
Elwarfally, Mahmoud Gebril. U.S. policy toward Libya, 1969–1982: the role of image. PPiU, 1985. 391 p. Micro 85–21,509
DAI, v. 46A, Mar. 1986: 2800–2801.

634
Elwedyani, Sulaiman Ghaith. A cross-sectional investigation of the production, recognition, and sensitivity of some Arab learners of English as a foreign language. DGU, 1982. 186 p. Micro 83–2768
DAI, v. 43A, Mar. 1983: 2983.

635
Emarah, Riad el-Sayed. Potential self-sufficiency in major Egyptian crops: necessary production and price policies as estimated by an econometric model. IaAS, 1982. 263 p. Micro 82–21,182
DAI, v. 43A, Oct. 1982: 1233.

71

636
Endargeeri, Mohammed Said. The impact of selected social and familial factors on the academic achievement of female students in Saudi Arabia. CLSU, 1986. DAI, v. 47A, Aug. 1986: 491.

637
Engroff, John W. The Arabic tradition of Euclid's *Elements*: Book V. MH, 1980. CDI, 1973–1982, v. 34: 464.

638
Entessar, Tahmineh. Revolution and leadership: a study of four countries [China, Russia, Egypt and Indonesia]. MoSU, 1983. 323 p.   Micro 83–25,360
DAI, v. 44A, Jan. 1984: 2236.

639
Eraqi, Abdulmohsen Mohammed. An investigation of educational television in Saudi Arabia. OrCS, 1986. 180 p.   Micro 86–23,452
DAI, v. 47A, Mar. 1987: 3337.

640
Erheil, Habis S. Trends and patterns in international tourism in Jordan. OCU, 1985. 145 p.   Micro 85–26,555
DAI, v. 46A, Apr. 1986: 3125.

641
Erian, Nabila Meleka. Coptic music: an Egyptian tradition. MdU-BC, 1986. 469 p.   Micro 86–21,595
DAI, v. 47A, Dec. 1986: 1918–1919.

642
Ernst, Carl W. Faith and infidelity in sufism: ecstatic expressions and their repercussions in medieval Islamic society. MH, 1981.
CDI, 1973–1982, v. 34: 475.

643
el-Ersan, Abdelmajid Ali. The making of Jordan's foreign policy under King Hussein. CCC, 1983. 199 p.   Micro 83–28,276
DAI, v. 44A, Feb. 1984: 2569.

644
Escowitz, Edward C. Mediterranean outflow salinity distribution and diffusion in the eastern North Atlantic. NNU-ES, 1978. 97 p.   Micro 81–28,152
DAI, v. 42B, Dec. 1981: 2286.

645
Esemuede, Samuel I. The role of monetary and fiscal policies in the economic development of Nigeria [and Saudi Arabia], 1966–1980. OCUCE, 1985. 260 p.
Micro 86–10,342
DAI, v. 47A, Sept. 1986: 1006.

646

Esfahani, Hadi Salehi. A system-wide analysis of the impact of policy on agricultural performance in Egypt. CU, 1984. 187 p.   Micro 85–12,810

DAI, v. 46A, Jan. 1986: 2026.

647

Eshky, Talal Majed Anwar. A descriptive analysis of the formation and development of the Arab States Broadcasting Union. MiDW, 1982. 256 p.

Micro 83–6873

DAI, v. 43A, May 1983: 3454–3455.

648

Essa, Laila Mohamed. Expectations of the head nurse's qualifications, leadership behavior and role in Egyptian hospitals. CoU-H, 1983. 212 p.

Micro 83–22,690

DAI, v. 44B, Dec. 1983: 1780.

649

al-Essa, Mohammed Omer. Formal and traditional education in Saudi Arabia: a comparative study of the goals and objectives of the primary level. OAU, 1986. 194 p.   Micro 87–15,305

DAI, v. 48A, Oct. 1987: 827.

650

Essatara, M'Barek. Zinc deficiency: experimental studies in the rat and epidemiological studies in Morocco. MnU, 1985. 277 p.   Micro 86–8884

DAI, v. 47B, Oct. 1986: 1346.

651

Essawi, Rihab Ahmed. A proposal for a modification of the preparation for school supervisors in the educational system of the West Bank. PPiU, 1987. 195 p.

Micro 87–19,293

DAI, v. 48A, Dec. 1987: 1386.

652

Etaibi, Ghalib Tulhab. The Gulf Cooperation Council: Arabia's model of integration. MChB, 1984. 269 p.   Micro 85–10,684

DAI, v. 46A, Sept. 1985: 783.

653

Ewald, Janet J. Leadership and social change on an Islamic frontier: the Kingdom of Taqali, 1780–1900. WU, 1982. 444 p.   Micro 83–4936

DAI, v. 44A, Aug. 1983: 552.

654

al-Eyoni, Saleh Mohammed A. H. F. A comparative study between opinions of science faculty and prospective science teachers regarding science training program at Saudi Arabian junior colleges. CoGrU, 1983. 188 p.

Micro 83–24,321

DAI, v. 44A, May 1984: 3341–3342.

655
Ez-Elarab, Mostafa Mohamed. An estimation of a complete demand system for Egyptian imports under a separable utility function. NcRS, 1982. 98 p.
Micro 82–26,649
DAI, v. 43A, Dec. 1982: 2033.

656
Ezzahiri, Brahim. Wheat leaf rust epidemiology in Morocco and the expression and inheritance of resistance in the cultivar area. MnU, 1986. 118 p.
Micro 87–6919
DAI, v. 47B, June 1987: 4723.

657
Ezzaki, Abdelkader. The effects of text structure on the comprehension and recall of [Moroccan] adult readers of English as a foreign language. PPT, 1984. 251 p.
Micro 84–19,756
DAI, v. 45A, Dec. 1984: 1701.

658
Fadaak, Tarek Ali. Urban housing policy evaluation in the Kingdom of Saudi Arabia. OrPS, 1984. 187 p.   Micro 84–20,068
DAI, v. 45A, Dec. 1984: 1888.

659
Fadan, Yousef Mohammed Osamah. The development of contemporary housing in Saudi Arabia, 1950–1983: a study in cross-cultural influence under conditions of rapid change. MCM, 1983.
CDI, 1983, v. 5: 127.

660
el-Faedy, Mahjoub Attia. Agricultural development in a petroleum-based economy: the Libyan case. UU, 1982. 227 p.   Micro 83–5435
DAI, v. 43A, Apr. 1983: 3419.

661
Faghrour, Daho. Revolutionary causality in theory and practice, case study: Algeria, 1830–1954. CoDU, 1984. 218 p.   Micro 84–18,359
DAI, v. 45A, Dec. 1984: 1837.

662
Faheem, Mohammed Eisa. Higher education and nation building: a case study of King Abdulaziz University. IU, 1982. 231 p.   Micro 82–18,462
DAI, v. 43A, Sept. 1982: 593–594.

663
Faik, Ala Yahya. Theatrical elements in religious storytelling of medieval Islamic culture. MiU, 1986. 154 p.   Micro 86–21,278
DAI, v. 47A, Dec. 1986: 1928.

664
al-Faiz, Abdullah Abdul Rahman. A cross-cultural study of student attitudes

involving Arabic schools in the United States. MoU, 1986. 164 p.
Micro 87–16,687
DAI, v. 48A, Nov. 1987: 1064.

665
Faizo, Lutfi Abdul-Rahman. The cycles of Arabic drama: authenticity versus Western imitation and influence. CoU, 1985. 296 p.　　　Micro 86–8600
DAI, v. 47A, Aug. 1986: 542.

666
el Faki, Salah el Din Hamid. An environment-based performance appraisal system for the public service in the Sudan. CLSU, 1983.
DAI, v. 43A, June 1983: 4034.

667
al-Faleh, Nasser Abdulrahman. Effects of lecture-demonstration and small group experimentation teaching methods on Saudi Arabian students' chemistry achievement and attitudes toward science learning. InU, 1981. 122 p.
Micro 81–19,040
DAI, v. 42A, Sept. 1981: 1083–1084.

668
Falemban, Ali Nawawi. Influences on the career and educational decisions of male and female secondary school graduates in Saudi Arabia. CLSU, 1986.
DAI, v. 47A, Oct. 1986: 1275–1276.

669
Fallatah, Mohammed A. S. The emergence of Pan-Arabism and its impact on Egyptian foreign policy, 1945–1981. IdU, 1986. 347 p.　　　Micro 87–1946
DAI, v. 47A, Apr. 1987: 3864–3865.

670
Faour, Muhammad Ali. Determinants of female age at first marriage in Jordan. MiU, 1983. 211 p.　　　Micro 84–2275
DAI, v. 44A, Apr. 1984: 3171.

671
el-Far, Ibrahim Abdel-Wikeil Morsy. An experimental study of effects of using diagnostic/prescriptive procedures on the mastery learning of the first-year algebra course required of preservice secondary school teachers in Egypt. PSt, 1981. 186 p.　　　Micro 82–5905
DAI, v. 42A, Apr. 1982: 4341.

672
Farah, Abdul-Aziz Mohamed. Child mortality and its correlates in Sudan. PU, 1981. 282 p.　　　Micro 81–27,020
DAI, v. 42A, Dec. 1981: 2877–2878.

673
Farah, Osman Mohamed. The bathymetry, oceanography, and bottom sedi-

ments of Dongonab Bay (Red Sea), Sudan. DeU, 1982. 163 p.

Micro 83–9883

DAI, v. 43B, June 1983: 3885.

674

Faraj, Abdulatif Hussein. Saudi Arabian educators' perceptions of educational goals for secondary schools. InU, 1981. 233 p.   Micro 81–28,007

DAI, v. 42A, Jan. 1982: 2995–2996.

675

al-Faraj, Taqi Naser. Mathematical models for planning the production, refining and marketing of crude oil and refined petroleum products [for Saudi Arabia]. TxU, 1986. 226 p.   Micro 87–159

DAI, v. 47B, Mar. 1987: 3936.

676

Fareed, Hassan Abu-Baker. The relationship between high school open climate and student alienation in the Western Province of Saudi Arabia. KU, 1983. 209 p.   Micro 83–17,937

DAI, v. 44A, Oct. 1983: 1049.

677

Fares, Abderrahim F. Salary and promotion determinants at two Middle Eastern universities [Kuwait University and University of Jordan]. TxLT, 1982. 149 p.

Micro 83–2159

DAI, v. 43A, Feb. 1983: 2729.

678

Farghal, Mohammed Ali. The syntax of *wh*-questions and related matters in Arabic. InU, 1986. 211 p.   Micro 87–7784

DAI, v. 48A, Aug. 1987: 380.

679

Farghaly, Ali Ahmed Sabry. Topics in the stntax of Egyptian Arabic. TxU, 1981. 237 p.   Micro 81–19,288

DAI, v. 42A, Sept. 1981: 1127.

680

Farooqi, Naimur Rahman. Mughal-Ottoman relations: a study of political and diplomatic relations between Mughal India and the Ottoman Empire. WU, 1986. 443 p.   Micro 86–5685

DAI, v. 47A, Sept. 1986: 1026.

681

Farrell, Eileen R. Ngoma ya Ushindani: competitive song exchange and the subversion of hierarchy in a Swahili Muslim town on the Kenya Coast. MH, 1980.

CDI, 1973–1982, v. 34: 522.

682

Fasheh, Violet M. Perceived needs for student services/programs in the four-year institutions of higher education in the West Bank. ICarbS, 1983. 275 p.

Micro 83–26,532

DAI, v. 44A, Jan. 1984: 2057–2058.

683

Fattah, Hala Mundhir. The development of the regional market of Iraq and the Gulf, 1800–1900. CLU, 1986. 273 p.   Micro 86–6453

DAI, v. 47A, July 1986: 286.

684

Fattah, Younis Mahmoud. The role of rural women in family decision making in Iraq. TU, 1981. 144 p.   Micro 82–3831

DAI, v. 42A, Mar. 1982: 4166–4167.

685

Fayad, Mona Shafik. The impact of the absurd on modern Arabic literature: a study of the influence of Camus, Ionesco and Beckett. IU, 1986. 245 p.

Micro 87–1480

DAI, v. 47A, May 1987: 4080.

686

al-Fayez, Abdulaziz Ibrahim. The national security of Kuwait: external and internal dimensions. MU, 1984. 522 p.   Micro 84–10,252

DAI, v. 45A, July 1984: 295–296.

687

Fedida, Michael. Honor, kinship, and marriage in Arab culture. ICU, 1984.
CDI, 1984, v. 5: 125.

688

Feintuch, Yossi. Washington and Jerusalem: the United States position on the status of Jerusalem, 1947–1967. GEU, 1985. 412 p.   Micro 86–5731

DAI, v. 47A, July 1986: 288.

689

Fellahi, Salah. An assessment of Algerian development. NSyU, 1985. 367 p.

Micro 86–17,316

DAI, v. 47A, Nov. 1986: 1865.

690

Fernandez, Damian J. Cuba's foreign policy in the Middle East, 1959–1985. FMU, 1986. 223 p.   Micro 86–19,477

DAI, v. 47A, Dec. 1986: 2303–2304.

691

el-Fiki, Abdel Momin Farag. The development of university education in the Socialist People's Libyan Arab Jamahiriya, 1955 to 1980. OrU, 1982. 403 p.

Micro 82–24,834

DAI, v. 43A, Dec. 1982: 1849.

692

Filemban, Kamal Nowawi. Faculty performance evaluation at King Abdulaziz University, Saudi Arabia: an exploratory study. FTaSU, 1986. 332 p.

Micro 86–16,883

DAI, v. 47A, Nov. 1986: 1545.

693

Filemban, Samir Noorudein. Verbal classroom interaction in elementary school mathematics classes in Saudi Arabia. OrCS, 1982. 125 p.　　Micro 82–6527

DAI, v. 42A, Apr. 1982: 4342.

694

Firestone, Reuven. The evolution of Islamic narrative exegesis in the Abraham-Ishmael legends. NNU, 1988. 357 p.

Letter from Elmer Holmes Bobst Library, New York University.

695

Fischer, Steven C. Production and pricing patterns in the international crude oil market. MH, 1985. 269 p.　　Micro 85–10,203

DAI, v. 46A, Oct. 1985: 1037.

696

Fisher, Carol G. The pictorial cycle of the *Siyer-i Nebi*: a late sixteenth century manuscript of the life of Muḥammad. MiEM, 1981. 397 p.

Micro 81–17,230

DAI, v. 42A, Sept. 1981: 897.

697

Fituri, Ahmed Said. Tripolitania, Cyrenaica, and Bilad as-Sudan: trade relations during the second half of the nineteenth century. MiU, 1982. 247 p.

Micro 83–4488

DAI, v. 43A, Apr. 1983: 3393.

698

Foerster, Sharan W. The effects of a U.S. educational experience on the traditional cultural values of Libyan students. TxU, 1981. 196 p.　　Micro 82–8169

DAI, v. 42A, May 1982: 4942.

699

Fordham, Glenn W. The psychological orientation towards growth in Lawrence Durrell's *The Alexandria Quartet*. TxDN, 1981. 173 p.　　Micro 81–18,082

DAI, v. 42A, Sept. 1981: 1159.

700

Fouad, Nawal A. Family planning behavior of Arab-American women. CU-Sf, 1987. 298 p.　　Micro 87–8446

DAI, v. 48B, Sept. 1987: 703.

701

Fouzan, Ebrahim Abdulaziz. The involvement of parents of educable mentally

retarded in their children's educational programs in Saudi Arabia. CSdU, 1986. 251 p.   Micro 87–10,632
DAI, v. 48A, Aug. 1987: 359.

702
Fox, Samuel E. The structure of the morphology of Cairene Arabic. ICU, 1982.
CDI, 1973–1982, v. 34: 637.

703
Fozan, Mohammed Nasser. Interest-free loans used by the Saudi government as a transfer mechanism of oil revenue to the private sector. AzU, 1986. 190 p.
Micro 86–13,814
DAI, v. 47A, Oct. 1986: 1428.

704
Fradkin, Robert A. Markedness theory and the verb systems of Russian and Arabic: aspect, tense and mood. InU, 1985. 305 p.   Micro 85–27,003
DAI, v. 46A, Apr. 1986: 3017.

705
Fraenkel, Eran. Skopje from the Serbian to Ottoman Empires: conditions for the appearance of a Balkan Muslim city. PU, 1986. 311 p.   Micro 86–14,795
DAI, v. 47A, Oct. 1986: 1456–1457.

706
Fraih, Insaf J. Aesthetic inquiry into Jordanian embroidery. NNU, 1985. 360 p.
Micro 86–3877
DAI, v. 46A, June 1986: 3575.

707
Fraihat, Muhammed Hassan A. Holistic education: an alternative approach to Arabic language instruction. MU, 1981. 272 p.   Micro 82–10,321
DAI, v. 42A, June 1982: 5011.

708
Fraijat, Ghaleb A. Educational planning process at the national level in Jordan.
PPiU, 1986. 166 p.   Micro 87–1961
DAI, v. 47A. Apr. 1987: 3685.

709
France, Judith E. AFL-CIO foreign policy: an Algerian example, 1954–1962.
InMuB, 1981. 206 p.   Micro 82–1899
DAI, v. 42A, Feb. 1982: 3719.

710
Franklin, Robert L. The Indian community in Bahrain: labor migration in a plural society. MH, 1985. 600 p.   Micro 86–2284
DAI, v. 47A, July 1986: 225.

711
Frayha, Nemer Mansour. Religious conflict and the role of social studies for

79

citizenship education in the Lebanese schools between 1920 and 1983. CSt, 1985. 396 p. Micro 85–22,144
DAI, v. 46A, Feb. 1986: 2176.

712
Fredericks, Brian E. The United States in Southwest Asia: the evolution of strategic framework, 1980–1985. DGW, 1986. 441 p. Micro 86–15,748
DAI, v. 47A, Oct. 1986: 1475.

713
Freeman, Larry E. The Saudi Arabian heat low: a numerical perspective. CoFS, 1984. 227 p. Micro 84–29,894
DAI, v. 45B, Apr. 1985: 3258.

714
Friedlander, Melvin A. The management of peace-making in Egypt and Israel, 1977–79. DAU, 1982. 629 p. Micro 82–24,886
DAI, v. 43A, Dec. 1982: 2087.

715
Friedman, Charles B. The construct validation of second language proficiency tests with different native language groups [Arabs included]. InU, 1984. 124 p.
Micro 84–17,166
DAI, v. 45A, Nov. 1984: 1373.

716
Friend, Robyn C. Some syntactic and morphological features of Suleimaniye Kurdish. CLU, 1985. 236 p. Micro 85–13,111
DAI, v. 46A, Oct. 1985: 964.

717
Fukuyuma, Yoshihiro F. Soviet threats to intervene in the Middle East, 1956–1973. MH, 1981.
CDI, 1973–1982, v. 34: 686.

718
Fusfeld, Warren E. The shaping of Sufi leadership in Delhi: the Naqshbandiyya Mujaddidiyya, 1750 to 1920. PU, 1981. 308 p. Micro 81–27,024
DAI, v. 42A, Dec. 1981: 2807.

719
Gaballa, Hassan el-Banna M. Case-marking and classical Arabic: a semantic and historiographic study. DeU, 1986. 397 p. Micro 86–29,279
DAI, v. 47A, Mar. 1987: 3411.

720
al-Gabbani, Mohammed Abdelaziz. Community structure, residential satisfaction and preferences in a rapidly changing urban environment: the case of Riyadh, Saudi Arabia. MiU, 1984. 338 p. Micro 84–12,083
DAI, v. 45A, Aug. 1984: 640.

721

Gaber, Julia E. Lamb of God or demagogue? A Burkean cluster analysis of the selected speeches of Minister Louis Farrakhan. OBgU, 1986. 186 p.

Micro 86–28,835

DAI, v. 47A, May 1987: 3908.

722

Gaber, Mohamed Mahmoud. Foreign direct investment in Egypt: a study of the impact and effectiveness of the Egyptian national policy, 1972–1979. NNU-B, 1983. 247 p.

Micro 86–9204

DAI, v. 47A, Aug. 1986: 611.

723

Gabir, Dafie'a Awad. Assessing organizational effectiveness: two Sudanese agri-business cases. OU, 1983. 242 p.

Micro 84–3517

DAI, v. 44A, May 1984: 3443–3444.

724

al-Gaeed, Ibrahim Hamad. An evaluative study of the English as a foreign language teacher preparation programs of Saudi Arabia as perceived by program students and graduates. InU, 1983. 176 p.

Micro 84–1542

DAI, v. 44A, Apr. 1984: 3036.

725

Gaffney, Patrick D. *Shaykh, khuṭba,* and *masjid*: the role of the local Islamic preacher in Upper Egypt. ICU, 1982.

CDI, 1983, v. 5: 145.

726

al-Gahtani, Thabit Masilith S. Sponsoring Saudi male graduates in the United States and their academic commitment: King Abdulaziz University case. ViU, 1981. 169 p.

Micro 82–19,061

DAI, v. 43A, Jan. 1983: 2322.

727

Gailani, Mohamed Bakhiet. Water activity in relation to microbiology during processing and storage of Sudanese dried beef (Sharmoot). OKentU, 1985. 152 p.

Micro 85–15,935

DAI, v. 46B, Feb. 1986: 2513–2514.

728

Gancz, Nechama. Israel's quest for American arms: a case study of a client-patron relationship, 1968–78. ViU, 1983. 328 p.

Micro 83–28,746

DAI, v. 44A, June 1984: 3802.

729

Ganji, Ghorbanali. A cross-national study of the correlates of civil strife in Middle Eastern nations, 1960–73. TxDN, 1981. 177 p.

Micro 81–18,084

DAI, v. 42A, Sept. 1981: 1297.

730
el-Garid, el-Taher M. Economic segmentation, kinship resources, and socio-economic achievement in Libya. UU, 1987. 258 p.
Letter from Marriott Library, University of Utah.

731
al-Garradi, Taher K. The image of al-Ma'rrī as infidel among medieval and modern critics. UU, 1987. 250 p.
Letter from Marriott Library, University of Utah.

732
al-Gatami, Munira Abdulwahab. A plan for implementing a model national rehabilitation program: task analysis, organization design, and prospective evaluation method, with special reference to the State of Kuwait. AzU, 1986. 172 p.   Micro 86-23,820
DAI, v. 47B, Jan. 1987: 2824.

733
el-Gattus, Mohamed Abdalla. Guidelines for adult education organization and administration in small population centers in Libya. CoGrU, 1981. 180 p.
Micro 81-19,795
DAI, v. 42A, Sept. 1981: 927.

734
Gawarecki, Susan L. Neotectonics of the Ras Issaran region, Gulf of Suez, Egypt. ScU, 1986. 271 p.   Micro 87-4627
DAI, v. 47B, May 1987: 4447.

735
Gaynor, William M. Optimal pricing and production of an exhaustible resource: the case of Saudi Arabian crude oil. MdU, 1983. 174 p.   Micro 84-19,490
DAI, v. 45A, Nov. 1984: 1486.

736
Gebril, Gelani Bashir. An investigation of adult education program content and need as perceived by adult basic education and trade union education partici-pants in three major metropolitan areas in Libya. KMK, 1982. 254 p.
Micro 82-21,839
DAI, v. 43A, Oct. 1982: 1010-1011.

737
Gellens, Sam I. Scholars and travelers: the social history of early Muslim Egypt, 218-487/833-1094. NNC, 1986. 226 p.   Micro 86-23,524
DAI, v. 47A, Jan. 1987: 2706.

738
Georgeski, Julie D. Nature of and differences in adjustment to and valuing of the American culture among refugees from Eastern Europe, the Middle East, and African countries. CSdI, 1987. 127 p.   Micro 87-20,628
DAI, v. 48A, Dec. 1987: 1547.

739
Gerami, Shahin. Export alliances as a mechanism of dependence control in the world-system: the case of OPEC. OkU, 1983. 198 p.   Micro 83–13,779
DAI, v. 44A, Aug. 1983: 593.

740
Gettu, Tegegnework. Conflict and accommodation in Ethio-Sudanese relations, 1956–1986. NNC, 1987. 414 p.   Micro 87–10,182
DAI, v. 48A, July 1987: 216.

741
Ghaban, Mahroos Ahmed. Education and individual modernity among Saudi students: a study of the impact of formal and cross-cultural education on modernizing attitudes and values. MiEM, 1986. 154 p.   Micro 87–471
DAI, v. 47A, Mar. 1987: 3295.

742
al-Ghabra, Shafeeq Nazem. Palestinians in Kuwait: the family and the politics of survival. TxU, 1987.
Letter from the General Libraries, University of Texas at Austin.

743
al-Ghamdi, Abdulazizi Sagr. An approach to planning a primary health care delivery system in Jeddah, Saudi Arabia. MiEM, 1981. 107 p.
Micro 82–2380
DAI, v. 42A, Feb. 1982: 3754.

744
al-Ghamdi, Abdullah Abdulghani. Action research and the dynamics of organizational environment in the Kingdom of Saudi Arabia. CLSU, 1982.
DAI, v. 43A, Sept. 1982: 918.

745
al-Ghamdi, Abdullah Moghram. A proposed in-service education model for middle and secondary school teachers in Saudi Arabia. InU, 1984. 298 p.
Micro 85–6077
DAI, v. 46A, July 1985: 115.

746
al-Ghamdi, Abdulrahim Mashini. The professional development of inservice teachers in Saudi Arabia: a study of the practice and needs. MiEM, 1982. 225 p.   Micro 83–3745
DAI, v. 43A, Mar. 1983: 2967.

747
Ghamdi, Ahmad M. Abboush. Public expenditure in Saudi Arabia: testing of Wagner's law and critical appraisal of development. CoFS, 1982. 197 p.
Micro 83–17,792
DAI, v. 44A, Oct. 1983: 1155.

748
al-Ghamdi, Ali Sagr. Attitudes on the impact of foreign labor force in Saudi society: the case of Jeddah city. MiEM, 1985. 284 p.   Micro 86–7043
DAI, v. 47A, Aug. 1986: 657.

749
al-Ghamdi, Hamdan A. A study of selected aspects of the academic pursuits of Saudi Arabian government master's degree scholarship students in the United States of America. TxHU, 1985. 251 p.   Micro 85–17,693
DAI, v. 46A, Mar. 1986: 2578.

750
al-Ghamdi, Mohammed Said Dammas. The impact of ecological factors upon the attitudes of Saudi students toward work values: a search for development approach. FTaSU, 1982. 207 p.   Micro 82–12,891
DAI, v. 42A, June 1982: 5239.

751
al-Ghamdi, Saleh Ziay M. Educational research in the university: a comparative study of Saudi Arabia and Morocco. TNJ, 1985. 507 p.   Micro 85–22,410
DAI, v. 46A, Feb. 1986: 2200.

752
al-Ghamdi, Seraj Mohsen. A study to explore the extent to which junior colleges meet the Saudi Arabian community diverse educational needs as perceived by administrators, teachers and students. PPiU, 1984. 220 p.   Micro 85–291
DAI, v. 45A, May 1985: 3244.

753
al-Ghamedi, AbdulKareem Abdulla. The influence of the environment on pre-Islamic socio-economic organization in southwestern Arabia. AzTeS, 1983. 310 p.   Micro 83–15,793
DAI, v. 44A, Sept. 1983: 799.

754
Ghanayem, Mohammad A. The theory of foreign direct investment in capital-rich, labor-short economies: the case for Saudi Arabia, Kuwait and United Arab Emirates. TxDaM, 1981. 104 p.   Micro 81–28,586
DAI, v. 42A, Jan. 1982: 3245.

755
Ghandhistani, Abdullah Hassan. Staff development inservice teacher training in written composition at an Islamic elementary school [Philadelphia, PA]: a program for preventing functional illiteracy. OCUCE, 1986. 134 p.
Micro 87–13,033
DAI, v. 48A, Sept. 1987: 632.

756
Ghandour, Mahmoud Mohamed. Planning for future: a ten-year projection of

four critical elements of the Kuwaiti educational system. KU, 1981. 250 p.

Micro 82–18,799

DAI, v. 43A, Sept. 1982: 604.

757

Ghandour, Mahmoud Mohamed. Effect on item reliability, difficulty, and discrimination of conventional versus complex "all-of-the-above" and "none-of-the-above" multiple choice items. KU, 1985. 153 p.　　　Micro 86–8397
DAI, v. 47A, Aug. 1986: 514.

758

Ghandour, Nabiha Habbab. Coverage of the Arab World and Israel in American news magazines between 1975 and 1981: a comparative content analysis. NNC-T, 1984. 257 p.　　　Micro 84–24,222
DAI, v. 45A, Feb. 1985: 2476.

759

Ghandoura, Abbas Hassan. Achievement effects of teacher comments on homework in mathematics classes in Saudi Arabia. OrCS, 1982. 139 p.

Micro 82–16,635

DAI, v. 43A, Aug. 1982: 388.

760

al-Ghanim, Abdul-Aziz Ghanim. A study of the academic, personal and social problems perceived by Kuwaiti undergraduate and graduate students in the United States. DGW, 1983. 163 p.　　　Micro 83–24,475
DAI, v. 44A, Jan. 1984: 2053–2054.

761

Ghanima, Sari Ahmad. The effects of a six-week exercise and rope jump program on AAHPERD health related physical fitness test scores of high school females in the Hashemite Kingdom of Jordan. FTaSU, 1986. 147 p.

Micro 86–26,794

DAI, v. 47A, Apr. 1987: 3694.

762

Ghareeb, Ghareeb Abdel-Fattah. An investigation of the relationship between depression and assertiveness in Egyptian depressed subjects. PPiU, 1983. 190 p.

Micro 84–11,698

DAI, v. 45A, Aug. 1984: 415.

763

Ghavamshahidi, Zohreh. Dissidence and conformity in Iranian politics: political culture and Islamic revolution. OkU, 1986. 409 p.　　　Micro 86–13,721
DAI, v. 47A, Oct. 1986: 1467.

764

Ghawanni, Mansour Ahmed. The factors influencing male secondary school students' choice of educational track in Saudi Arabia: science versus the arts. MiEM, 1985. 355 p.　　　Micro 86–7079
DAI, v. 47A, Aug. 1986: 402.

765

al-Ghazali, Abdullah. al-ʿUrḍī's *Maʿādin al-dhahab* and the scholarly life of eleventh/seventeenth century Aleppo. UU, 1982. 501 p.   Micro 83–5433
DAI, v. 43A, June 1983: 3928–3929.

766

Ghazali, Mohammed N. A portfolio approach to the oil surplus problem: Saudi Arabia as a study case. CCC, 1985. 171 p.   Micro 85–15,193
DAI, v. 46A, Nov. 1985: 1337.

767

Ghaznawi, Hassan Ismail. The development and management of hospitals in the western region of Saudi Arabia. LNT, 1982. 194 p.   Micro 82–16,733
DAI, v. 43B, Nov. 1982: 1449.

768

Ghazwi, Fahmi Salim. Modernization and social change in family life in Jordan, 1961–1981. ViU, 1985. 399 p.   Micro 85–26,885
DAI, v. 46A, Apr. 1986: 3166.

769

Gheiadi, Ibrahim Mohammad. Attitudes toward American-Soviet policies in the Middle East: an analysis of the opinions of Arab journalists. PU, 1982. 328 p.
Micro 83–7315
DAI, v. 43A, May 1983: 3699.

770

Gherfal, Ibrahim Rajab. The application of principles of reinforcement to the teaching of English as a second language in a developing country: an experiment with Libyan male preparatory school students from culturally diverse rural and urban communities. DCU, 1982. 146 p.   Micro 82–13,750
DAI, v. 43A, July 1982: 147–148.

771

Ghodbane, Mabrouk. The Algerian policy of foreign borrowing and its development strategy: a dependency theory perspective. NAlU, 1985. 419 p.
Micro 85–26,836
DAI, v. 46A, Apr. 1986: 3149–3150.

772

Ghonaim, Ahmed Ali A. A study of the relationship between organizational climate, job satisfaction, and educational district size, and the differences in the perception by male administrators and teachers in Saudi Arabia. MiEM, 1986. 322 p.   Micro 86–25,022
DAI, v. 47A, Jan. 1987: 2393.

773

Ghowail, Thanaa Ibrahim. The acoustic phonetic study of the two pharyngeals /ḥ,ʿ/ and the two laryngeals /ʔ,h/ in Arabic. InU, 1987. 196 p.
Micro 87–17,850
DAI, v. 48A, Nov. 1987: 1189.

774
Ghuloum, Mohammed Haider. A model of the monetary sector of Kuwait. CCC, 1984. 209 p.   Micro 84–11,908
DAI, v. 45A, Aug. 1984: 589.

775
el-Gibaly, Saad Ahmed Abd-Alla. A normative curriculum model for accounting in the comprehensive high school with application to the future comprehensive high schools of Egypt. InU, 1982. 226 p.   Micro 83–1059
DAI, v. 43A, Feb. 1983: 2536.

776
Gilbert, Carmen C. The reading strategies used by selected adult Spanish and Arabic readers in their native language and in English. IU, 1984. 272 p.
                                                                Micro 84–22,067
DAI, v. 45A, Jan. 1985: 2049–2050.

777
Ginsburg, Alix E. Jerusalem diminished: aspects of Jerusalem in the contemporary Hebrew short story (in the works of David Schachar, Aharon Apelfeld, Amos Oz and A. B. Yehoshua). MWalB, 1984. 272 p.   Micro 84–20,767
DAI, v. 45A, Dec. 1984: 1770.

778
Girgis, Sami Said. Plan for developing a Christian community to serve the needs of immigrants from the Arab world in Jersey City, New Jersey. NjMD, 1981. 131 p.   Micro 81–19,828
DAI, v. 42A, Sept. 1981: 970.

779
Gittes, Katharine S. The frame narrative: history and theory. CU-S, 1983. 218 p.
                                                                Micro 83–19,117
DAI, v. 44A, Nov. 1983: 1444.

780
Gochenour, David T. The penetration of Zaydi Islam into early medieval Yemen. MH, 1984. 366 p.   Micro 84–19,446
DAI, v. 45A, Dec. 1984: 1784.

781
Godfrey, John B. Overseas trade and rural change in nineteenth century Morocco: the social region and agrarian order of the Shawiya. MdBJ, 1985. 481 p.
                                                                Micro 85–18,488
DAI, v. 46A, Dec. 1985: 1714.

782
Godlewska, Anne M. C. Compilation and the Napoleonic mapping of Egypt: an historical reconstruction. MWC, 1985. 587 p.   Micro 85–19,164
DAI, v. 46A, Feb. 1986: 2404.

783

Gohaidan, Mohamed Soliman Sultan. Organizational innovations in developing countries: the case of Saudi Arabia. CU-SB, 1981. 272 p.   Micro 82–15,855
DAI, v. 43A, Aug. 1982: 320.

784

el-Gohary, Osamah Mohammed Noor. Mosque design in light of psychoreligious experience. PU, 1984. 576 p.   Micro 84–22,900
DAI, v. 45A, Jan. 1985: 1893.

785

Gold, Isadore J. The United States and Saudi Arabia, 1933–1953: postimperial diplomacy and the legacy of British power. NNC, 1984. 340 p.
Micro 84–27,398
DAI, v. 45A, Apr. 1985: 3205–3206.

786

Goldberg, Ellis J. Tinker, tailor, and textile worker: class and politics in Egypt, 1930–1954. CU, 1983. 450 p.   Micro 84–13,402
DAI, v. 45A, Sept. 1984: 932.

787

Goldman, Shalom L. The Joseph story in Jewish and Islamic lore. NNU, 1986. 189 p.   Micro 87–6314
DAI, v. 47A, June 1987: 4403.

788

Gomaa, Amina Serour. The *Mishnah, Tractate Qiddushin*; a translation from Hebrew to Arabic, with introduction and commentary. NNU, 1982. 245 p.
Micro 82–27,185
DAI, v. 43A, Jan. 1983: 2372–2373.

789

Gomaa, Salwa Sharawi. Egyptian diplomacy in the seventies: a case study in leadership. PPiU, 1986. 223 p.   Micro 86–20,241
DAI, v. 47A, Dec. 1986: 2304.

790

al-Gorashi, Masaud Khedder. Saudi Arabians' perceptions of their doctoral degrees. TNJ, 1987. 273 p.   Micro 87–14,409
DAI, v. 48A, Sept. 1987: 570–571.

791

Gordon, Joel S. Towards Nasser's Egypt: the consolidation of the July Revolution and the end of the Old Regime, 1952–1955. MiU, 1987. 552 p.
Micro 87–20,219
DAI, v. 48A, Dec. 1987: 1524–1525.

792

Gouryh, Admer G. The plays of Walīd Ikhlāṣī: a study in theme and structure.

NNCU-G, 1983. 503 p.   Micro 83–19,768
DAI, v. 44A, Nov. 1983: 1246.

793
el Gousi, Abdelmonein Mahmoud. *Ribā*, islamic law and interest. PPT, 1982.
303 p.   Micro 83–11,594
DAI, v. 44A, July 1983: 198.

794
Grabler, Susan L. From concessionaire to *shaykh*: the shaping of colonial economic
policy in Sudan, 1898–1930. WU, 1986. 434 p.   Micro 86–14,369
DAI, v. 47A, Dec. 1986: 2278.

795
Granara, William E. Political legitimacy and *jihād* in Muslim Sicily. PU, 1986.
254 p.   Micro 87–3208
DAI, v. 47A, Apr. 1987: 3849.

796
Grant, Earl E. Folk religion in Islam: its historical emergence and missiological
significance. CPFT, 1987. 759 p.   Micro 87–14,604
DAI, v. 48A, Oct. 1987: 951.

797
Gregory, Robert T. Geology and isotope geochemistry of the Samail Ophiolite
Complex, southeastern Oman mountains. CPT, 1981. 368 p.
                                                       Micro 81–18,604
DAI, v. 42B, Nov. 1981: 1789.

798
Greiner, Theodore H. The planning, implementation and evaluation of a project
to protect, support and promote breastfeeding in the Yemen Arab Republic.
NIC, 1983. 660 p.   Micro 83–28,625
DAI, v. 44B, Mar. 1984: 2710.

799
Groiss, Arnon. Religious particularism and national integration: changing per-
ceptions of the political self-identity among the Greek-Orthodox Christians of
Greater Syria, 1840–1914. NjP, 1986. 217 p.   Micro 85–29,774
DAI, v. 46A, Apr. 1986: 3135.

800
Gruenbaum, Ellen R. Health services, health, and development in Sudan: the
impact of the Gezira Irrigated Scheme. CtU, 1982. 402 p.   Micro 82–16,407
DAI, v. 43A, Aug. 1982: 492.

801
Grummon, Stephen R. The rise and fall of the Arab Shaykhdom of Bushire,
1750–1850. MdBJ, 1985. 316 p.   Micro 85–18,489
DAI, v. 46A, Feb. 1986: 2419.

802
Guhl, Nora L. The economic determinants of fertility in metropolitan Egypt: the role of child labor. ICU, 1986.
DAI, v. 47A, Nov.1986: 1892.

803
el Guindi, Mohamed Abdel Salam M. M. A microassay for human transferrin and human iron absorption studies on fortification of Egyptian bread. KU, 1986.
278 p.   Micro 87–11,219
DAI, v. 48B, Aug. 1987: 390.

804
Gumati, Yousef Daw. Crustal extension, subsidence, and thermal history of the Sirte Basin, Libya. ScU, 1985. 219 p.   Micro 86–4263
DAI, v. 47B, July 1986: 108.

805
Gunn, Leslie J. The socialist experiment in Tunisia, 1961–1969. CLSU, 1987.
DAI, v. 48A, Aug. 1987: 475.

806
al-Gurashi, Hassan Dhaifallah. Proposed goals for adult basic education programs in the western province of Saudi Arabia as perceived by teachers and administrators. CoGrU, 1982.   Micro 82–13,265
DAI, v. 43A, July 1982: 45–46.

807
Gustaniya, Issam Ibrahim. An analysis of the barriers to the learning process of senior high school students in the Makkah School District in Saudi Arabia (including implications which impact on the Community/Junior College in Saudi Arabia). CMalP, 1984. 216 p.   Micro 84–25,690
DAI, v. 45A, Feb. 1985: 2410.

808
Gwynne, Rosalind W. The *Tafsīr* of Abū ʿAlī al-Jubbāʾī: first steps toward a reconstruction, with texts, translation, biographical introduction and analytical essay. WaU, 1982. 311 p.   Micro 82–12,544
DAI, v. 42A, June 1982: 5138.

809
al-Habeeb, Musa Mohammed Saleh. Evaluation of instructional supervision of English programs at the intermediate and secondary schools in Saudi Arabia. WU, 1981. 199 p.   Micro 82–6817
DAI, v. 43A, July 1982: 60–61.

810
Habeeb, Rakan Abdulkareem. The role of the Saudi broadcasting system in the utilization of the classical form of the Arabic language in preserving culture. MiDW, 1985. 246 p.   Micro 86–5001
DAI, v. 47A, July 1986: 19.

811
Haberer, Rose B. Status, power, and influence of women in an Arab village in Israel. InLP, 1985. 607 p.   Micro 86-6547
DAI, v. 47A, July 1986: 225-226.

812
Habib, Nagy Mikhail. Structural changes in a developing economy and monetary control: the case of Egypt. InU, 1981. 214 p.   Micro 81-28,010
DAI, v. 42A, Jan. 1982: 3245.

813
Habibi, Nader. The economic consequences of the interest-free Islamic banking systems. MiEM, 1987. 202 p.   Micro 87-14,331
DAI, v. 48A, Dec. 1987: 1502-1503.

814
al-Hachami, Naji Obaid M. A simulation cost-effectiveness model for public education in Iraq. FTaSU, 1983. 183 p.   Micro 83-23,821
DAI, v. 44A, Dec. 1983: 1633.

815
Hadad, Mohamed Ahmed Elhag. Characterization and selection of rhizobia for use as inoculants for groundnuts in Sudan. IaAS, 1984. 127 p.
    Micro 84-23,708
DAI, v. 45B, Jan. 1985: 1966.

816
al-Haddad, Abdullah Esa. An investigation of the possible correlation of teacher evaluation grades reporting teacher effectiveness to the Ministry of Education and students' achievement scores in the subject areas of the curriculum at the elementary level of the public schools in Kuwait. CoGrU, 1984. 123 p.
    Micro 84-29,821
DAI, v. 45A, Apr. 1985: 3057.

817
Haddad, Afaf Shukri. Quality of life of Jordanian college students. CLU, 1986. 152 p.   Micro 86-21,069
DAI, v. 47A, Dec. 1986: 2025.

818
el-Haddad, Awad Yousef. The feasibility of agricultural settlement projects in the Jabal al-Akhdar, Libya: an example of the Wadi al-Kharrubah Agricultural Settlement Project. MiEM, 1985. 262 p.   Micro 86-3403
DAI, v. 47A, Aug. 1986: 625.

819
Haddad, Ghassan F. Problems and issues in the phonology of Lebanese Arabic. IU, 1984. 356 p.   Micro 84-22,072
DAI, v. 45A, Jan. 1985: 2083.

820
al-Haddad, Mohammad Sulieman. The effect of detribalization and sedentarization on the socio-economic structure of the tribes of the Arabian Peninsula: Ajman tribe as a case. KU, 1981. 275 p.   Micro 82–18,737
DAI, v. 43A, Sept. 1982: 853.

821
Haddad, Samir A. The shift in field dependence/independence of Jordanian children after living in the United States. MiDW, 1983. 145 p.
Micro 84–5973
DAI, v. 44A, June 1984: 3587.

822
al-Hadethy, Waleed Hassan. Educational theatre in Iraq: elementary and secondary levels, late 19th century to 1985. CoU, 1986. 399 p.
Micro 86–18,919
DAI, v. 47A, Dec. 1986: 1927.

823
al-Hadhod, Dalal Abdulwahed. Leadership behavior of elementary public school principals as perceived by teachers and principals in the State of Kuwait. CLSU, 1984.
DAI, v. 46A, Feb. 1986: 2135–2136.

824
Hadidi, Muna S. Competencies necessary for teachers of visually handicapped students in Jordan as perceived by teacher educators, administrators, principals, and teachers. OU, 1985. 125 p.   Micro 85–26,178
DAI, v. 46A, Mar. 1986: 2660.

825
Hadiji, Mouldi. The history and *Dīwān* of Balḥārith. DGU, 1983. 244 p.
Micro 84–1499
DAI, v. 44A, Apr. 1984: 3078.

826
Hadjipavlou-Trigeorgis, Maria C. Identity conflict resolution in divided societies: the case of Cyprus. MBU, 1987. 355 p.   Micro 87–18,242
DAI, v. 48A, Nov. 1987: 1305–1306.
Deals also with Lebanon.

827
Haeri, Shahla. Contracts as models for sexual unions: temporary marriage, *mut'a*, in contemporary Iran. CLU, 1985. 350 p.   Micro 85–350
DAI, v. 46A, Jan. 1986: 1989.

828
Hafez, Abdullah Ibrahim M. The relationship between the cerebral lateralization for Arabic language and achievement in science [in Jeddah, Saudi Arabia]. OrCS, 1984. 98 p.   Micro 83–26,446
DAI, v. 44A, Feb. 1984: 2429.

829

Hafiz, Omar Zohair. Foreign trade model for Saudi Arabia: an econometric approach. CaQInU, 1981. 204 p.   Micro 81-28,066
DAI, v. 42A, Jan. 1982: 3231.

830

Hagahmed, Gamaleldin Osman. Development play, a Q-methodological study of the role of television in the Sudan. MoU, 1985. 190 p.   Micro 86-11,739
DAI, v. 47A, Sept. 1986: 700.

831

Haghighi, Mohammad. The impact of the Islamic economic doctrines on modern business institutions with emphasis on Iran. CoGrU, 1982. 301 p.
Micro 82-21,863
DAI, v. 43A, Nov. 1982: 1608-1609.

832

Hagopian, Hagop Y. The extent of Middle Eastern content taught in world history programs in public secondary schools in Georgia. AU, 1983. 143 p.
Micro 83-14,028
DAI, v. 44A, Aug. 1983: 370-371.

833

Haider, Mohammed Ishaq. The impact of Egyptian agricultural policies on farm income and resource use. CoFS, 1982. 209 p.   Micro 82-27,922
DAI, v. 43A, Jan. 1983: 2405.

834

Haifa, Said Jamil. The monetary approach to the balance of payments: an analysis of the balance of payments of the major oil exporting countries [Iraq, Kuwait, Libya and Saudi Arabia]. CaQMM, 1984.
DAI, v. 45A, Apr. 1985: 3182.

835

Haile, Reesom. Africa on television: U.S. network television coverage of African affairs, 1977-1980. NNU, 1987. 145 p.   Micro 87-20,123
DAI, v. 48A, Dec. 1987: 1346.

836

al-Haj Hussein, Raef T. An empirical examination of power and conflict in Jordanian food distribution channels. AU, 1985. 226 p.   Micro 85-19,369
DAI, v. 46A, Jan. 1986: 2011.

837

Hajjar, Jeanette Moghabghab. A translation of the seventeenth century Arabic manuscript *Kitāb ad-dalāla al-lāmi'a*, with an introduction that explains its significance in the history of the Middle East. MWalB, 1981. 405 p.
Micro 81-26,879
DAI, v. 42A, Dec. 1981: 2807.

838

al-Hajjeh, Anis Ahmad. Managerial leadership and work-related values of American and Middle Eastern nationals: a cross-cultural study. CSdI, 1984. 101 p.
Micro 84–19,093
DAI, v. 45A, Dec. 1984: 1850.

839

al-Hajji, Yacoub Yousef. Attitudes of students and science teachers toward science laboratory work in the middle schools in Kuwait. MBU-E, 1983. 125 p.
Micro 83–9716
DAI, v. 43A, June 1983: 3866.

840

Hakeem, Farid Hasan. An investigation of the effect of testing as an aid in the instructional process on the EFL students' learning of grammar [in Medina, Saudi Arabia]. KU, 1984. 122 p.
Micro 84–24,329
DAI, v. 45A, Feb. 1985: 2375.

841

Hakim, Kawther Noori. Arabic negation: a functional analysis. CSfU, 1986. 164 p.
Micro 87–1922
DAI, v. 47A, Apr. 1987: 3688.

842

Hallaq, Wael Bahjat. The gate of *ijtihād*: a study in Islamic legal history. WaU, 1983. 112 p.
Micro 83–19,415
DAI, v. 44A, Nov. 1983: 1555.

843

Hallawani, Ebtesam Abdul-Rahman. Working women in Saudi Arabia: problems and solutions. CCC, 1982. 205 p.
Micro 82–28,749
DAI, v. 43A, Jan. 1983: 2448.

844

al-Hamad, Turki Hamad Turki. Political order in changing societies; Saudi Arabia: modernization in a traditional context. CLSU, 1985.
DAI, v. 46A, Apr. 1986: 3142.

845

al-Hamad, Youssef Mohammad. Home/school cooperation as perceived by primary school teachers and administrators in the Kuwaiti educational system. MiEM, 1986. 241 p.
Micro 87–428
DAI, v. 47A, June 1987: 4242.

846

Hamade, Samir Najm. Educational environment relating to the productivity and publication patterns of social scientists in the Middle East. PPD, 1987. 186 p.
Micro 87–14,601
DAI, v. 48A, Sept. 1987: 497.

847

al-Hamadi, Abdullah Mohammed. An approach for teacher participation in curriculum planning in the State of Qatar. NBuU, 1984. 196 p.

Micro 85–3679

DAI, v. 46A, Aug. 1985: 337.

848

Hamarneh, Mustafa B. Social and economic transformation of Trans-Jordan, 1921–1946. DGU, 1985. 242 p.　　　　　　　　Micro 86–13,934

DAI, v. 47A, Nov. 1986: 1855.

849

Hamblin, William J. The Fatimid army during the early Crusades. MiU, 1985. 130 p.　　　　　　　　　　　　　　　Micro 85–12,418

DAI, v. 46A, Oct. 1985: 1068.

850

al-Hamdan, Jasem Mohammad Nasir. A study of faculty evaluation at Kuwait University. OAU, 1984. 426 p.　　　　　　　Micro 85–4160

DAI, v. 45A, June 1985: 3555.

851

Hamdi, Moh'd Nazih Abdel-Qader. Relations of Jordanian children's school performance to parental involvement with children's achievement and parental model of helping as perceived by children. CLU, 1983. 144 p.

Micro 83–26,733

DAI, v. 44A, Feb. 1984: 2360–2361.

852

Hamdi, Narjes Abdel-Gader. Differences in pictorial perception between American and Arab children ages six and seven years old. CLSU, 1981.

DAI, v. 42A, Dec. 1981: 2449–2450.

853

Hamed, Abdulwahed Khaled. Capital absorptive capacity of non-oil sectors in Saudi Arabia. WMUW, 1984. 354 p.　　　　　Micro 85–16,885

DAI, v. 46A, Feb. 1986: 2376.

854

Hamed, Faisal Hassan. Privatization of state-owned enterprises [in Saudi Arabia]. FTaSU, 1986. 265 p.　　　　　　　Micro 87–2237

DAI, v. 47A, Apr. 1987: 3867.

855

Hamed, Osama Ahmad. The state as an agent of economic development: Egypt, 1952–1970. CLU, 1987. 134 p.　　　　　　Micro 87–13,866

DAI, v. 48A, Sept. 1987: 703.

856

Hamed, Said Abd el Aal. An analysis of support resources used to help solve the

problems faced by Egyptian students and their families in the United States. MoSU, 1985. 160 p. Micro 85–20,112
DAI, v. 46A, Jan. 1986: 1836.

857
Hamid, Abdel Halim M. A descriptive analysis of Sudanese colloquial Arabic phonology. IU, 1984. 274 p. Micro 85–2161
DAI, v. 45A, May 1985: 3339.

858
Hamid, Abdel Rahim Nur Eldin. African political rhetoric: an analysis of persuasive strategies in the discourse of President Gaafar M. Nimeiri of the Sudan, 1970–1980. InLP, 1983. 238 p. Micro 84–361
DAI, v. 44A, Mar. 1984: 2622.

859
al-Hamid, Mohammed Muejeb. The negative implications of a *rentier* society on academic achievement: a case study of Saudi Arabia. CLU, 1986. 290 p.
Micro 86–14,062
DAI, v. 47A, Oct. 1986: 1275.

860
Hamied, Jabur Majied. Training needs assessment of cooperative supervisors in Wasit Province of Iraq. WU, 1986. 278 p. Micro 86–13,389
DAI, v. 47A, Oct. 1986: 1153.

861
Hamilton, James D. The macroeconomic effects of petroleum supply disruptions. CU, 1983. 260 p. Micro 83–28,904
DAI, v. 44A, Feb. 1984: 2525.

862
Hamilton, John A. Epics of the lone will: a study of *Travels in Arabia Deserta* and *Seven Pillars of Wisdom*. MH, 1979.
CDI, 1973–1982, v. 34: 135.

863
al-Hammad, Abdul-Muhsen Abdullah. A study of cracks and other deficiencies encountered in prestressed concrete pipes, effectiveness of repair procedures, and its impact on future expansion of the SWC [Sea-Water Cooling] Project in Jubail, Saudi Arabia. KU, 1985. 212 p. Micro 85–29,190
DAI, v. 46B, Apr. 1986: 3539.

864
Hammad, Ahmad Zaki Mansur. Abū Ḥāmid al-Ghazālī's juristic doctrine in *al-Muṣṭafá min ʿilm al-uṣūl*, with a translation of volume one of *al-Muṣṭafá min ʿilm al-uṣūl*. ICU, 1987. 784 p.
Letter from University of Chicago Library.

865
Hammad, Alam. The development of a system dynamics model for the world

96

petroleum tanker industry [and the Suez Canal]. DGW, 1977. 274 p.

Micro 77–29,516

DAI, v. 38A, Jan. 1978: 4267.

866

Hammad, Hal Jamal. Child-rearing attitudes and practices of Jordanian mothers of four-year-old preschoolers in Amman. ULA, 1982. 216 p.

Micro 83–13,545

DAI, v. 44A, Aug. 1983: 380.

867

Hammad, Khalil Nayef. Foreign aid and economic development: the case of Jordan. ICarbS, 1981. 188 p. Micro 82–6457

DAI, v. 42A, Apr. 1982: 4520–4521.

868

Hammoud, Mohamed Salah-Dine. Arabicization in Morocco: a case study in Language planning and language policy attitudes. TxU, 1982. 313 p.

Micro 82–17,874

DAI, v. 43A, Sept. 1982: 792.

869

al-Hamoudi, Khalid Abdulrahman. An evaluation of the current national agricultural data base in Saudi Arabia: an information system approach. MiEM, 1984. 234 p. Micro 84–15,199

DAI, v. 45B, Oct. 1984: 1067.

870

Hamroush, Hany Ahmed. Archaeological geochemistry of Hierakonpolis in the Nile Valley, Egypt. ViU, 1985. 355 p. Micro 86–15,607

DAI, v. 47B, Nov. 1986: 1898.

871

Hamshari, Omar Ahmad Mohammad. Job satisfaction of professional librarians: a comparative study of technical and public service departments in academic libraries in Jordan. MiU, 1985. 161 p. Micro 86–448

DAI, v. 46A, May 1986: 3179–3180.

872

Hamza, Mohammad Riyad. A comparative study between two groups concerning the identification and validation of competencies needed by industrial teacher educators at the University of Technology in Iraq. TU, 1985. 144 p.

Micro 85–11,383

DAI, v. 46A, Sept. 1985: 689.

873

Hamzeh, Ahmad Nizar. Conflict in Lebanon: a survey of opinions and attitudes. CLSU, 1986.

DAI, v. 47A, Dec. 1986: 2299–2300.

874
el-Har, Ahmed M. Ibn Rushd's (Averroës') doctrine of the agent intellect. MoSU, 1982. 219 p. Micro 82–23,663
DAI, v. 43A, Nov. 1982: 1574.

875
Harb, Ahmad Musa. Half-way between north and south: an archetypal analysis of the fiction of Tayeb Salih. IaU, 1986. 213 p. Micro 86–22,770
DAI, v. 47A, Jan. 1987: 2573–2574.

876
al-Hareky, Saad M. A study of the effectiveness of modern educational technology on the mathematics performance of elementary students in Saudi Arabia. PSt, 1983. 203 p. Micro 84–9010
DAI, v. 45A, Sept. 1984: 734–735.

877
Hares, Abdullatif K. Education and national integration in Lebanon. NNC-T, 1985. 257 p. Micro 86–11,680
DAI, v. 47A, Sept. 1986: 857.

878
al-Harethi, Zayed O. Z. A study of attitudes and attitude change of Saudi students in the United States toward some social issues. MnU, 1985. 292 p.
Micro 86–6206
DAI, v. 47B, July 1986: 428.

879
Harik, Judith P. "Nasserism" in the Andes?: an analysis of the government of Peruvian General Juan Velasco Alvarado, 1968–1975. IaU, 1981. 365 p.
Micro 81–28,402
DAI, v. 42A, Jan. 1982: 3285.

880
Hariri, Hashim Bakur. School climate, competency and training of principals in intermediate schools in Saudi Arabia. CoGrU, 1982. 174 p.
Micro 82–13,271
DAI, v. 43A, July 1982: 31.

881
Hariri, Khaled Ibrahim. International commercial fishing arrangements and their implications for fisheries development in the north west Indian Ocean region. WaU, 1982. 346 p. Micro 82–18,227
DAI, v. 43B, Sept. 1982: 572.

882
Hariry, Mohamed Mahdi Ismail Jamal. A study of the production and evaluation of training materials for the training of pre-service male teachers in the operation of AV equipment in Saudi Arabia. CoU, 1983. 221 p. Micro 84–8048
DAI, v. 45A, July 1984: 58.

883

al-Harithi, Sa'id Khadher al-Orabi. The mass media in Saudi Arabia: present concept, functions, barriers and selected strategy for effective use in nation-building and social awareness. OU, 1983. 392 p.   Micro 84–152
DAI, v. 44A, Mar. 1984: 2614.

884

Harrison, Robert T. Road to Suez: Gladstone and the Egyptian Crisis of 1882. CLSU, 1987.
DAI, v. 48A, Oct. 1987: 999.

885

al-Harthi, Ali Hossein. A study of faculty development needs as perceived by administrators and faculty members in Saudi Arabian universities. TxHU, 1985. 201 p.   Micro 86–7007
DAI, v. 47A, Sept. 1986: 719.

886

Harvey, Donald. British imperialism in the Middle East of World War One: a psychosocial history of the Arab Revolt. TxU, 1982. 279 p.
Micro 82–27,662
DAI, v. 43A, Jan. 1983: 2418.

887

Harwell, Deanna J. A descriptive survey study of the health problems, health status and health behaviors of Middle Eastern students utilizing the Student Health Center at the University of Toledo using a multiple methods design. OTU, 1983. 222 p.   Micro 83–28,552
DAI, v. 44A, Feb. 1984. 2367.

888

Hasan, Bassam Mostafa. Historical development of community colleges in Jordan. OkS, 1986. 117 p.   Micro 87–9717
DAI, v. 48A, July 1987: 32.

889

el-Hasan, Nayef Khaled. The complex poem in new Arabic poetry, 1950–1985. PU, 1985. 285p.   Micro 86–3632
DAI, v. 46A, June 1986: 3733.

890

Hasan, Perween. Sultanate mosque-types in Bangladesh: origins and development. MH, 1984. 480 p.   Micro 84–19,351
DAI, v. 45A, Jan. 1985: 1896.

891

Hasan, Sana. Bureaucracy and political participation in "modern" Egypt. MH, 1984. 492 p.   Micro 84–19,352
DAI, v. 45A, Jan. 1985: 2242–2243.

892
Hashem, Abd-el-Raheem Mobarak. Egyptian food system development: simulation of alternative strategic plans for Egyptian food security. KMK, 1986.
268 p.   Micro 86–17,107
DAI, v. 47A, Nov. 1986: 1825.

893
Hashem, Abdullah Aklah. An analytical survey of in-service training needs of secondary level biology teachers in Kuwait. CoGrU, 1982. 178 p.
                                                                          Micro 82–6170
DAI, v. 42A, Apr. 1982: 4385.

894
Hashem, Mhboub Edmond. Images of, and attitudes toward, the Arabs and the Israelis in the American prestige press [*Newsweek, Time, U.S. News and World Report*]—June 1, 1980–May 31, 1983: a content analysis. FTaSU, 1984. 318 p.
                                                                          Micro 85–1829
DAI, v. 45A, May 1985: 3238.

895
Hashim, Ibrahim Mohamed. Meadow use by wild ungulates in the Dinder National Park, Sudan. NmLcU, 1984. 103 p.   Micro 84–9290
DAI, v. 45B, July 1984: 11.

896
Hashim, Kamal M. Sentential complements in Egyptian colloquial Arabic. DGU, 1980. 133 p.   Micro 81–16,525
DAI, v. 42A, Aug. 1981: 686.

897
Hashim, Wahid Hamza. The impact of modernization on Middle Eastern politics.
AzU, 1987. 309 p.   Micro 87–12,876
DAI, v. 48A, Sept. 1987: 736.

898
al-Hashimi, Mohammad Ahmed. An econometric study of the industrial production function in Iraq for 1970–1979. TU, 1983. 171 p.   Micro 83–19,309
DAI, v. 44A, Oct. 1983: 1160.

899
Hassan, Ahmed R. Leadership behavior of physical education department heads in Egypt. CLSU, 1986.
DAI, v. 47A, Jan. 1987: 2395.

900
Hassan, Arafa Ahmed. The status of environmental education in the Egyptian secondary schools as perceived by science and social science teachers and administrative personnel. MiEM, 1984. 299 p.   Micro 85–7499
DAI, v. 46A, Oct. 1985: 857.

901
Hassan, Hassan Shakir. An evaluation of extension's educational program impact on farmers of the Blue Nile integrated agriculture development project, Sudan, 1984. MdU, 1984. 169 p. Micro 85–14,534
DAI, v. 46A, Nov. 1985: 1167.

902
al-Hassan, Mohsin Shaikh Ali. The viewing habits of preschool Saudi children living in the United States watching "Sesame Street" programs. PPT, 1986. 169 p. Micro 86–11,802
DAI, v. 47A, Sept. 1986: 717.

903
al-Hassan, Naser Yousef. Heroism in Old English and Classical Arabic poetry: a comparative study of four battle poems. InU, 1982. 324 p. Micro 83–826
DAI, v. 43A, Feb. 1983: 2674.

904
Hassan, Nawal Ahmed. Child-rearing practices of Palestinian mothers of five-year-old children in the refugee camps in Jordan. OrU, 1983. 234 p.
Micro 84–8171
DAI, v. 45A, July 1984: 76.

905
Hassan, Sabir Mohamed. The impact of the export sector on the domestic economy of the Sudan. NSyU, 1982. 245 p. Micro 83–1643
DAI, v. 43A, Mar. 1983: 3057.

906
Hassan, Shafiq Falah. Arab preschool children's request modifications: the effect of listeners' age and speakers' age and gender. WU, 1984. 88 p.
Micro 84–24,509
DAI, v. 45A, May 1985: 3307–3308.

907
Hassan, Yahya Abdel Kader. Design model for the development of a prototype theme/amusement park to be located at the Suez Canal Region, the Arab Republic of Egypt. TU, 1983. 135 p. Micro 84–2735
DAI, v. 44A, Apr. 1984: 3159.

908
Hassassian, Manuel S. Political opposition in the national movement of Palestine. OCU, 1986. 218 p. Micro 86–22,285
DAI, v. 47A, Feb. 1987: 3175.

909
Hatem, Tarek Abdel Kader. The impact of international banks on development: a case study, Egypt. CoU, 1986. 194 p. Micro 87–352
DAI, v. 47A, Mar. 1987: 3472.

910

Hattar, Haneh Suleiman. Stressors, ethnic identity, self-concept and health of Jordanian-American adolescents. CU-Sf, 1987. 268 p.   Micro 87–8447
DAI, v. 47B, June 1987: 4820.

911

Hattox, Ralph S. Coffee-houses and urban society in the Mamluk and Ottoman lands in the fifteenth and sixteenth centuries. NjP, 1982. 218 p.
Micro 82–21,574
DAI, v. 43A, Oct. 1982: 1249–1250.

912

Hazu, Tuma Wadi. The effect of cultural affinity on language dominance of Arab minority students in selected American public schools. FTaSU, 1982. 127 p.
Micro 82–14,928
DAI, v. 43A, Aug. 1982: 352.

913

Heath, Peter. The thirsty sword: structure and composition in *Sīrat 'Antar ibn Shaddād*. MH, 1981.
CDI, 1973–1982, v. 35: 235.

914

Heck, Gene W. Cairo or Baghdad... ? A critical re-examination of the role of Egypt in the Fatimid dynasty's imperial design. MiU, 1986. 349 p.
Micro 86–21,295
DAI, v. 47A, Dec. 1986: 2276.

915

al-Hedaithy, Saleh Sulaiman Abdulla. Survey of Saudi Arabian soils for the etiologic agent of Histoplasmosis. AzTeS, 1983. 90 p.   Micro 83–22,536
DAI, v. 44B, Nov. 1983: 1351.

916

al-Heeti, Khalaf Nassar. Judgment analysis technique applied to readability prediction of Arabic reading material. CoGrU, 1984. 175 p.
Micro 84–11,458
DAI, v. 45A, Oct. 1984: 1080.

917

Hegazey, Elmorsy Elsaid. The contribution of oil to the economic development in Kuwait, 1962–1982: a macroeconometric approach. CtU, 1985. 203 p.
Micro 85–12,148
DAI, v. 46A, Oct. 1985: 1047–1048.

918

al-Hegelan, Abdelrahman Abdelaziz. Innovation in the Saudi Arabian bureaucracy: a survey analysis of senior bureaucrats. FTaSU, 1984. 193 p.
Micro 84–19,206
DAI, v. 45A, Dec. 1984: 1855.

919

Hegland, Mary E. Imam Knomaini's village: recruitment to revolution. NBiSU, 1986. 909 p.   Micro 86–8718
DAI, v. 47A, Aug. 1986: 568.

920

Heiat, Abbas. An econometric study of an oil-exporting country: the case of Iran. OrPS, 1987. 160 p.   Micro 87–19,378
DAI, v. 48A, Dec. 1987: 1516.

921

Heichal, Gabriella T. Decision making during crisis: the Korean War and the Yom Kippur War. DGW, 1984. 219 p.   Micro 84–10,484
DAI, v. 45A, July 1984: 292–293.

922

Heikkinen, Eleanor K. Textual transmission and teaching in tenth-century Islamic Spain. MH, 1981.
CDI, 1985, v. 5: 193.

923

al-Hemaisan, Mohammed Ibrahim. Science achievement, attitudes toward science, learning motivation, and divergent creativity of Saudi Arabian middle school male students identified as academically gifted or non-gifted. InU, 1985. 173 p.   Micro 85–26,980
DAI, v. 46A, Apr. 1986: 2985–2986.

924

Henderson, Robert T. Basic perceptual and cognitive processes employed by Arabic-speaking students in the development of reading skills in English as a second language. PPiU, 1983. 212 p.   Micro 84–11,759
DAI, v. 45A, Aug. 1984: 508–509.

925

Hermansen, Marcia K. Shah Wali Allah's theory of religion in *Ḥujjat Allāh al-bāligha*, with a translation of volume 1 of *Ḥujjat Allāh al-bāligha*. ICU, 1982.
CDI, 1983, v. 5: 183.

926

Hevi-Yiboe, Laetitia A. P. Perceived competencies and attitudes of Sudanese undergraduate students. IaAS, 1987. 130 p.   Micro 87–16,775
DAI, v. 48A, Oct. 1987: 852.

927

Hiatt, Joseph M. Between desert and town: a case study of encapsulation and sedentarization among Jordanian Bedouin. PU, 1981. 275 p.
Micro 82–7977
DAI, v. 42A, May 1982: 4864–4865.

928

Hijab, Izzat Mohammed. Mass media in Jordan: a historical analysis of the evolution of press, radio and television. MnU, 1985. 211 p.

Micro 85–19,277

DAI, v. 46A, Jan. 1986: 1768.

929

Hilal, Batie Khalifa. Economic growth in Iraq with special emphasis on the contribution of labor force to growth during the period 1960–1984. OAU, 1987. 237 p. Micro 87–15,313

DAI, v. 48A, Oct. 1987: 995.

930

Hilal, Mohamed Mahmoud. An evaluation of Egypt's debt servicing capacity as compared with selected large debt nations. CSdI, 1986. 177 p.

Micro 86–16,710

DAI, v. 47A, Nov. 1986: 1832–1833.

931

Himmerich, Maurice F. Deification in John of Damascus. WMM, 1985. 208 p.

Micro 85–16,275

DAI, v. 46A, Dec. 1985: 1664.

932

al-Himyari, Abbas Hussien. Managing water resources in the Tigris and Euphrates drainage basin: an inquiry into the policy process. TxDN, 1984. 320 p.

Micro 84–23,849

DAI, v. 45A, Jan. 1985: 2251.

933

al-Hinai, Muhammad Talib. Multinational management and the constraints of culture, law, and economy: experiences in Saudi Arabia and the Emirates. CSdI, 1978. 116 p. Micro 85–12,558

DAI, v. 46A, Oct. 1985: 1028.

934

al-Hindi, Zakariyya Yahya Lal. The status of instructional media in the education of the teachers for the handicapped at the Special Education Training Institute in Saudi Arabia. PPiU, 1987. 257 p. Micro 87–19,278

DAI, v. 48A, Dec. 1987: 1437.

935

el-Hmaisat, Hamad Abdel-Qader. Barriers and facilitators encountered in the use of instructional media by Jordanian general secondary level teachers in the public schools of Amman. MiEM, 1985. 255 p. Micro 85–13,896

DAI, v. 46A, Nov. 1985: 1256.

936

Hobbs, Joseph J. Bedouin reconciliation with the Egyptian Desert. TxU, 1986. 283 p. Micro 86–18,492

DAI, v. 47A, Nov. 1986: 1842.

937
Hodges, Christopher B. Low income countries [Egypt and Morocco] and the world wheat trade. MnU, 1983. 194 p.   Micro 83–18,078
DAI, v. 44A, Sept. 1983: 818.

938
Hodieb, Mostafa A. Egyptian internal auditors' objectivity: how it is influenced by managers. ScU, 1985. 133 p.   Micro 85–18,028
DAI, v. 46A, Dec. 1985: 1678.

939
Hoffman, Eva R. The emergence of illustration in Arabic manuscripts: classical legacy and Islamic transformation. MH, 1982. 393 p.   Micro 82–22,643
DAI, v. 43A, Nov. 1982: 1326.

940
Hoffman, Michael L. Urban planning and the underdevelopment of a Third World city: Meknes, Morocco, 1912–1956. WU, 1984. 247 p.
Micro 84–14,240
DAI, v. 45A, Nov. 1984: 1549–1550.

941
Hoffman-Ladd, Valerie J. The religious life of Muslim women in contemporary Egypt. ICU, 1986.
CDI, 1986, v. 5: 247.

942
al-Holeibi, Abdullatif Hamad. Actual and ideal functions of the college dean as perceived by deans and faculty members at King Faisal University, Saudi Arabia. OkS, 1985. 158 p.   Micro 85–28,075
DAI, v. 46A, Apr. 1986: 2933–2934.

943
Homiedan, Abdullah Hamad. Utilizing the theory of articulatory settings in the teaching of English pronunciation to Saudi students learning English as a second language. KU, 1985. 205 p.   Micro 85–29,184
DAI, v. 46A, Apr. 1986: 3018.

944
Hopper, May Habboush. Comparative analysis of ethnic identity, self-concept and attitudes toward women among Lebanese and Palestinians. FU, 1983. 161 p.
Micro 83–24,974
DAI, v. 44A, Jan. 1984: 2093.

945
Horne, Amelia D. Maternal age at last birth and reproductive span: an analysis of Egyptian fertility. NcU, 1985. 139 p.   Micro 86–5666
DAI, v. 47B, July 1986: 44.

946
Hossain, Abu Ali Mokerrom. The international labor migration to the Middle

East: the impact and consequences for the social structure of a sender country, the case of Bangladesh. CU-Riv, 1986. 297 p.   Micro 87–6991
  DAI, v. 47A, June 1987: 4524.

947

al-Hossaini, Mohammed Abdullah. A study of Saudi elementary school administrative communication and organizational climate in the District of Riyadh. MoU, 1985. 190 p.   Micro 85–29,635
  DAI, v. 46A, May 1986: 3199.

948

Hothali, Abdullah Mohsen. Evaluation of the elementary social studies teacher training programs at Makkah and Taif junior colleges in Saudi Arabia. PPiU, 1985. 152 p.   Micro 86–17,222
  DAI, v. 47A, Nov. 1986: 1697–1698.

949

Houiti, Ahmed. Industrialization and economic development: the experience of post-independence Algeria, 1962–1984. DAU, 1986. 306 p.

Micro 86–26,317

  DAI, v. 47A, Feb. 1987: 3207.

950

al-Houthy, Ibrahim Mohammed. A study of factors influencing secondary school students' career choice and their attitudes toward the teaching profession: the case of the Yemen Arab Republic. FTaSU, 1986. 157 p.   Micro 87–2227
  DAI, v. 47A, June 1987: 4242–4243.

951

Hu, Mannshya G. IMF conditionality and stabilization policies: Sudan, Brazil and Mexico. NTR, 1986. 187 p.   Micro 86–19,979
  DAI, v. 47A, Dec. 1986: 2256.

952

al-Hudaithy, Abdullah Soliman. An analysis of the role of the Agricultural Bank and extension services on the changing pattern of agriculture in Al Qassim Region of Saudi Arabia. CoGrU, 1983. 123 p.   Micro 83–28,483
  DAI, v. 44A, Feb. 1984: 2577.

953

Huffard, Evertt W. Thematic dissonance in the Muslim-Christian encounter: a contextualized theology of honor. CPFT, 1985. 371 p.   Micro 85–12,592
  DAI, v. 46A, Oct. 1985: 1001.

954

Hulais, Hamdi Yousef. The interactional variation of motivational factors, abilities and support in relation to perceived intensity of stress conditions among medical students [at King Abdulaziz University, Jeddah, Saudi Arabia]. KMK, 1982. 209 p.   Micro 83–4335
  DAI, v. 43A, Apr. 1983: 3169–3170.

955

al-Hulwah, Mohammed Ibraheem. OPEC as an actor in world politics: a study in its internal and external dimensions. CU-SB, 1981. 308 p.   Micro 82–6221
DAI, v. 42A, Apr. 1982: 4574.

956

al-Humaidy, Abdullah Mohammad. Guidelines for establishing an open university in the Arab Gulf states. MiEM, 1986. 263 p.   Micro 87–429
DAI, v. 47A, Mar. 1987: 3325.

957

al-Humiari, Amin Abdallah. Influence of planting and infestation dates on fall armyworm damage to some Yemeni sorghum varieties. AzU, 1985. 105 p.
Micro 85–29,394
DAI, v. 46B, May 1986: 3701.

958

Hummert, James R. Childhood growth and morbidity in a medieval population from Kulubnarti in the Batn el Hajar of Sudanese Nubia. CoU, 1983. 237 p.
Micro 84–905
DAI, v. 44A, Mar. 1984: 2816.

959

Hunley, Roy E. The Rahad Boderlands study: the distribution of development resources through social practice in eastern Sudan. NBiSU, 1987. 335 p.
Micro 86–26,733
DAI, v. 47A, Feb. 1987: 3092.

960

Hunter, Janice K. Image of Arabs in Florida Community College social science textbooks. FU, 1982. 110 p.   Micro 83–13,644
DAI, v. 44A, Aug. 1983: 454.

961

Hunzai, Faqir. The concept of *tawḥīd* in the thought of Ḥamīd al-Dīn al-Kirmānī (d. after 411/1021). CaQMM, 1986. 309 p.
Letter from McGill University Libraries.

962

Hurst, Thomas R. The Syriac letters of Timothy I (727–823): a study in Christian-Muslim controversy. DCU, 1986. 285 p.   Micro 86–13,464
DAI, v. 47A, Oct. 1986: 1369.

963

Husain, Mir Zohair. The politics of Islamic revivalism: a case study of Pakistan under Z. A. Bhutto, 1972–77. PU, 1985. 607 p.   Micro 85–23,430
DAI, v. 46A, Feb. 1986: 2425–2426.

964

al-Husain, Zaid Abdullmohsein. Development planning: a realistic approach for

Saudi Arabia. CoGrU, 1981. 443 p.   Micro 82–2707
DAI, v. 42A, Feb. 1982: 3351.

965
al-Husayn al-Amiri, Abdallah Muhammad. at-Ṭūfi's refutation of traditional
Muslim juristic sources of law and his view on the priority of regard for human
welfare as the highest legal source or principle. CU-SB, 1982. 217 p.
                                                                     Micro 83–3343
DAI, v. 43A, Apr. 1983: 3343.

966
Husein, Hasan Ibrahim. Economic, social and spatial mobility: the case of the
Palestinians. NNCU-G, 1986. 234 p.   Micro 86–14,681
DAI, v. 47A, Oct. 1986: 1492.

967
al-Hussain, Abdullah Ali. An analysis of the science curriculum in public secondary schools in Saudi Arabia as perceived by Saudi science students in the
United States. OrU, 1983. 232 p.   Micro 83–25,253
DAI, v. 44A, Jan. 1984: 2107.

968
Hussain, Maqitul. In search of an identity—Muslims in contemporary India: a
sociological analysis. NjR, 1982. 280 p.   Micro 82–21,674
DAI, v. 43A, Oct. 1982: 1305.

969
Hussein, Bashir Salih. Coverage of government opinion and opposing opinion in
two Sudanese newspapers before and after the nationalization of the press,
1968–1983. OAU, 1985. 244 p.   Micro 85–18,578
DAI, v. 46A, Jan. 1986: 1766.

970
al-Hussniyah, Abdulrahman Ali Raqa. Perceptions of Saudi students of public
administration curricula in the United States and their perceptions of selected
administrative practices in Saudi Arabia. CLavC, 1985. 180 p.
                                                                     Micro 85–11,739
DAI, v. 46A, Oct. 1985: 1081.

971
Huyette, Summer S. Political adaptation in Sa'udi Arabia: a study of the Council
of Ministers. NNC, 1984. 340 p.   Micro 84–27,414
DAI, v. 45A, Apr. 1985: 3202–3203.

972
Ibnattya, Abdelhai Andaloussi. Effects of cork oak (*Quercus suber* L.) canopy cover
on seasonal herbage production, foliar cover, and nutritive quality in the
Mamora National Forest of Morocco. OrCS, 1984. 211 p.   Micro 85–993
DAI, v. 45B, May 1985: 3392.

973
Ibnouf, Mohamed Ahmed Osman. An economic analysis of mechanized food production schemes in the central plains of the Sudan. MiEM, 1985. 236 p.
Micro 86–7089
DAI, v. 47A, Aug. 1986: 604.

974
Ibrahim, Abdallah Ali. Evolution of government and society in Tripolitania and Cyrenaica (Libya), 1835–1911. UU, 1982. 390 p.   Micro 82–13,384
DAI, v. 43A, July 1982: 233–234.

975
al-Ibrahim, Abdulla Ali. Regional and urban development in Saudi Arabia. CoU, 1982. 424 p.   Micro 82–29,805
DAI, v. 43A, Jan. 1983: 2398–2399.

976
Ibrahim, Ahmed Mohamed Mohamed. A computer literacy program for pre-service secondary school mathematics teachers in Egypt. PPiU, 1986. 314 p.
Micro 87–7605
DAI, v. 47A, June 1987: 4314.

977
Ibrahim, Ali Mohamed. The dependability of needs assessment data: an application of generalizability theory to the ratings of educational goals [in the Sudan]. CLU, 1984. 141 p.   Micro 84–11,875
DAI, v. 45A, Aug. 1984: 499.

978
Ibrahim, Bakur Mohammad. A proposal for satellite communications utilization in higher education in the Kingdom of Saudi Arabia. MiDW, 1986. 220 p.
Micro 87–6170
DAI, v. 47A, June 1987: 4221–4222.

979
al-Ibrahim, Farouk Yassin. Adjustment problems facing Syrian students and their families in New York. NNC-T, 1983. 136 p.   Micro 83–13,354
DAI, v. 44A, July 1983: 82.

980
Ibrahim, Fawzi Bahzad. Bahrain Stock Exchange: a structured model-organization and mechanism. CSdI, 1984. 225 p.   Micro 84–14,953
DAI, v. 45A, Sept. 1984: 905.

981
Ibrahim, Ibrahim Mirghani. The role of international joint ventures in the development of the Sudan. MH, 1983.
CDI, 1985, v. 5: 214.

982
al-Ibrahim, Khaled Ibrahim. An investigation of differences among elementary

social studies teachers in Riyadh, Saudi Arabia, in their use of, attitudes toward, and perception of their ability to use the problem solving method. CoGrU, 1984. 164 p. Micro 84–18,113
DAI, v. 45A, Nov. 1984: 1360–1361.

983
Ibrahim, Mahmood. The social and economic background of the Umayyad caliphate: the role of Muʻāwiya ibn Abī Sufyān. CLU, 1981. 410 p.
Micro 81–20,976
DAI, v. 42A, Oct. 1981: 1745–1746.

984
Idiong, Calixtus S. The role of Arab states in the decolonization of Africa, South of the Sahara, from 1955 to 1982. DHU, 1985. 484 p. Micro 85–28,734
DAI, v. 46A, Apr. 1986: 3150.

985
Igweonwu, Isaac C. The politics of transformation: Nigeria, OPEC and the multinational corporations. MU, 1984. 413 p. Micro 84–18,892
DAI, v. 45A, Dec. 1984: 1860.

986
al-Imad, Leila Sami. The Fatimid vizierate, 969–1172. NNU, 1986. 183 p.
Micro 86–14,488
DAI, v. 47A, Oct. 1986: 1456.

987
Imam-Jomeh, Iraj. Petroleum-based accumulation and the state form in Iran: aspects of social and geographical differentiation, 1953–1979. CLU, 1985. 423 p. Micro 85–19,109
DAI, v. 46A, Jan. 1986: 2099.

988
Indurthy, Rathnam. The Arab-Israeli conflict and the Persian Gulf as a sub-system, 1948–72. KU, 1985. 898 p. Micro 85–29,102
DAI, v. 46A, Apr. 1986: 3150.

989
Inoguchi, Kuniko Yokota. The political economy of non-oil exporting LDCS: the oil crisis as the threshold of exploratory change. CtY, 1982. 313 p.
Micro 82–21,410
DAI, v. 43A, May 1983: 3699.

990
Irani, George Emile. The papacy and the Middle East: the role of the Holy See in the Arab-Israeli conflict, 1962–1982. CLSU, 1985.
DAI, v. 46A, May 1986: 3480.

991
Irshied, Omar Musleh. The phonology of Arabic: Bani Hassan, a Bedouin Jor-

danian dialect. IU, 1984. 179 p.   Micro 85–2190
    DAI, v. 45A, May 1985: 3339.

992
Isa, Abdulla Saleh. Proposed standards for university libraries in Saudi Arabia.
PPiU, 1982. 210 p.   Micro 82–19,919
    DAI, v. 43A, Oct. 1982: 962.

993
al-Isa, Muhammad S. Developing a methodology to predict high accident loca-
tions on rural highways in Saudi Arabia using speed distribution characteristics.
MiEM, 1984. 183 p.   Micro 85–3180
    DAI, v. 45B, June 1985: 3883.

994
Ishaya, Arian Beit. Class and ethnicity in rural California: the Assyrian community of Modesto-Turlock, 1910–1985. CLU, 1985. 267 p.   Micro 86–3956
    DAI, v. 47A, July 1986: 321–322.

995
al-Ismaeel, Abdulwahab Umar. Selected social studies teaching strategies in
Saudi Arabian secondary schools. KU, 1981. 132 p.   Micro 82–18,793
    DAI, v. 43A, Dec. 1982: 1808.

996
Ismail, Ahmed Mohamed el-Saman. Ralph W. Tyler and curriculum evaluation
with reference to Egyptian education. CtU, 1984. 337 p.   Micro 85–9508
    DAI, v. 46A, Sept. 1985: 599.

997
Issa, Mahmoud Sayed Abdou. Modernization and the fertility transition: Egypt,
1975. PU, 1981. 434 p.   Micro 81–17,795
    DAI, v. 42A, Sept. 1981: 1329.

998
Issa-Fullata, Moustafa Mohammed. An experimental study for modernizing
instruction through educational technology: the case of Saudi Arabia. NBuU,
1982. 263 p.   Micro 83–3200
    DAI, v. 43A, Mar. 1983: 2861–2862.

999
Isteitiya, Samir Sharif. The phonetics and phonology of classical Arabic described
by al-Jurjānī's *al-Muqtaṣad*. MiU, 1984. 179 p.   Micro 84–22,256
    DAI, v. 45A, Jan. 1985: 2083–2084.

1000
Jabr, Soliman Mohammed. Individualizing geography instruction in Saudi Arabian secondary schools. KU, 1981. 223 p.   Micro 81–28,727
    DAI, v. 42A, Jan. 1982: 2997.

1001
Jacobberger, Patricia A. Remote sensing in arid regions: three case studies (Southwestern Kansas; Meatiq Dome, Eastern Desert, Egypt; and Kharga Depression, Western Desert, Egypt). MoSW, 1982. 134 p.   Micro 83–2342
DAI, v. 43B, Mar. 1983: 2835.

1002
Jakubowska, Longina A. Urban Bedouin: social change in a settled environment.
NSbSU, 1985. 375 p.   Micro 86–9830
DAI, v. 47A, Oct. 1986: 1384.

1003
Jalali-Tehrani, Seyed Mohammad Mohsen. Religious commitment as a factor in personality integration [of Muslim and Christian males]—a factor in mental health. CSfSI, 1985. 105 p.   Micro 85–28,569
DAI, v. 46B, Apr. 1986: 3629.

1004
Jalbert, Paul L. Structures of "News Speak:" U.S. network television coverage of the Lebanon War, summer 1982. MBU, 1984. 214 p.   Micro 84–18,791
DAI, v. 45A, Dec. 1984: 1563.

1005
Jallad, Saud Saadeh. The role of an educational technology center in the development of teacher education in the Yemen Arab Republic. DCU, 1981. 246 p.
      Micro 81–21,272
DAI, v. 42A, Oct. 1981: 1448.

1006
Jambi, Abdussalam Ali. The relationship between the perceived leader behavior of departmental chairpersons and faculty morale at the College of Education, King Saud University in Riyadh, Saudi Arabia. OkU, 1984. 202 p.
      Micro 84–13,978
DAI, v. 45A, Sept. 1984: 762.

1007
Jamil, Muhammad Faris. Islamic *wirāqah* (stationery) during the early Middle Ages. MiU, 1985. 300 p.   Micro 85–12,437
DAI, v. 46A, Oct. 1985: 974.

1008
Jan, Mohammed Saleh Ali. An investigation of the problems of the English program in the intermediate boys' schools of Saudi Arabia. MiEM, 1984. 333 p.
      Micro 85–7505
DAI, v. 46A, Aug. 1985: 314.

1009
Jan, Najmudein Abdulghafour. Between Islamic and Western education: a case study of Umm al-Qura University, Makkah, Saudi Arabia. MiEM, 1983. 140 p.   Micro 84–7201
DAI, v. 44A, June 1984: 3557–3558.

1010
Jandora, John W. Buṭrus al-Bustānī: ideas, endeavors, and influence. ICU, 1981. CDI, 1973–1982, v. 35: 518.

1011
al-Janobi, Ali Hassan. The perceptions of Saudi Arabian students in the U.S.A. to their general secondary education certificate examinations and some relationships to selected demographic variables. OrU, 1984. 152 p.
Micro 84–24,003
DAI, v. 45A, Jan. 1985: 2034.

1012
al-Jarallah, Ahmed J. Impact of industrialization on the small-sized town of Jubail, Saudi Arabia. CoGrU, 1983. 182 p.   Micro 84–8142
DAI, v. 45A, Sept. 1984: 944.

1013
Jarawan, Eva Muawwad. Development and verification of role-specific competencies for hospital administrators in Lebanon. GASU, 1984. 201 p.
Micro 84–29,301
DAI, v. 45A, Mar. 1985: 2928.

1014
Jarbawi, Ali Bassam. Modernism and secularism in the Arab Middle East. OCU, 1981. 317 p.   Micro 82–1233
DAI, v. 42A, Feb. 1982: 3738.

1015
Jasem, Iesa Mohammad. Word frequency count in "spontaneous" conversations of five year old Kuwaiti Arabic speaking children. MiEM, 1984. 153 p.
Micro 85–3224
DAI, v. 46A, Aug. 1985: 347.

1016
al-Jasir, Abdullah Saleh. An analytical and descriptive comparison of international communication systems in the United States and the Soviet Union as adapted for use in Saudi Arabia. OkU, 1982. 240 p.   Micro 82–15,898
DAI, v. 43A, Aug. 1982: 296.

1017
al-Jasser, Jasser Abdulrahman. Comparative effect of native English-speaking instructors (NESI) and nonnative English-speaking instructors (NNESI) on performance of the freshman students at King Saud University. KU, 1983. 77 p.   Micro 84–3606
DAI, v. 44A, May 1984: 3308.

1018
al-Jasser, Muhammad Sulaiman. The role of financial development in economic development: the case of Saudi Arabia. CU-Riv, 1986. 338 p.
Micro 86–23,026
DAI, v. 47A, Jan. 1987: 2679.

1019
Jastaniah, Abdulaziz Saddiq. The Islamic state in light of the Qur'ān and *Sunnah*. CCC, 1982. 143 p. Micro 82-6207
DAI, v. 42A, Apr. 1982: 4578.

1020
Jastaniah, Abdulla Rashad. Industrial safety and technologicalization: an analysis of the management of industrial safety programs in Saudi Arabia. IaCfT, 1982. 288 p. Micro 83-13,586
DAI, v. 44A, Oct. 1983: 1147.

1021
Jbara, Taysir Yunes. al-Ḥājj Muḥammad Amīn al-Ḥusaynī, Muftī of Jerusalem: the Palestine years, 1921-1937. NNU, 1982. 292 p. Micro 83-7832
DAI, v. 43A, May 1983: 3676.

1022
Jbeily, Kamil Assaad. A profile of the needs and concerns of English-speaking public secondary science teachers from five geographic regions of the Republic of Lebanon. TxU, 1987. 276 p. Micro 87-17,443
DAI, v. 48A, Nov. 1987: 1164.

1023
al-Jefri, Abdulrahim Houssain. Relationships between traditional and modern values held by Saudi Arabians and perceptions of life satisfaction in old age. FU, 1985. 141 p. Micro 85-23,800
DAI, v. 46A, Mar. 1986: 2778.

1024
al-Jehani, Nasir Mohammed. Sociostylistic stratification of Arabic in Makkah. MiU, 1985. 186 p. Micro 85-12,350
DAI, v. 46A, Oct. 1985: 962.

1025
al-Jenabi, Muhammed Nassif Jasim. Manpower planning for agricultural development: the role of agricultural higher education institutions in Iraq. PPiU, 1981. 132 p. Micro 82-13,128
DAI, v. 43A, July 1982: 50.

1026
Jennings, Anne M. Power and influence: women's associations in an Egyptian Nubian village. CU-Riv, 1985. 215 p. Micro 85-20,633
DAI, v. 46A, Jan. 1986: 1990.

1027
Jensen, Mehri Samandari. The impact of religion, socio-economic status, and degree of religiosity on family planning among Moslems and Baha'is in Iran: a pilot survey research. CoGrU, 1981. 108 p. Micro 82-13,272
DAI, v. 43A, July 1982: 273-274.

1028
el Jerary, Abdallah Taher. The design of a mass media training program: the formulation of a paradigm for the developing nations with particular application to the Libyan example. WU, 1981. 319 p.   Micro 81–24,607
DAI, v. 42A, Jan. 1982: 2907.

1029
al-Jerian, Abdullah A. The production factors of a traditional Red Sea fishery and its bioeconomics. MiU, 1985. 135 p.   Micro 86–396
DAI, v. 46B, May 1986: 3645.

1030
Jessup, Suzanne E. B. The effects of knowledge of moral development stage theory and a request to fake on the defining issues test scores of adolescents in a multinational American school in Kuwait. KMK, 1983. 92 p.   Micro 84–7677
DAI, v. 45A, July 1984: 158–159.

1031
al-Jibouri, Sadia Jabouri Joudi. Size, technology, and organizational structure in the manufacturing industry of a developing country: Iraq. MsSM, 1983. 273 p.
Micro 84–10,658
DAI, v. 45A, Aug. 1984: 571–572.

1032
al-Jilani, Ahmed Abbas. Environmental impact on organizational design in Saudi Arabia. FTaSU, 1985. 227 p.   Micro 85–13,354
DAI, v. 46A, Oct. 1985: 1081.

1033
al-Jindi, Alia Abdullah Ibraheem. The status of educational media in the preparation of female teachers in Saudi Arabia. PPiU, 1987. 272 p.
Micro 87–19,279
DAI, v. 48A, Dec. 1987: 1437.

1034
Jitmoud, Linda K. K. An intellectual historical study of Islamic *jihād* during the life of Muhammad and in the twentieth century. InMuB, 1985. 279 p.
Micro 85–25,203
DAI, v. 46A, Mar. 1986: 2720–2721.

1035
Jiyad, Mohammed Mossa. A linguistic evaluative study of the textbooks used to teach English in Libya. TxU, 1982. 326 p.   Micro 82–17,889
DAI, v. 43A, Sept. 1982: 707.

1036
Johnson, Kathryn V. The unerring balance: a study of the theory of sanctity (*wilāyah*) of 'Abd al-Wahhāb al-Sha'rānī. MH, 1985. 476 p.   Micro 86–2289
DAI, v. 47A, July 1986: 216.

1037
Joma, Hussain M. A needs analysis study for the establishment of a community college educational system in the United Arab Emirates. MiKW, 1982. 139 p.
Micro 83–5531
DAI, v. 43A, Apr. 1983: 3198.

1038
Judeh, Hikmat Adib. A study of the attitudes of Jordanian educators in higher education toward the presence of women in scientific and technical fields of study in Jordanian institutes of higher education. DGW, 1985. 242 p.
Micro 85–16,228
DAI, v. 46A, Dec. 1985: 1543.

1039
al-Jufry, Mohamed Ghazaly. A study of banking sector management training provisions in response to the Saudanization policy. CSdI, 1983. 149 p.
Micro 84–447
DAI, v. 44A, Mar. 1984: 2866.

1040
al-Juhani, Abdullah Muhammad. Recruting public servants in the Kingdom of Saudi Arabia. CCC, 1985. 210 p.   Micro 85–17,260
DAI, v. 46A, Dec. 1985: 1752.

1041
al-Juhany, Uwaidah Metaireek. The history of Najd prior to the Wahhabis: a study of social, political and religious conditions in Najd during three centuries preceding the Wahhabi reform movement. WaU, 1983. 320 p.
Micro 83–19,382
DAI, v. 44A, Oct. 1983: 1171.

1042
al Jumaily, Fathia H. Rural migration and juvenile delinquency in Iraq: a case study of Medenat al Thowrah in Baghdad. NBuU, 1984. 140 p.
Micro 84–26,015
DAI, v. 45A, Feb. 1985: 2659.

1043
al-Jurf, Reima Sado. An ethnographic study of reading comprehension instruction in EFL classrooms in secondary schools in Saudi Arabia. IaU, 1986. 386 p.
Micro 86–22,737
DAI, v. 47A, Jan. 1987: 2522.

1044
Justice, David B. The semantics of form in Arabic, in the mirror of European languages. CU, 1981. 622 p.   Micro 82–11,978
DAI, v. 42A, June 1982: 5107.

1045
al-Juwayer, Ibrahim Ibn Mubarak. Development and family in Saudi Arabia: an

exploratory study on the views of university students in Riyadh. FU, 1984.
281 p.   Micro 84–20,987
DAI, v. 45A, Jan. 1985: 2254.

1046
Kabatilo, Ziad Salah. A pilot description of indigenous signs used by deaf persons
in Jordan. MiEM, 1982. 204 p.   Micro 83–8958
DAI, v. 44A, July 1983: 136.

1047
Kabbali, Ahmed. Compensatory growth studies in native Moroccan breeds of
sheep. MnU, 1987. 76 p.   Micro 87–10,305
DAI, v. 48B, July 1987: 10.

1048
Kabbara, Mahmoud Farouk. 'Abd al-Nāṣir's Egypt and the Soviet Union: an
Egyptian view, 1952–1970—the impact of differences between Arab socialist
and Marxist-Leninist ideologies. AzU, 1981. 551 p.   Micro 81–16,811
DAI, v. 42A, Aug. 1981: 811.

1049
Kabli, Talal Hassan. Selected factors influencing the use of instructional media by
elementary school male teachers in al-Medina District in Saudi Arabia. MiEM,
1986. 210 p.   Micro 87–484
DAI, v. 47A, Apr. 1987: 3738.

1050
Kadjar, Shapoor Masood. Psychopathology of fanaticism: a case study in the
fanaticism of the Islamic Iranian revolution. CLSU, 1981.
DAI, v. 42A, Apr. 1982: 4301.

1051
Kadom, Wajeha Thabit. A comparison of influences that motivate a desire in
women participants age 15–45 from rural and urban areas of Iraq to continue
their education after completing People's School. KMK, 1984. 212 p.
                                                        Micro 85–6795
DAI, v. 46A, July 1985: 48–49.

1052
Kafafi, Laila Hussein. Age at marriage and cumulative fertility in rural Egypt.
NcD, 1983. 140 p.   Micro 83–21,566
DAI, v. 44A, Nov. 1983: 1590.

1053
al Kahem, Hmoud Fares. The freshwater fishes of Arabia: systematics and conservation. CoFS, 1983. 225 p.   Micro 84–8887
DAI, v. 45B, July 1984: 64.

1054
Kalaji, Fadwa Naim. Analysis of savings behavior in the countries of the Arab

world. PPiU, 1985. 186 p.   Micro 85–21,513
DAI, v. 46A, Feb. 1986: 2378.

1055
Kallan, Jeffrey E. The assimilation of internal migrants to large cities of the Third
World: a comparative study. NcU, 1986. 198 p.   Micro 87–11,124
DAI, v. 48A, Aug. 1987: 485.

1056
Kamal, Abdulaziz Abdulrahman. A study of attitudes, social adjustment and
educational problems of Qatari students pursuing higher education in the
United States. MnU, 1984. 178 p.   Micro 84–18,493
DAI, v. 45A, Nov. 1984: 1344.

1057
Kamal, Fawaz. A study of the political aspects of the Druze law. PPDrop, 1981.
158 p.   Micro 81–20,775
DAI, v. 42A, Dec. 1981: 2797–2798.

1058
Kamel, Boshra Naguib. Arguing in English as a second language: a study of the
speech act performance of Arabic speakers. IU, 1983. 250 p.   Micro 84–9965
DAI, v. 45A, July 1984: 104.

1059
Kamel Hafez, Nermine. Illiteracy in Egypt: a problem study and a language
analysis of literacy primers used by radio and television. TxU, 1983. 348 p.
                                                        Micro 83–29,836
DAI, v. 44A, Mar. 1984: 2751–2752.

1060
al-Kamookh, Ali Abdulrahman. A survey of the English language teachers'
perceptions of the English language teaching methods in the intermediate and
secondary schools of the eastern province in Saudi Arabia. KU, 1981. 135 p.
                                                        Micro 82–18,794
DAI, v. 43A, Dec. 1982: 1808.

1061
Kamp, Kathryn A. Architectural indices of socio-economic variability: an ethno-
archaeological case study from Syria. AzU, 1982. 403 p.   Micro 82–17,498
DAI, v. 43A, Sept. 1982: 852.

1062
Kanbar, Wadih K. Continuity and spatial change in Arab-Islamic cities. NNC,
1984. 280 p.   Micro 87–3044
DAI, v. 47A, Apr. 1987: 3889.

1063
al-Kandari, Jasem Yousef. Alienation in the workplace: a comparative study

between Kuwaiti and non-Kuwaiti workers. CoU, 1983. 161 p.

Micro 84–870

DAI, v. 44A, Mar. 1984: 2745.

1064

Kane, Constance F. A comparative study of social welfare decentralization in Egypt and Israel. MWalB, 1985. 265 p.　　　　　Micro 85–9076

DAI, v. 46A, Sept. 1985: 810–811.

1065

Kanungsukkasem, Vijit. A measurement and comparison of selected physical fitness components and anthropometrical characteristics of American, Middle Eastern, and East and Southeast Asian male students at Oklahoma State University. OkS, 1983. 246 p.　　　　　Micro 83–25,819

DAI, v. 44A, Jan. 1984: 2084.

1066

Karake, Zeinab A. A macroeconometric comparative analysis of the effects of Eastern European and Western technologies on less developed countries: the case of Egypt. DGW, 1987. 320 p.　　　　　Micro 87–13,518

DAI, v. 48A, Sept. 1987: 708.

1067

Karam, Ebraheem Mohammad Hassan. A proposed alternative program for secondary schools of the state of Kuwait. AzU, 1981. 213 p.　Micro 81–16,686

DAI, v. 42A, Aug. 1981: 647.

1068

Karaman, Aykut. The ecology of the built environment: toward designing for "genius loci" [near the Gulf]. PU, 1983. 182 p.　　　　Micro 84–6680

DAI, v. 45A, July 1984: 1.

1069

Karasek, Richard M. Structural and stratigraphic analysis of the Paleozoic Murzuk and Ghadames Basins, western Libya. ScU, 1981. 164 p.

Micro 81–23,422

DAI, v. 42B, Nov. 1981: 1790–1791.

1070

Karimi, Khalid Ali Mansour. University in transition, a study in institutional development: a case study of Umm al-Qura University, Mecca, Saudi Arabia. InU, 1983. 208 p.　　　　　Micro 83–28,103

DAI, v. 44A, Apr. 1984: 2991–2992.

1071

al-Karni, Ali Saad M. Student perceptions of the extracurricular activities program at King Saud University. MiEM, 1986. 158 p.　　　Micro 87–430

DAI, v. 47A, Mar. 1987: 3248.

1072

Karra, Mihira V. Zinc, calcium and magnesium in human lactation: a compari-

119

son of mineral levels in milk of American and Egyptian women and growth of their infants. InLP, 1986. 219 p.	Micro 86–22,167
DAI, v. 47B, Dec. 1986: 2380.

1073
Kashefinejad, Djavad. Investment strategy of Middle Eastern OPEC countries (MEOPEC). CCC, 1982. 264 p.	Micro 82–12,352
DAI, v. 42A, June 1982: 5180–5181.

1074
al-Kassabi, Majid Abdullah. A management training model for engineers in Saudi Arabia. MoRM, 1985. 143 p.	Micro 86–6797
DAI, v. 47A, Aug. 1986: 580.

1075
Kassis, Jihad Georges. U.S. Foreign policy-making in Middle East crises: the 1973-74 oil embargo. InNd, 1981. 339 p.	Micro 81–18,574
DAI, v. 42A, Sept. 1981: 1304–1305.

1076
Kastens, Kim A. Structural causes and sedimentological effects of "cobblestone topography" in the eastern Mediterranean Sea. CU-S, 1981. 223 p.
Micro 82–3027
DAI, v. 42B, Mar. 1982: 3609–3610.

1077
Katheb, Abdulrahman H. Enad. The effects of media use and reliance on cognitions and perceptions of the Arab-Israeli conflict. OAU, 1986. 242 p.
Micro 86–17,990
DAI, v. 47A, Jan. 1987: 2354.

1078
Kattan, Robert Anton Said. The impact of government expenditures in the transformation process of a traditional economy: a case study of Saudi Arabia. DGW, 1982. 321 p.	Micro 82–11,770
DAI, v. 42A, June 1982: 5203.

1079
Katz, Cindi. "If there weren't kids there wouldn't be fields": children's environmental learning, knowledge and interactions in a changing socio-economic context in rural Sudan. MWC, 1986. 584 p.	Micro 87–7533
DAI, v. 47A, June 1987: 4481.

1080
Katz, David J. *Kāfir* to Afghan: religious conversion, political incorporation and ethnicity in the Väygal Valley, Nuristan. CLU, 1982. 364 p.
Micro 82–19,698
DAI, v. 43A, Oct. 1982: 1214.

1081
Kaud, Nasser Ibrahim. Optimal oil extraction, exploration and investment in an

underdeveloped oil-exporting country: the Saudi case. WaU, 1985. 166 p.
Micro 85–21,609
DAI, v. 46A, Jan. 1986: 2018.

1082
Kaufold, Howard S. OPEC portfolio investment, oil supply and worldwide inflation. NjP, 1981. 137 p. Micro 81–18,338
DAI, v. 42A, Sept. 1981: 1256.

1083
Kavoossi, Masoudadin. The impact of oil revenues on foreign policy: a comparative analysis of Iran and Kuwait, 1974–1978. DCU, 1983. 368 p.
Micro 83–6545
DAI, v. 43A, May 1983: 3700.

1084
Kawtb, Kawther Ibrahim Mohamed. Teaching beginning reading to students of English as a foreign language in Egypt: a comparative study. PPiU, 1981. 188 p.
Micro 82–8682
DAI, v. 42A, May 1982: 4779.

1085
Kayed, Isam M. H. The influence of Arabic grammar on edited and nonedited English used by Arabs. MoU, 1985. 242 p. Micro 86–7916
DAI, v. 47A, Aug. 1986: 522.

1086
Kayed, Zuhair Abdelkarim. Income tax theory and its practice in Jordan. CLSU, 1981.
DAI, v. 42A, Feb. 1982: 3749–3750.

1087
al-Kaylani, Majid Irsan. Ibn Taymīya on education: an analytical study of Ibn Taymīya's views on education. PPiU, 1981. 217 p. Micro 82–2221
DAI, v. 42A, Feb. 1982: 3494.

1088
Kazaleh, Fadwa Ann. Biculturalism and adjustment: a study of Ramallah-American adolescents in Jacksonville, Florida. FTaSU, 1986. 245 p.
Micro 86–9672
DAI, v. 47A, Aug. 1986: 448.

1089
Kazan, Fayad el-Abd. Relations between mass media and attitudes toward modernity and psychological stress of university students and civil servants in four Arabian Gulf countries. PPT, 1987. 565 p. Micro 87–11,358
DAI, v. 48A, Aug. 1987: 242.

1090
al-Kazi, Lubna Ahmad. The dilemma of ultra-rapid development: reliance on

migrant labour in the oil rich Gulf States. TxU, 1983. 334 p.

Micro 84–14,335

DAI, v. 45A, Sept. 1984: 945.

1091

al-Kazmi, Zohair Ahmed. Student perceptions of parental influence in choice of college and academic field of study at King Abdulaziz University in Saudi Arabia. MiEM, 1981. 198 p. Micro 81–17,205

DAI, v. 42A, Aug. 1981: 565.

1092

Kechichian, Joseph A. The Gulf Cooperation Council: search for security in the Persian Gulf. ViU, 1985. 596 p. Micro 86–15,597

DAI, v. 47A, Dec. 1986: 2305.

1093

Keck, Lois T. The role of migration in maintaining and changing an ethnic identity: the case of the Egyptian-Americans in the Washington-Baltimore metropolitan region. NBiSU, 1986. 238 p. Micro 86–17,882

DAI, v. 47A, Nov. 1986: 1791.

1094

Keegan, John M. The phonology and morphology of Moroccan Arabic. NNCU-G, 1986. 279 p. Micro 86–29,706

DAI, v. 47A, Mar. 1987: 3413.

1095

Kelley, Edward R. Mark Tobey and the Baha'i Faith: new perspectives on the artist and his paintings. TxU, 1983. 252 p. Micro 84–14,395

DAI, v. 45A, Oct. 1984: 978.

1096

Kelsay, John E. Religion and morality in Islam: a proposal concerning ethics in the formative period. ViU, 1985. 388 p. Micro 86–15,600

DAI, v. 47A, Nov. 1986: 1769.

1097

Kendall, Patrick. The impact of market structure and political instability on the official price of OPEC crude, 1972–1983. PPT, 1987. 160 p.

Micro 87–11,359

DAI, v. 48A, Aug. 1987: 448.

1098

Kensara, Ehsan Mohammed. Factors influencing the use of educational media technology by Saudi student-teachers from the College of Education at Umm al-Qura University. PPiU, 1987. 219 p. Micro 87–19,300

DAI, v. 48A, Dec. 1987: 1439.

1099

Keophumihae, Sanguan. Oil dependence and Thai foreign policy behavior

during the Arab-Israeli war of October 1973. IDeKN, 1985. 348 p.
Micro 86–4330
DAI, v. 46A, June 1986: 3795–3796.

1100
Keshavjee, Rafique Habiib. The quest for gnosis and the call of history: modernization among the Ismailis of Iran. MH, 1981.
CDI, 1973–1982, v. 35: 711.

1101
Kestenberg-Amighi, Janet T. The Zoroastrians: persistence of a small minority group in Moslem Iran. MoU, 1984. 468 p. Micro 85–12,224
DAI, v. 46A, Oct. 1985: 1015.

1102
Khader, Mahmoud Mohammad. Designing a model for an art teacher education program for Jordan. FTaSU, 1983. 296 p. Micro 84–4741
DAI, v. 44A, May 1984: 3250.

1103
el-Khafaifi, Hussein Mabrok. The role of the Cairo Academy in coining Arabic scientific terminology: an historical and linguistic evaluation. UU, 1985. 226 p.
Micro 85–24,161
DAI, v. 46A, Mar. 1986: 2678.

1104
Khairy, Majduddin Omar. Jordan and the world system: incorporation and resistance. MdU, 1980. 230 p. Micro 81–16,495
DAI, v. 42A, Aug. 1981: 882.

1105
al-Khalaf, Abdullah Hamad. Specification and calibration of Bagnold's model for sand transport: Urayq Al Buldan dune field, central Saudi Arabia. InU, 1986.
264 p. Micro 86–27,972
DAI, v. 47A, Feb. 1987: 3153.

1106
Khalaf, Jassim Muhammad. The Kuwait National Assembly: a study of its structure and function. NAlU, 1984. 276 p. Micro 85–1705
DAI, v. 46A, Sept. 1985: 784.

1107
Khalaf, Mahmud Mohammed. The relationship between economic development and the legal system: the historical case of the Arabs. CLSU, 1986.
DAI, v. 48A, Oct. 1987: 1008.

1108
Khalaf, Rima. The distribution of the trade effects of the Arab Common Market. OrPS, 1984. 218 p. Micro 84–7807
DAI, v. 44A, June 1984: 3758.

1109

Khalaf, Sulayman Najm. Family, village and the political party: articulation of social change in contemporary rural Syria. CLU, 1981. 635 p.

Micro 81–20,988

DAI, v. 42A, Oct. 1981: 1701–1702.

1110

Khalafalla, Elfatih Shaaeldin. The development of peripheral capitalism in Sudan, 1898–1978. NBuU, 1981. 228 p. Micro 81–22,178

DAI, v. 42A, Oct. 1981: 1720.

1111

al-Khalidi, Abdullah Motad. Job content and context factors related to satisfaction and dissatisfaction in three occupational levels of the public sector in Saudi Arabia. FTaSU, 1983. 296 p. Micro 83–23,822

DAI, v. 44A, Dec. 1983: 1917–1918.

1112

al-Khalifah, Abdullah H. M. Ecological expansion in Saudi Arabia: a case study in socioeconomic development. TxU, 1985. 256 p. Micro 85–29,814

DAI, v. 46A, Apr. 1986: 3168.

1113

Khalifeh, Issam Ali. A stratigraphic and ceramic analysis of the Late Bronze and Iron Age periods from Area II, Sounding X, A/B-8/9, at Sarepta (Modern Sarafand), Lebanon. PU, 1981. 757 p. Micro 82–7985

DAI, v. 43A, July 1982: 233.

1114

Khalifeh, Suha Maher. The history of organized sports in Jordan. FMU, 1986. 237 p. Micro 86–19,484

DAI, v. 47A, Dec. 1986: 2077–2078.

1115

Khalil, Ali Mohammed. Transcendental production function, productivity and technical change in Iraqi manufacturing: an economic analysis. NTR, 1986. 137 p. Micro 87–8527

DAI, v. 47A, June 1987: 4475.

1116

Khalil, Aziz M. Communicative error evaluation: a study of American native speakers' evaluations and interpretations of deviant utterances written by Arab EFL learners. IU, 1984. 170 p. Micro 85–2202

DAI, v. 45A, May 1985: 3339.

1117

Khalil, Helmy Mohamed. A development plan of mechanical engineering programs for Egypt. MoU, 1980. 175 p. Micro 82–2645

DAI, v. 42A, Feb. 1982: 3534.

1118

al-Khalil, Mowaffaq Ali. Oil and economic development in OPEC countries, with case studies about Iraq and Algeria. FTaSU, 1984. 312 p.   Micro 85–5282
DAI, v. 46A, July 1985: 193.

1119

Khalil, Saadeh Abdel Rahim. The relationship between teacher perceptions of ideal and actual supervisory behavior and teacher satisfaction with supervision in Jordan. OrU, 1983. 243 p.   Micro 84–3739
DAI, v. 44A, May 1984: 3267.

1120

Khan, Frances Surdar Banon. Sufi motifs and themes in the imagery patterns of Ghalib's Urdu Ghazal. WU, 1982. 831 p.   Micro 82–14,744
DAI, v. 43A, Oct. 1982: 1148.

1121

Khan, Hafiz A. Ghaffar. Shāh Walī Allāh: an analysis of his metaphysical thought. PPT, 1987. 399 p.   Micro 87–11,361
DAI, v. 48A, Aug. 1987: 417.

1122

Khan, Shahrukh Rafi. Profit and loss sharing: an economic analysis of an Islamic financial system. MiU, 1983. 282 p.   Micro 83–14,306
DAI, v. 44A, Aug. 1983: 535.

1123

Khan, Waqar Masood. Towards an interest free Islamic economic system: a theoretical analysis of prohibiting debt financing. MBU, 1984. 162 p.

Micro 84–4684

DAI, v. 44A, May 1984: 3431–3432.

1124

Khassawneh, Anis Saker. The social setting of administrative behavior in Jordan. CCC, 1987. 185 p.   Micro 87–5182
DAI, v. 47A, May 1987: 4187.

1125

Khateeb, Mohammed Shahhat. Relating technical education to industrial manpower requirements in the Kingdom of Saudi Arabia. CLSU, 1985.
DAI, v. 46A, Mar. 1986: 2595–2596.

1126

al Khateeb, Talal A. The relationship of teacher salary and other selected variables to student achievement in Iraqi preparatory schools in Baghdad. PPiU, 1982. 103 p.   Micro 83–12,546
DAI, v. 44A, July 1983: 69.

1127

Khater, Tony. Lebanese politics and the Palestinian resistance movement, 1967–

1976. NBuU, 1982. 306 p.   Micro 82–14,191
DAI, v. 43A, July 1982: 254.

1128
el-Khatib, Adib. Housing in Nablus: socioeconomic characteristics and housing
satisfaction of three Palestinian sub-groups. NNCU-G, 1985. 309 p.
                                                           Micro 85–15,622
DAI, v. 46A, Nov. 1985: 1402.

1129
Khatib, Basel Raouf. The politics of Arab and Persian nationalisms in the Gulf.
CLSU, 1981.
DAI, v. 43A, July 1982: 258–259.

1130
Khatib, Hashem Anwar. The foreign policy of Jordan. CLSU, 1986.
DAI, v. 47A, Mar. 1987: 3553.

1131
al-Khatib, Hussein Helal Muhammad. Economic evaluation of vocational education in Jordan. IU, 1986. 332 p.   Micro 87–1428
DAI, v. 47A, June 1987: 4369.

1132
Khattab, Mohamed Kamel. The importance of telecommunications media used
in conjunction with non-formal education and rural community centers for
rural development in Saudi Arabia. WU, 1982. 202 p.   Micro 83–1870
DAI, v. 43A, Apr. 1983: 3148.

1133
al-Khattabi, Abdulhamid Awaid. The current status of geographic education in
the elementary school as perceived by geography teachers and supervisors in
Saudi Arabia. CoDU, 1986. 268 p.   Micro 86–17,661
DAI, v. 47A, Nov. 1986: 1586–1587.

1134
Khayat, Abdulaziz Abdulla. A study of institutional environment at King Ab-
dulaziz University as perceived by upper division students. MiEM, 1981. 203 p.
                                                           Micro 81–26,518
DAI, v. 42A, Dec. 1981: 2526–2527.

1135
al Khayyat, Aly A. A modified Gaussian plume dispersion model suitable for the
climate of Saudi Arabia. WaPS, 1984. 97 p.   Micro 85–4218
DAI, v. 45B, June 1985: 3886.

1136
Khazali, Mohammad Mohmoud. Modernity: a study of Adonis' ['Alī Aḥmad
Sa'īd] theory and poetry. TxU, 1983. 207 p.   Micro 83–19,619
DAI, v. 44A, Oct. 1983: 1081.

1137
el-Khazen, Farid Elias. The disintegration of the Lebanese confessional system, 1867–1976. MdBJ, 1987. 886 p. Micro 87–16,622
DAI, v. 48A, Nov. 1987: 1312.

1138
Kheir, Ahmed I. M. Government policy on higher education in the Sudan, 1970 to 1985. TxHU, 1986. 211 p. Micro 87–53
DAI, v. 47A, Mar. 1987: 3263.

1139
Kherbachi, Hamid. Structural change and employment in Algeria. NTR, 1984. 168 p. Micro 84–26,524
DAI, v. 45A, Feb. 1985: 2576.

1140
Khered, Muhammad Omar Hasan. Measuring the syntactic maturity in the written English of Arab students at four proficiency levels and establishing an EFL index of development. KU, 1983. 215 p. Micro 83–17,940
DAI, v. 44A, Oct. 1983: 1010.

1141
Khogali, Mohamed Elamien. Peanut harvest losses in Sudan. MiEM, 1984. 165 p.
Micro 85–3229
DAI, v. 45B, June 1985: 3873.

1142
Kholafa, Said Ahmed M. An economic analysis of foreign assets, money supply, and inflation in Saudi Arabia, 1963–1983. ULA, 1985. 147 p.
Micro 85–23,701
DAI, v. 46A, Mar. 1986: 2755.

1143
Kholaif, Ali Ibrahim. The Hijaz Vilayet, 1869–1908: the sharifate, the *hajj*, and the Bedouins of the Hijaz. WU, 1986. 177 p. Micro 86–14,375
DAI, v. 47A, Dec. 1986: 2286.

1144
Khosrowshahi, Manouchehr Rostamy. Management of communal conflict in the Middle East: the case of the Kurds. TxDN, 1983. 264 p. Micro 84–4325
DAI, v. 44A, May 1984: 3481.

1145
al-Khouli, Saiyed Fathi Ahmed. Forecasting manpower skills by occupation and nationality in a petrodollar-surplus economy: the case of Saudi Arabia. CoU, 1985. 469 p. Micro 85–22,639
DAI, v. 46A, Feb. 1986: 2395.

1146
Khoury, Radwan Mitry. Perceived effects of inservice training for teachers in

Jordan on selected objectives. MiU, 1982. 211 p.   Micro 83-4522
DAI, v. 43A, Apr. 1983: 3295-3296.

1147
al-Khulaifi, Ibrahim Mohammed. An investigation of the viewing bahavior toward *Iftaḥ yā Simsim* by Kuwaiti kindergarteners. OU, 1984. 155 p.
                                                                 Micro 85-3979
DAI, v. 46A, July 1985: 68.

1148
Khuthaila, Hend Majid. Developing a plan for Saudi Arabian women's higher
education. NSyU, 1981. 321 p.   Micro 81-23,916
DAI, v. 42A, Nov. 1981: 1991.

1149
Khuthaila, Khalid Majid. Saudi Arabia's development: a dependency theory
perspective. NSyU, 1984. 288 p.   Micro 85-755
DAI, v. 45A, May 1985: 3459.

1150
Kianian S. A., M. Amin. Estimation and projection of the demand for refined
petroleum products in Iran. CoU, 1983. 249 p.   Micro 84-8044
DAI, v. 45A, July 1984: 246.

1151
Kiener, Ronald C. The Hebrew paraphrase of Saadia Gaon's *Kitāb al-amānāt wa'l-
i'tiqādāt*. PU, 1984. 391 p.   Micro 84-17,320
DAI, v. 45A, Nov. 1984: 1433.

1152
Kiewe, Amos. An analysis by rhetorical models of the Sadat-Begin peace negotia-
tion from inception to completion. OAU, 1984. 268 p.   Micro 84-16,357
DAI, v. 45A, Oct. 1984: 985.

1153
el-Kikhia, Mansour Omar. Political process and political economy in the Third
World: a case study of Libya. CU-SB, 1986. 402 p.   Micro 87-9108
DAI, v. 48A, July 1987: 215.

1154
Kilgore, Lynn. Degenerative joint disease in a medieval Nubian population. CoU,
1984. 242 p.   Micro 85-8954
DAI, v. 46A, Aug. 1985: 462.

1155
Kim, Ho-Dong. The Muslim rebellion and the Kashghar Emirate in Chinese
Central Asia, 1864-1877. MH, 1986. 326 p.   Micro 86-20,493
DAI, v. 47A, Dec. 1986: 2281.

1156
Kim, Yung Myung. The political economy of military rule: a comparative study

of Brazil, South Korea, Peru and Egypt. NBuU, 1985. 400 p.

Micro 85–18,758

DAI, v. 46A, Jan. 1986: 2060.

1157

Kimball, Charles A. Striving together in the way of God: Muslim participation in Christian-Muslim dialogue. MH, 1987. 475 p.　　Micro 87–19,767

DAI, v. 48A, Dec. 1987: 1475.

1158

al-Kinani, Hatim O. Jafer. Faculty participation in the decision making process in Iraqi universities. CoGrU, 1986. 191 p.　　Micro 87–7032

DAI, v. 47A, June 1987: 4243.

1159

Kingseed, Cole C. Eisenhower and Suez: a reappraisal of presidential activism and crisis management. OU, 1983. 262 p.　　Micro 83–18,382

DAI, v. 44A, Oct. 1983: 1167.

1160

Kisnawi, Mahmoud Mohammed. Attitudes of students and fathers toward vocational education: the role of vocational education in economic development in Saudi Arabia. CoU, 1981. 342 p.　　Micro 82–9834

DAI, v. 42A, May 1982: 4808.

1161

Klailat, Ahlam. Palestinian and Jordanian educational aspirations and expectations. WU, 1981. 195 p.　　Micro 81–15,996

DAI, v. 42A, Sept. 1981: 1333.

1162

Klare, Michael T. Arms, oil and intervention: U.S. military strategy in the Persian Gulf during the Nixon era. OCUG, 1976. 178 p.　　Micro 85–1532

DAI, v. 45A, May 1985: 3443.

1163

Kleem, Ferris A. The Cleveland Maronite Lebanese and education. MiDW, 1982. 397 p.　　Micro 82–16,152

DAI, v. 43A, Sept. 1982: 774.

1164

Kleibo, Ali M. The desire for progress: a structural anthropological analysis of contemporary Arabic knowledge as embedded in Tawfīq el-Ḥakīm's *Oeuvres*. PPT, 1986. 199 p.　　Micro 86–27,471

DAI, v. 47A, Feb. 1987: 3092.

1165

al-Knawy, Saud M. M. A study of leadership bahavior as perceived and expected by deans, heads of departments, and faculty members in three selected institutions of higher learning in Saudi Arabia. OkS, 1985. 223 p.

Micro 85–28,844

DAI, v. 46A, Apr. 1986: 2934.

1166
Knezevich, Linda C. The administration and management of the Patriarchate of Antioch. NNU, 1985. 336 p.   Micro 86–4063
DAI, v. 46A, June 1986: 3752.

1167
Knipp, Margaret M. Women, Western education and change: a case study of the Hausa-Fulani of northern Nigeria. IEN, 1987. 466 p.   Micro 87–10,356
DAI, v. 48A, July 1987: 164.

1168
Knott, Charlotte A. The development of housing and housing policy in Tunis. DGU, 1983. 286 p.   Micro 84–25,178
DAI, v. 45A, Feb. 1985: 2623.

1169
Kobrin, Nancy. Moses on the margin: a critical transcription and semiotic analysis of eight Aljamiado legends of the Morisco figura of Muuçáa. MnU, 1984. 490 p.

Micro 84–13,797

DAI, v. 45A, Sept. 1984: 838.

1170
Koch, Barbara J. Repetition in discourse: cohesion and persuasion in Arabic argumentative prose. MiU, 1981. 261 p.   Micro 82–4686
DAI, v. 42A, Mar. 1982: 3983.

1171
Koehler, Robert P. Sedimentary environment and petrology of the Ain Tobi Formation, Tripolitania, Libya. TxHR, 1982. 299 p.   Micro 82–16,332
DAI, v. 43B, Aug. 1982: 366.

1172
Kohli, Zohra. Education in post-colonial Algeria: analysis of educational reforms and policies. MBU, 1987. 254 p.   Micro 87–9643
DAI, v. 48A, July 1987: 19.

1173
al-Korashi, Salim. A survey of the Math and Science Center Programs of the Ministry of Education of Saudi Arabia. PPiU, 1987. 222 p.   Micro 87–19,280
DAI, v. 48A, Dec. 1987: 1385.

1174
Kouache, Hocine. Peasants, dependency, and underdeveloped areas of Algeria: the case of Beni-Chebana. MiEM, 1985. 239 p.   Micro 86–3441
DAI, v. 46A, June 1986: 3677.

1175
Koura, Aly Abdulsamea. Verbal interaction patterns of selected English as a foreign language teachers in Egyptian secondary schools. DGW, 1986. 210 p.
Micro 86–18,311
DAI, v. 48A, Aug. 1987: 294.

1176
Kramer, Martin S. The congress in modern Islam: on the origins of an innovation.
NjP, 1982. 372 p.
Micro 82–7144
DAI, v. 42A, Apr. 1982: 4544–4545.

1177
Kressel, Neil J. American public opinion and mass media coverage of the Arab-Israeli conflict, 1948–1982. MH, 1983. 329 p.
Micro 83–22,390
DAI, v. 44B, Dec. 1983: 2014.

1178
Krieger, Laurie E. Body notions, gender roles, and fertility regulating method use in Imbaba, Cairo. NcU, 1984. 285 p.
Micro 84–25,491
DAI, v. 45A, Feb. 1985: 2573.

1179
Kshedan, Hadi Salem. The spatial structure of Tripoli, Libya: an example of a Third World socialist city. OkU, 1984. 180 p.
Micro 84–13,979
DAI, v. 45A, Jan. 1985: 2219.

1180
Kuipers, Florence G. A comparative lexicon of three modern Aramaic dialects.
DGU, 1983. 337 p.
Micro 84–1503
DAI, v. 44A, Apr. 1984: 3050.

1181
Kukali, Nabil Elias. A multiple regression analysis of job satisfaction of workers who have graduated from business and industrial schools in Jordan. WyU, 1984. 234 p.
Micro 85–8871
DAI, v. 46A, Oct. 1985: 959.

1182
Kuko, Mustafa Hamza. An evaluation and analysis of the effects of regional economic development on internal migration in the Sudan. CU-Riv, 1984. 342 p.
Micro 85–5270
DAI, v. 46A, July 1985: 232.

1183
Kumamoto, Robert D. International terrorism and American foreign relations, 1945–1976. CLU, 1984. 410 p.
Micro 84–20,199
DAI, v. 45A, Dec. 1984: 1845.

1184
Kumasaka, Yuzo. A comparison of the slowdown in productivity growth after the

two oil crises: Japan and the U.S.A. PU, 1984. 440 p.   Micro 84-17,325
DAI, v. 45A, Nov. 1984: 1465.

1185
Kurashi, Mohammed Farid Yasin. The social responsibility of the multinational corporations operating in Saudi Arabia. CCC, 1984. 386 p.
Micro 85-23,016
DAI, v. 46A, Mar. 1986: 2746.

1186
Kurdi, Abdulrahman Abdulkadir. The Islamic state: a perspective of the Islamic holy revelation. AzU, 1983. 276 p.   Micro 83-23,743
DAI, v. 44A, Dec. 1983: 1911.

1187
Kurdi, Mafaz Abdul Mohsen. Saudi Arabia: perspective on oil, foreign policy, and the Arab-Israeli conflict, 1970–1980. CCC, 1982. 210 p.
Micro 82-20,587
DAI, v. 43A, Dec. 1982: 2088.

1188
Kurdi, Mahgoub Ahmad. The encounter of religions: an analysis of the problem of religion in southern Sudan, 1899–1983. PPT, 1986. 286 p.
Micro 86-11,885
DAI, v. 47A, Sept. 1986: 939.

1189
Kushigian, Julia A. Three versions of Orientalism in contemporary Latin American literature: [Severo] Sarduy, [Jorge Luis] Borges and [Octavio] Paz. CtY, 1984. 200 p.   Micro 85-9711
DAI, v. 46A, Oct. 1985: 993.

1190
Kutubkhanah, Ismael Khaleel. Rural community development in Saudi Arabia: a study of participation, opinions, and evaluations of the Development Center's programs and services by Wadi Fatma villagers. MiEM, 1986. 265 p.
Micro 86-13,306
DAI, v. 47A, Oct. 1986: 1506–1507.

1191
LaBianca, Oystein S. Sedentarization and nomadization: food system cycles at Hesban and vicinity in Transjordan. MWalB, 1987. 411 p.
Micro 87-15,746
DAI, v. 48A, Oct. 1987: 969.

1192
Lacey, Robert K. Man and society in the *Luzūmiyyāt* of al-Maʿarrī. MH, 1984. 350 p.   Micro 85-3546
DAI, v. 45A, June 1985: 3651.

1193
Laffey, Robert M. United States policy toward and relations with Syria, 1941 to 1949. InNd, 1981. 200 p. Micro 81–18,576
DAI, v. 42A, Sept. 1981: 1271–1272.

1194
LaFouge, Jean-Pierre. Études sur les modèles littéraires et ideologiques des récits algériens d'Eugène Fromentin. InU, 1986. 308 p. Micro 86–17,809
DAI, v. 47A, Nov. 1986: 1742.

1195
Lafraie, Najibullah. Ideology of revolution: a normative study of the Islamic revolution in Iran. DHU, 1986. 451 p. Micro 86–29,150
DAI, v. 47A. Mar. 1987: 3548.

1196
Lahood, Gabriel. A comparative analysis of the concept of agency in Aristotle and Avicenna. NBuU, 1985. 259 p. Micro 86–9127
DAI, v. 47A, Aug. 1986: 558.

1197
Lalehparvaran, Parvin. A content analysis of *The New York Times* and *St. Louis Post-Dispatch* coverage of the Arab-Israeli conflict from June 6, 1982-February 12, 1983. OkS, 1984. 107 p. Micro 85–4368
DAI, v. 45A, June 1985: 3469.

1198
Lampe, Gerald E. Ibn al-Muqaffa': political and legal theorist and reformer. MdBJ, 1986. 133 p.
Personal knowledge.

1199
Landenberger, Margaret. United States diplomatic efforts on behalf of Moroccan Jews, 1880–1906. MnCS, 1981. 264 p. Micro 82–1686
DAI, v. 42A, Feb. 1982: 3710.

1200
Laouisset, Djamel-Eddine. The growth of the Algerian iron and steel industry. FMU, 1983. 164 p. Micro 83–28,150
DAI, v. 44A, Feb. 1984: 2525.

1201
Larsen, Ulla M. A comparative study of the levels and the differentials of sterility in Cameroon, Kenya and Sudan. NjP, 1985. 231 p. Micro 85–20,747
DAI, v. 46A, Mar. 1986: 2819.

1202
Larson, Bryant L. The Moslems of Soviet Central Asia: Soviet and Western perceptions of a growing political problem. MnU, 1983. 291 p.
Micro 83–18,089
DAI, v. 44A, Sept. 1983: 834.

1203
Lau, Linda D. Muṣʿab b. al-Zubayr and his governorate of Iraq [655–692 A.D.]. InU, 1981. 120 p.   Micro 82–2952
DAI, v. 42A, Feb. 1982: 3705.

1204
Launer, Harold M. Social control and customary law among the Gaam (Ingessana) of Blue Nile Province, Sudan. ICarbS, 1983. 228 p.   Micro 84–14,020
DAI, v. 45A, Sept. 1984: 879.

1205
Lawson, Fred H. Social origins of aggressive foreign policy: the case of Muhammad ʿAlī's Egypt, 1800–1835. CLU, 1982. 364 p.   Micro 82–19,714
DAI, v. 43A, Oct. 1982: 1283.

1206
al-Lawzi, Sulieman Ahmed. Planning, budgeting, and development in Jordan: an examination of how these policy processes function in a poor and uncertain environment. TxDN, 1987. 271 p.   Micro 87–13,933
DAI, v. 48A, Sept. 1987: 743.

1207
Layne, Linda L. The production and reproduction of tribal identity in Jordan. NjP, 1986. 357 p.   Micro 86–29,435
DAI, v. 47A, Mar. 1987: 3467.

1208
Layoun, Mary N. The non-Western novel: ideology and the genre as immigrant. CU, 1985. 339 p.   Micro 85–25,026
DAI, v. 46A, May 1986: 3346.

1209
Le Gall, Michel F. Pashas, bedouins and notables: Ottoman administration in Tripoli and Benghazi, 1881–1902. NjP, 1986. 278 p.   Micro 86–26,173
DAI, v. 47A, Feb. 1987: 3165.

1210
Le Coat, Nanette C. Neither fable nor science: Volney's writings on travel and history [*Le voyage en Égypte et en Syrie*]. MdBJ, 1986. 287 p.   Micro 86–1277
DAI, v. 47A, July 1986: 196.

1211
Lefebvre, Jeffrey A. Client dependency and donor dependency: American arms transfers to the Horn of Africa, 1953–1986. CtU, 1986. 454 p.
                                              Micro 86–19,128
DAI, v. 47A, Nov. 1986: 1868.

1212
Lenker, Michael K. The importance of the *riḥla* for the Islamization of Spain. PU, 1982. 388 p.   Micro 82–17,145
DAI, v. 43A, Sept. 1982: 835–836.

1213

Lenzen, Cherie J. The Byzantine/Islamic occupation at Caesarea Maritima as evidenced through the pottery. NjMD, 1983. 769 p.　　Micro 83–17,854
DAI, v. 44A, Oct. 1983: 1138.

1214

Lerrick, Alison. *Taghribat Banī Hilāl al-Ḍiyāghim*: variation in the oral epic poetry of Najd. NjP, 1984. 494 p.　　Micro 84–17,427
DAI, v. 45A, Nov. 1984: 1415.

1215

Lewis, Maureen A. The socioeconomic determinants of infant mortality in Jordan: an econometric approach. MdBJ, 1985. 261 p.　　Micro 85–10,427
DAI, v. 46A, Sept. 1985: 766.

1216

Lewis-Ruggiero, Brenda M. Cross-cultural perceptions of justice [of Muslim males born and raised in the Middle East and living in the United States]. CLU, 1987. 206 p.　　Micro 87–19,991
DAI, v. 48A, Dec. 1987: 1530.

1217

Lieb, Diana. Conflict resolution—theory and practice: a case study of the Egyptian/Israeli Peace Treaty, 1973–1979. NNU, 1982. 331 p.　　Micro 82–27,206
DAI, v. 43A, Jan. 1983: 2445.

1218

al-Lihiedan, Saleh Ibrahim. Factors involved in the adoption and rejection of instructional design ideas in Saudi Arabian universities. MiEM, 1985. 312 p.
Micro 86–7044
DAI, v. 47A, Nov. 1986: 1651.

1219

Lillios, Anna. Love in Lawrence Durrell's *Alexandria Quartet*. IaU, 1986. 240 p.
Micro 87–7997
DAI, v. 47A, June 1987: 4398.

1220

Lin, Gi-Yu. A disequilibrium analysis of three macroeconomies after two OPEC shocks: U.S., Germany, and Japan. ICIU, 1983. 112 p.　　Micro 84–338
DAI, v. 44A, June 1984: 3766.

1221

Lindley, Wilber T. The tag end of diplomacy: American policy in the Near East, 1949–1953. TxFTC, 1985. 284 p.　　Micro 85–29,997
DAI, v. 46A, May 1986: 3469–3470.

1222

Litsky, Elliott B. The Murphy-Weygand agreement: the United States and French North Africa, 1940–1942. NNF, 1986. 441 p.　　Micro 86–15,698
DAI, v. 47A, Oct. 1986: 1461.

1223
Livnat, Michal A. Focus constructions in Somali. IU, 1984. 176 p.
                                                        Micro 85–2225
DAI, v. 45A, May 1985: 3339–3340.

1224
Lockman, Zachary. Class and nation: the emergence of the Egyptian workers'
movement. MH, 1983. 689 p.   Micro 83–22,401
DAI, v. 44A, Dec. 1983: 1888.

1225
Loderer, Claudio F. Theory and evidence about the structure of the international
oil market, 1974–1980: a collection of related essays. NRU, 1983. 165 p.
                                                        Micro 83–21,685
DAI, v. 44A, Nov. 1983: 1518.

1226
Long, Roger D. Liaquat Ali Khan [1895–1951]: from National Agriculturalist
Party to Muslim League. CLU, 1985. 428 p.   Micro 85–25,859
DAI, v. 46A, Mar. 1986: 2783.

1227
Lowe, Lisa M. French literary Orientalism: representations of "others" in the texts
of Montesquieu, Flaubert, and Kristeva. CU-SC, 1986. 164 p.
                                                        Micro 86–19,255
DAI, v. 47A, Dec. 1986: 2151.

1228
El Lozy, Mahmoud Ahmed. Four Egyptian playwrights: translations and critical
essays. CU-SB, 1986. 696 p.   Micro 86–29,649
DAI, v. 47A, June 1987: 4237.

1229
Lutfi, Huda. A study of al-Quds in the late fourteenth century based primarily on
the Haram estate inventories and related documents. CaQMM, 1983. 528 p.
Letter from McGill University Libraries.

1230
McAllister, Carol L. Matriliny, Islam, and capitalism: combined and uneven
development in the lives of Negeri Sembilan women. PPiU, 1987. 600 p.
                                                        Micro 87–19,258
DAI, v. 48A, Dec. 1987: 1487–1488.

1231
McAuliffe, Jane D. Perceptions of the Christians in Qur'ānic *tafsīr*. CaOTU, 1984.
DAI, v. 46A, Nov. 1985: 1313.

1232
Maccaferri, James T. Ottoman foreign policy and the British occupation of

Egypt: the Hasan Fehmi Pasha Mission of 1885. CLU, 1983. 345 p.
Micro 84–8838
DAI, v. 45A, July 1984: 269.

1233
McCullough, James S. Financing local government services in developing countries: case studies of implementing innovation [Tunisia]. NcU, 1983. 220 p.
Micro 83–26,235
DAI, v. 44A, Jan. 1984: 2268.

1234
McDonnell, Mary B. The conduct of *ḥajj* from Malaysia and its socioeconomic impact on Malay society: a descriptive and analytical study, 1860–1981. NNC, 1986. 671 p.
Micro 86–23,573
DAI, v. 47A, Jan. 1987: 2701.

1235
McFadden-Preston, Claudette. The rhetoric of Minister Louis Farrakhan: a pluralistic approach. OU, 1986. 242 p.
Micro 87–3587
DAI, v. 47A, June 1987: 4233.

1236
Macheski, Ginger E. Replacing people with petroleum: energy and labor in U.S. agriculture, 1900 to 1978. MiEM, 1986. 239 p.
Micro 86–25,046
DAI, v. 47A, Jan. 1987: 2746.

1237
McHugh, Neil. Holymen of the Blue Nile: religious leadership and the genesis of an Arab Islamic society in the Nilotic Sudan, 1500–1850. IEN, 1986. 493 p.
Micro 86–27,375
DAI, v. 47A, Feb. 1987: 3159.

1238
Mack, Deborah L. Legal change and social structure: the politics of law in eastern Sudan. IEN, 1986. 245 p.
Micro 86–27,372
DAI, v. 47A, Feb. 1987: 3092.

1239
MacKenzie, Neil D. A topographical study of Cairo under the Ayyubids. MiU, 1986. 424 p.
Micro 87–2787
DAI, v. 47A, Apr. 1987: 3854.

1240
MacLean, Derryl N. Religion and society in Arab Sind. CaQMM, 1985.
DAI, v. 46A, May 1986: 3467.

1241
Macmillan, Ewen G. Priorities underlying the evolution of an Arabic short vowel system: Cantineau's Rweli idiolects as exponents of the chronological ordering of linguistic shifts. NjP, 1985. 158 p.
Micro 85–26,828
DAI, v. 46A, Apr. 1986: 3019.

1242
Madanat, Eugeny M. A study for improvement of reading achievement in Arabic language in primary public schools in Jordan. MiU, 1981. 308 p.
Micro 81-16,189
DAI, v. 42A, Aug. 1981: 542.

1243
Madanat, Suheil Sleh. Self-help housing: an option for Jordan. NSyU, 1984. 209 p.   Micro 85-3333
DAI, v. 45A, June 1985: 3764.

1244
Madison, Billy B. The Addis Ababa Agreement on the problem of southern Sudan: a study to evaluate the distribution of benefits among social groups in the southern Sudan and to determine the impact of this distribution on the region's political stability. CoDU, 1984. 359 p.   Micro 86-26,348
DAI, v. 47A, Feb. 1987: 3180-3181.

1245
Madison, Marlyn A. A trilateral appraoch to development cooperation: Afro-Arab solidarity [after 1973]. CU, 1985. 261 p.   Micro 85-25,041
DAI, v. 46A, Mar. 1986: 2802.

1246
Madjid, Nurcholish. Ibn Taymiyya on *kalām* and *falsafa*: a problem of reason and revelation in Islam. ICU, 1984.
CDI, 1984, v. 5: 260.

1247
Magnuson, Douglas K. Islamic reform in contemporary Tunisia: a comparative ethnographic study. RPB, 1987. 365 p.   Micro 87-15,533
DAI, v. 48A, Oct. 1987: 969.

1248
el-Magrahi, Milad A. British policy toward Egypt, 1875-1885: British imperial expansion and Egyptian nationalist response. WaU, 1982. 246 p.
Micro 82-18,219
DAI, v. 43A, Sept. 1982: 891.

1249
Magsood, Sultan Said. A study of the undergraduate academic advising program at Umm al-Qura University, Saudi Arabia, as perceived by students and faculty advisers. MiEM, 1985. 275 p.   Micro 86-25,048
DAI, v. 47A, Jan. 1987: 2402.

1250
Maguire, Eunice G. D. The capitals and other granite carvings at Justinian's Church on Mount Sinai. MH, 1986. 814 p.   Micro 87-2400
DAI, v. 47A, Apr. 1987: 3596.

1251
Mahadin, Radwan Salim. The morphophonemics of the standard Arabic tricon-
sonantal verbs. PU, 1982. 427 p.　　　　　　　　　　Micro 82-17,148
DAI, v. 43A, Sept. 1982: 789.

1252
Mahafza, Sameh Mohammad Mustafa. The historical development and external
influence on the university education system in Jordan: the case of the University of Jordan. NBuU, 1987. 372 p.　　　　　　　　　Micro 87-10,733
DAI, v. 48A, Aug. 1987: 321.

1253
Mahdi, Abbas Abid. Elementary school principals' leadership behavior as per-
ceived by themselves and their teachers in Baghdad City, Iraq. CLSU, 1984.
DAI, v. 44A, June 1984: 3562.

1254
Mahdi, Niran Hashim. An analytical study of the pre-service teacher education
program at the University of Baghdad for prospective teachers of English in
Iraq. TU, 1985. 144 p.　　　　　　　　　　　　　　Micro 85-11,391
DAI, v. 46A, Sept. 1985: 681.

1255
Mahdy, Fadel Hasson. Investment criteria for development projects in Iraq. AzU,
1984. 95 p.　　　　　　　　　　　　　　　　　　　Micro 85-468
DAI, v. 45A, May 1985: 3268.

1256
al-Mahmoud, Abdalla Yousef A. A comparison of mathematics achievement of
Jordanian, Canadian, and American students. DAU, 1986. 99 p.
　　　　　　　　　　　　　　　　　　　　　　　　Micro 86-25,125
DAI, v. 47A, May 1987: 4009.

1257
Mahmoud, Ahmad Jaser. The impact of the foreign migrants on national integra-
tion of the United Arab Emirates. MoU, 1985. 241 p.　　Micro 86-7924
DAI, v. 47A, Aug. 1986: 644.

1258
Mahmoud, Amal Abdul-Ghany. A functional analysis of written compositions of
Egyptian students of English and the applications of the notional-functional
syllabus for the teaching of writing. DGU, 1982. 204 p.　　Micro 83-21,349
DAI, v. 44A, Nov. 1983: 1439.

1259
Mahmoud, Mahgoub el-Tigani. The impact of partial modernization on the
emigration of Sudanese professionals and skilled workers. RPB, 1983. 513 p.
　　　　　　　　　　　　　　　　　　　　　　　　Micro 83-26,008
DAI, v. 44A, Jan. 1984: 2266.

1260
Mahmoud, Mahmoud Karem. The establishment of a nuclear weapon free zone in the Middle East: policy, problems and prospects. ScU, 1984. 270 p.
Micro 84–19,066
DAI, v. 45A, Jan. 1985: 2249.

1261
Maiman, Solaiman Ibrahim. Assessment of Piagetian cognitive abilities required for the twelfth grade male science students in Saudi Arabia to understand selected chemistry concepts taught to them. CoGrU, 1983. 120 p.
Micro 83–28,502
DAI, v. 44A, May 1984: 3343.

1262
Makar, Sizostris Hanna. The People's Republic of China's policy towards the Arab world in the 1970's. NNU, 1985. 296 p.   Micro 86–4067
DAI, v. 46A, June 1986: 3853–3854.

1263
Makhamreh, Muhsen Abdallah. Determinants of labor-management disputes and their settlement in the private sector in Jordan. OU, 1981. 176 p.
Micro 82–7220
DAI, v. 42A, Apr. 1982: 4562.

1264
Makhdom, Mohammed Annas M. Qadhy. The effect of an advance organizer on the reading and retention of foreign [Saudi] students in the United States. FU, 1983. 92 p.   Micro 84–15,140
DAI, v. 45A, Oct. 1984: 1083.

1265
Makinson, Carolyn. Sex differentials in infant and child mortality in Egypt. NjP, 1986. 318 p.   Micro 86–29,436
DAI, v. 47A, Mar. 1987: 3571.

1266
Makki, Elrabih Massoud. The Lebanese dialect of Arabic: southern region. DGU, 1983. 150 p.   Micro 84–1505
DAI, v. 44A, Apr. 1984: 3050.

1267
Makky, Ghazy Abdul Wahed. Characteristics of pilgrim accomodations in Mecca and recommendations for improvements. MiEM, 1981. 267 p.
Micro 81–26,526
DAI, v. 42A, Dec. 1981: 2858–2859.

1268
Makli, Adnan Hussain. Proposed theoretical framework for planning farmer training programs for rural development in Iraq. WU, 1983. 400 p.
Micro 84–2037
DAI, v. 45A, July 1984: 55.

1269
Malhuf, Mohamed Bashir. A demographic study of public residential and part-residential facilities for the mentally retarded persons in the Socialist People's Libyan Arab Jamahiriya. WU, 1985. 226 p.   Micro 85–19,773
DAI, v. 46A, Apr. 1986: 2999.

1270
al-Malik, Ibrahim Mohammed. Development planning in Saudi Arabia: the impact of the oil recession on structure, process, values, and policy outcomes. MoSU, 1987. 319 p.   Micro 87–15,055
DAI, v. 48A, Oct. 1987: 1012.

1271
Malkawi, Fathi Hasan. A case study of chemistry teaching and learning in a tenth grade classroom in Jordan. MiEM, 1984. 315 p.   Micro 85–7517
DAI, v. 46A, Aug. 1985: 392.

1272
Malki, Fouad Mohammed Said. A study of educational personnel attitudes toward vocational education in Jeddah, Saudi Arabia. PPiU, 1986. 177 p.
Micro 87–7575
DAI, v. 47A, June 1987: 4370.

1273
Malpezzi, Stephen J. Rent control and housing market equilibrium: theory and evidence from Cairo, Egypt. DGW, 1986. 271 p.   Micro 86–27,833
DAI, v. 47A, Feb. 1987: 3124.

1274
el Malti, Mohammed. The architecture of colonialism, Morocco, 1912–1932: an inquiry into the determinants of French colonial architecture. PU, 1983. 139 p.
Micro 83–26,283
DAI, v. 44A, May 1984: 3187.

1275
al Mana, Suaad Abdulaziz. Poetic necessity from the perspective of the medieval Arab critics and rhetoricians. MiU, 1986. 291 p.   Micro 86–12,460
DAI, v. 47A, Sept. 1986: 924.

1276
Mandell, Brian S. Mediation in the Middle East: alternatives in American policy and practice, 1969–1975. CaOTU, 1984.
DAI, v. 45A, Mar. 1985: 2986.

1277
al-Manea, Azeezah A. Historical and contemporary policies of women's education in Saudi Arabia. MiU, 1984. 233 p.   Micro 84–12,084
DAI, v. 45A, Aug. 1984: 353.

1278
Mani', Saleh Abdul-Rehman. Associative diplomacy: a study of the European

community's approach toward the Arab World. CLSU, 1981.
DAI, v. 44A, Aug. 1983: 569.

1279
Manser, Richard L. Roosevelt and China: from Cairo to Yalta. PPT, 1987. 364 p.
Micro 87–16,382
DAI, v. 48A, Oct. 1987: 1005.

1280
al-Mansour, Abdulaziz Mohammad. Attitudes of elementary teachers in Saudi Arabia toward teaching science in grades 4–6. InU, 1983. 136 p.
Micro 84–1556
DAI, v. 44A, Apr. 1984: 3026–3027.

1281
Mansour, Mansour Hasan. The spread and the domination of the Malki school of law in North and West Africa, eighth-fourteenth century. ICIU, 1981. 302 p.
Micro 82–20,021
DAI, v. 43A, Oct. 1982: 1255.

1282
Mansour, Mohamed Salah al-Din. An economic analysis of the world market for Egyptian cotton. OrCS, 1984. 134 p.   Micro 85–999
DAI, v. 45A, May 1985: 3417.

1283
Mansour, Taha A. International labor migration: the case of Jordan. OCU, 1983. 178 p.   Micro 84–6103
DAI, v. 45A, Aug. 1984: 574.

1284
el Mansouri, Mahmoud Mouhamed. A goal programming personnel management system for education and technical training in Libya. TxU, 1982. 262 p.
Micro 82–17,855
DAI, v. 43B, Sept. 1982: 843.

1285
Mansur, Milud Abdulkrim. Geology and linears of Libya. IdU, 1981. 276 p.
Micro 81–19,882
DAI, v. 42B, Sept. 1981: 944.

1286
Mansurnoor, Iik. *'Ulamā'*, villagers, and change: Islam in central Madura. CaQMM, 1987. 475 p.
Letter from McGill University Libraries.

1287
Marcus, Abraham. People and property in eighteenth-century Aleppo. NNC, 1979. 360 p.   Micro 82–4516
DAI, v. 42A, Mar. 1982: 4109.

1288
Marcus, Michael Alan. Townsmen and tribesmen: identity, history, and social change in eastern Morocco. NNU, 1983. 352 p.   Micro 83–24,832
DAI, v. 44A, Jan. 1984: 2190–2191.

1289
Marghalani, Mohammed A. A systematic design of a proposed model for school library media center programs in Saudi Arabia. PPiU, 1986. 234 p.
Micro 87–2071
DAI, v. 47A, Apr. 1987: 3600.

1290
el-Marghani, Abdulkrim Mohamed. Libyan settlements and migration adjustment. CoFS, 1982. 252 p.   Micro 82–27,918
DAI, v. 43A, Jan. 1983: 2468.

1291
Mar'i, Mariam Mahmood. Sex role perceptions of Palestinian males and females in Israel. MiEM, 1983. 144 p.   Micro 84–595
DAI, v. 44A, May 1984: 3269.

1292
Marquez, Jaime R. International transmission of oil price effects and the derivation of optimal oil prices. PU, 1983. 448 p.   Micro 83–26,311
DAI, v. 44A, Jan. 1984: 2199–2200.

1293
Mart, Joseph. A tectonic model of an incipient spreading center and its margins: the northern Read Sea and the Dead Sea rift. TxCM, 1984. 180 p.
Micro 84–28,785
DAI, v. 45B, Mar. 1985: 2855.

1294
Martin, David L. al-Fanā' (mystical annihilation of the soul) and al-baqā' (subsistence of the soul) in the work of Abū al-Qāsim al-Junayd al-Baghdādī. CLU, 1984. 312 p.   Micro 84–20,211
DAI, v. 45A, Dec. 1984: 1779.

1295
Martin, Debra L. Paleophysiological aspects of bone remodeling in the meroitic, x-group and Christian populations from Sudanese Nubia. MU, 1983. 209 p.
Micro 84–1083
DAI, v. 44A, Apr. 1984: 3109.

1296
Martin, Rebecca. Wild men and Moors in the Castle of Love: the Castle-Siege tapestries in Nuremberg, Vienna, and Boston. NcU, 1983. 368 p.
Micro 84–6931
DAI, v. 44A, June 1984: 3526.

1297
Martinez, Francisco J. Eastern Christian apocalyptic in the early Muslim period: Pseudo-Methodius and Pseudo-Athanasius. DCU, 1985. 637 p.

Micro 85–15,093

DAI, v. 46A, Nov. 1985: 1375.

1298
al-Mashal, Mashal Dakheel. The Kuwait Finance House: viability and growth as an interest-free financial institution. CSdI, 1987. 319 p. Micro 87–14,638
DAI, v. 48A, Oct. 1987: 978.

1299
Mashat, Soraya Hassan. A rhetorical analysis of the image of Saudi women in two specific cross-cultural media messages. PSt, 1985. 195 p. Micro 85–16,063
DAI, v. 46A, Dec. 1985: 1431.

1300
al-Mashhadany, Ahmad Abid. A program planning framework for the agriculture extension service in Iraq. WU, 1981. 297 p. Micro 81–11,621
DAI, v. 42B, Aug. 1981: 453.

1301
Masoud, Khalid Saad. Perceived responsibility, authority, and delegation of department chairpersons compared to perceptions of faculty in Saudi Arabian universities. TxDN, 1986. 468 p. Micro 87–5146
DAI, v. 48A, July 1987: 21.

1302
Masri, Husni Fahmi. A study of the student personnel program of an-Najah National University, Nablus, and recommendations. OAU, 1983. 218 p.

Micro 83–19,006

DAI, v. 44A, Mar. 1984: 2688.

1303
el-Masri, Zienab Ismael. The demand for money in developing economies: the case of Libya, Saudi Arabia, and Iraq. MoU, 1982. 179 p.

Micro 83–26,778

DAI, v. 44A, Jan. 1984: 2198–2199.

1304
Masters, Bruce A. The merchants of Aleppo, 1630–1730: the commercial and financial life of an Ottoman Arab city. ICU, 1982.
CDI, 1983, v. 5: 275.

1305
Mat, Isma'il Bin. Adat and Islam in Malaysia: a study in legal conflict and resolution. PPT, 1985. 365 p. Micro 85–9386
DAI, v. 46A, Sept. 1985: 720.

1306
Matar, Fatima Khalifa. An investigation of the professional needs of science

144

teachers in socondary schools in Bahrain. OrU, 1986. 204 p.

Micro 86–13,361

DAI, v. 47A, Oct. 1986: 1270.

1307

Matar, Zeina. The *Faraj al-mahmūm* of Ibn Ṭāwūs: a thirteenth century work on astrology and astrologers. NNU, 1987. 726 p.   Micro 87–12,765
DAI, v. 48A, Sept. 1987: 661.

1308

Matejka, Jacquelin C. Political participation in the Arab world: the *majlis* mechanism. TxU, 1983. 269 p.   Micro 84–14,412
DAI, v. 45A, Oct. 1984: 1198.

1309

al-Matouq, Ahmad Muhammad. al-Sharīf al-Murtaḍá's contribution to the theory of plagiarism in Arabic poetry. PU, 1987. 254 p.   Micro 87–13,997
DAI, v. 48A, Sept. 1987: 660–661.

1310

Mattair, Thomas R. U.S. foreign policy and revolutionary conflict in the Third World: the Carter Administration's Arab-Israeli policy. CU, 1986. 495 p.

Micro 87–18,081

DAI, v. 48A, Dec. 1987: 1535.

1311

Mattar, Philip. The Mufti of Jerusalem: Muḥammad Amīn al-Ḥusaynī, a founder of Palestinian nationalism. NNC, 1981. 219 p.   Micro 83–27,262
DAI, v. 44A, Feb. 1984: 2549.

1312

Mavrakis, Rafik Mohamed. Urban design principles and guidelines for the development of cities in North Africa and the Middle East. WaU, 1984. 347 p.
Letter from University of Washington Libraries.

1313

May, Kathleen M. Arab-American immigrant parents' social networks and health care of children. CU-Sf, 1985. 234 p.   Micro 86–600
DAI, v. 47B, July 1986: 134.

1314

Mayers, Marilyn A. A century of psychiatry: the Egyptian mental hospitals. NjP, 1984. 360 p.   Micro 84–9500
DAI, v. 45A, July 1984: 271–272.

1315

al-Mazroa, Suliman Abdullah. Public administration trends and prospects in the context of development in Saudi Arabia. CCC, 1980. 434 p.

Micro 82–20,577

DAI, v. 43A, Dec. 1982: 2091.

1316
al-Mazroe, Hafeez Mohamed Hafez. A comparison between Piagetian cognitive level and physics achievement for twelfth grade students in Saudi Arabia. CoGrU, 1982. 133 p. Micro 82–13,266
DAI, v. 43A, July 1982: 129.

1317
el Medani, Khalil Abdalla. Macro policies and micro-level analysis of agricultural development in Funj Region, Sudan. CU-Riv, 1986. 346 p.
Micro 86–13,847
DAI, v. 47A, Oct. 1986: 1383.

1318
al-Medfa, Nurah Abdulrahman. Factors contributing to the drop-out rate from adult evening elementary school centers: Sharjah City, Sharjah Emirate of the United Arab Emirates. CLSU, 1984.
DAI, v. 45A, May 1985: 3260–3261.

1319
Medley, Joseph E. Economic growth and development: a critique of Samir Amin's conception of capital accumulation and development. MU, 1981. 219 p.
Micro 81–18,026
DAI, v. 42A, Sept. 1981: 1263–1264.

1320
al-Mehawes, Mohammed Abdulrahman. Saudi Arabian graduate returnees: their readjustment, stress and coping to adapt and re-integrate into Saudi Arabia. CoDU, 1984. 256 p. Micro 84–11,922
DAI, v. 45A, Aug. 1984: 422.

1321
Mehdi, Mohamed Farhat. The interference of Arabic in the use of English prepositions. TxU, 1981. 232 p. Micro 82–8213
DAI, v. 43A, July 1982: 158.

1322
Mehrez, Samia Emad el Din. Bricolage as hypertextuality: a study of narrative structure and narrative modes in the works of contemporary Egyptian writer Gamal al-Ghitany. CLU, 1985. 205 p. Micro 85–13,141
DAI, v. 46A, Nov. 1985: 1272.

1323
Mehros, Sadiq Saeed. Saudi Arabia as an actor in world affairs: a study in the political role of oil and wealth in Saudi Arabian foreign relations behavior, 1965–1984. CLSU, 1985.
DAI, v. 46A, Nov. 1985: 1392.

1324
Meier, Candice S. Reality and truth in *The Alexandria Quartet*. IaDmD, 1983. 144 p. Micro 83–16,257
DAI, v. 44A, Sept. 1983: 761.

1325
Meissner, Jeffrey R. Tribes at the core: legitimacy, structure and power in Zaydi
Yemen. NNC, 1987. 466 p. Micro 87–10,208
DAI, v. 48A, July 1987: 165.

1326
Menconi, Evelyn A. An analysis of [American] teachers' perceptions of the Arab
world. MBU-E, 1981. 198 p. Micro 81–26,734
DAI, v. 42A, Dec. 1981: 2603.

1327
Menning, Ralph R. The collapse of "global diplomacy": Germany's descent into
isolation, 1906–1909. RPB, 1986. 237 p. Micro 86–17,597
DAI, v. 47A, Nov. 1986: 1852–1853.

1328
Merebah, Saad A. A. Cooperative learning in science: a comparative study in
Saudi Arabia. KMK, 1987. 256 p. Micro 87–15,228
DAI, v. 48A, Oct. 1987: 892.

1329
Merghelani, Abdul-Rahman Amin. Saracenism on the British stage, 1580–1642:
a formula for distance. CoU, 1982. 284 p. Micro 82–21,102
DAI, v. 43A, Oct. 1982: 975.

1330
Meriwether, Margaret L. The notable families of Aleppo, 1770–1830: networks
and social structure. PU, 1981. 401 p. Micro 81–27,049
DAI, v. 42A, Dec. 1981: 2808.

1331
Merryman, James L. Ecological stress and adaptive response: the Kenya Somali
in the twentieth century. IEN, 1984. 286 p. Micro 84–11,169
DAI, v. 45A, Aug. 1984: 567.

1332
Merryman, Nancy H. Economy and ecological stress: household strategies of
transitional Somali pastoralists in Northern Kenya. IEN, 1984. 338 p.
Micro 84–23,277
DAI, v. 45A, Jan. 1985: 2164.

1333
Mertz, Gordon J. Atmospheric and oceanic 40- to 50-day oscillations in the source
region of the Somali Current. CaBVaU, 1985.
DAI, v. 47B, Oct. 1986: 1673.

1334
Merzouk, Abdelaziz. Relative erodibility of nine selected Moroccan soils as related to their physical, chemical and mineralogical properties. MnU, 1985.
165 p. Micro 86–2901
DAI, v. 46B, June 1986: 4073.

1335
Metawie, Hani A. Egyptianizing theatre in Egypt, 1963–1970: a descriptive and critical examination of the clash between a quest for authenticity and a tendency to assimilate Western metatheatre. FTaSU, 1985. 361 p.
Micro 86–5781
DAI, v. 47A, July 1986: 22.

1336
Meyer, Walter D. An analysis of the monsoon boundary layer over the Arabian Sea employing fast-response, aerial turbulence data. MoSU, 1982. 221 p.
Micro 82–23,703
DAI, v. 43B, Dec. 1982: 1881–1882.

1337
Mezbache, Azzedine. American and French managers's self-perceived abilities for effective functioning in another culture [Saudi Arabia]: a comparative study. CSdI, 1986. 161 p.
Micro 87–2406
DAI, v. 47B, Apr. 1987: 4332.

1338
Meziane, Mohammed. Toward computing in Algerian higher education: assessment, perceptions and alternatives. CSdI, 1987. 198 p.
Micro 87–19,618
DAI, v. 48A, Dec. 1987: 1405.

1339
Miari, Mahmoud Hussein. Attitudes of educated Arabs in Israel toward Arab-Jewish coexistence. NSbSU, 1983. 263 p.
Micro 84–5393
DAI, v. 44A, June 1984: 3830.

1340
Miari, Samir M. The Arabs in Israel: a national minority and cheap labor force, a split labor market analysis. ICU, 1987. 238 p.
Micro 87–4852
DAI, v. 47A, May 1987: 4198.

1341
Michalak, Laurence O. The changing weekly markets of Tunisia: a regional analysis. CU, 1983. 283 p.
Micro 84–13,510
DAI, v. 45A, Sept. 1984: 880.

1342
Michelmore, Christina W. Student politics in Egypt, 1922–1952. PU, 1983. 293 p.
Micro 84–6696
DAI, v. 44A, June 1984: 3775.

1343
Miesse, Thomas W. Investment and economic development in Egypt: a study of local entrepreneurs and business patterns during the Open Door Policy. MiDW, 1984. 242 p.
Micro 84–14,518
DAI, v. 45A, Sept. 1984: 881.

1344
Mikdadi, Mohammad Fakhri Ahmad. An investigation of oral reading miscues generated by bilingual college students reading expository materials in Arabic and English. InU, 1985. 231 p.   Micro 85–27,024
DAI, v. 46A, June 1986: 3667.

1345
Mikhail-Ashrawi, Hanan Daud. The contemporary literature of Palestine: poetry and fiction. ViU, 1982. 435 p.   Micro 83–7417
DAI, v. 44A, Aug. 1983: 484.

1346
Miller, Christine D. The effects of socioeconomic development upon a model of women's fertility decision making in a Tunisian community. CU-I, 1985. 336 p.
Micro 85–27,426
DAI, v. 46A, Apr. 1986: 3164.

1347
Miller, James A. Imlil: a modern Moroccan geography. TxU, 1981. 342 p.
Micro 81–19,343
DAI, v. 42A, Sept. 1981: 1314.

1348
Miller, Larry B. Islamic disputation theory: a study of the development of dialectic in Islam from the tenth through fourteenth centuries. NjP, 1984. 265 p.
Micro 84–28,182
DAI, v. 45A, Mar. 1985: 2899.

1349
Miller, Max E. Interlanguage simplification and metropolitanization [of a native Arabic speaker]. TxU, 1981. 180 p.   Micro 81–28,662
DAI, v. 42A, Jan. 1982: 3139.

1350
Milyani, Ahmed Mahmoud. A robust phonetic digit recognition system for digits spoken in American English and Arabic. OkS, 1981. 307 p.   Micro 82–3126
DAI, v. 42B, Mar. 1982: 3780.

1351
Milyani, Hisham M. The budgetary process in Saudi Arabia. FTaSU, 1983. 165 p.   Micro 83–14,410
DAI, v. 44A, Aug. 1983: 573–574.

1352
Mir, Mustansir. Thematic and structural coherence in the Qur'an: a study of [Amin Ahsan] Islahi's concept of *naẓm*. MiU, 1983. 209 p.   Micro 83–14,336
DAI, v. 44A, Aug. 1983: 508.

1353
Miraglia, Dina D. An analysis of ethnic identity among Yemenite Jews in the

greater New York area. NNC, 1983. 270 p.   Micro 83–27,264
DAI, v. 44A, Feb. 1984: 2506.

1354
Mirfendereski, Guive. The Tamb Islands controversy, 1887–1971: a case study in claims to territory in international law. MMeT-F, 1985. 798 p.
Letter from Wessell Library, Tufts University.

1355
Mirghani, Hussein Mohammed. The benefits and costs of malaria control: the case of the Gezira Scheme of the Sudan. NSyU, 1985. 198 p.
    Micro 85–24,429
DAI, v. 46A, Mar. 1986: 2767–2768.

1356
Miri, Mohammed Raja Abdullah. American Zionism, Arab oil, and the Middle East conflict. TxHU, 1983. 419 p.   Micro 84–7658
DAI, v. 44A, June 1984: 3802.

1357
Misallati, Abdalla Salem Omer. Tripoli, Libya, structure and functions as an Arab-Islamic city. KyU, 1981. 349 p.   Micro 84–1364
DAI, v. 44A, Mar. 1984: 2885–2886.

1358
Miski, Abdelhamid. Prognosis of academic achievement in library and information science in Morocco: comparison of examinatorial and nonexaminatorial prediction models. PPiU, 1986. 144 p.   Micro 87–2069
DAI, v. 47A, Apr. 1987: 3600.

1359
el-Miskin, Tijani. Authorial disavowal as negotiation of textuality [in Arabic]: towards a theory of originary discourse. InU, 1984. 264 p.   Micro 85–1426
DAI, v. 45A, May 1985: 3344.

1360
Mitchell, Raye M. The development and validation of a reading attitude assessment instrument for junior high school students [within the Arabian American Oil Company (ARAMCO) school system in Saudi Arabia]. GU, 1984. 140 p.
    Micro 85–4623
DAI, v. 45A, June 1985: 3594–3595.

1361
Mitchell, Timothy P. As if the world were divided in two: the birth of politics in turn-of-the-century Cairo. NjP, 1984. 264 p.   Micro 84–9124
DAI, v. 45A, July 1984: 293–294.

1362
Mitiche, Nora Fatima. An investigation of selected lexical items in Kabyl Berber. TxU, 1985. 173 p.   Micro 86–9396
DAI, v. 47A, Aug. 1986: 521.

1363
Mittelman, Roy. The Meknes mellah and Casablancan Ville nouvelle: a comparative study of two Jewish communities in transformation. PPT, 1987. 297 p.
Micro 87–16,386
DAI, v. 48A, Oct. 1987: 945–946.

1364
al-Mizjaji, Ahmad Dawood. The public attitudes toward the bureaucracy in Saudi Arabia. FTaSU, 1982. 220 p.   Micro 83–9266
DAI, v. 43A, June 1983: 4032.

1365
Mizrahi, Judith. Sources of diversity in [Egyptian, Iraqi, Moroccan and Syrian] Sephardim. NNU, 1987. 529 p.   Micro 87–20,134
DAI, v. 48B, Dec. 1987: 1801–1802.

1366
el-Mneizel, Abdalla Falah. Development and psychometric analysis of a Jordanian adaptation of the Kaufman Assessment Battery for Children (K-ABC). AU, 1987. 249 p.   Micro 87–20,687
DAI, v. 48A, Dec. 1987: 1440.

1367
al-Moammar, Abdallah Abdulaziz F. The manpower dilemma of Saudi Arabia. CU-I, 1983. 217 p.   Micro 83–27,913
DAI, v. 44A, Feb. 1984: 2586.

1368
Modaimeegh, Ibrahim A. A study on the Middle East and the evolution of the balance of bargaining power between multinationals and host-developing countries. MH, 1985.
CDI, 1985, v. 5: 318.

1369
Modaress, Mostafa. Study of instructional technology programs in universities of OPEC countries in the Middle East. KU, 1986. 240 p.   Micro 87–11,249
DAI, v. 48A, Nov. 1987: 1177.

1370
Mofti, Farooq Abbas. Urban housing design in the context of Saudi Arabia's cultural and physical conditions: potentials and constraints. NTR, 1981. 308 p.
Micro 82–10,670
DAI, v. 42A, June 1982: 5278.

1371
al-Mogarry, Mohammed S. Modal choice elasticities and cost of misallocation of freight transportation on the Riyadh-Dammam corridor [Saudi Arabia]. InU, 1986. 152 p.   Micro 87–7771
DAI, v. 47A, June 1987: 4479.

1372
Mogassbi, Mohamed Massud. Perceptions of the higher education system and manpower development in Libya. DGW, 1984. 385 p.   Micro 85–931
DAI, v. 45A, May 1985: 3290.

1373
al-Mogel, Abdulrahman Ibrahim. Factors associated with the adoption of recommended farm practices among wheat growing farmers in al-Hasa, Saudi Arabia. MoU, 1984. 110 p.   Micro 85–561
DAI, v. 45A, May 1985: 3265.

1374
Mohamed, Abdelaziz Mustafa. Evaluating management training programs: the case of Sudan's Young Executive Program (YEP). PPiU, 1984. 207 p.
Micro 85–11,019
DAI, v. 46A, Sept. 1985: 749.

1375
Mohamed, Abdelhalim Hamid. Resource allocation and enterprise combination in a risky environment: case study of the Gezira Scheme, Sudan. OkS, 1984. 169 p.   Micro 85–15,280
DAI, v. 46A, Nov. 1985: 1360–1361.

1376
Mohamed, Adam Azzain. Regional resource allocations in the Sudan, 1971–1980. FTaSU, 1981. 161 p.   Micro 82–5734
DAI, v. 42A, Apr. 1982: 4571.

1377
Mohamed, Aida Abdel-Hamid. Comparative study: the cultural influences upon the drawings of schizophrenic patients in Egypt and the United States. MdU, 1982. 177 p.   Micro 82–26,490
DAI, v. 43A, Dec. 1982: 1799–1800.

1378
Mohamed, Faiza el Sayed. Sex role stereotyping in Arabic elementary reading textbooks in Egypt. PPiU, 1985. 158 p.   Micro 85–24,088
DAI, v. 46A, Mar. 1986: 2546.

1379
Mohamed, Mohamed Mahrous. A comparative evaluative study of two models for rehabilitation of the hearing impaired persons in Egypt. MiEM, 1982. 270 p.   Micro 82–16,571
DAI, v. 43A, Aug. 1982: 368.

1380
Mohamed, Omer Mohamed Ali. The international regime of the River Nile. CLSU, 1982.
DAI, v. 43A, Apr. 1983: 3412.

1381

Mohammad, Mahmoud Dawood. The semantics of tense and aspect in English and Modern Standard Arabic. DGU, 1982. 224 p.   Micro 83-2774
DAI, v. 43A, Mar. 1983: 2984.

1382

Mohammad, Majid Mahdi. Reading difficulty of Iraqi non-textbook reading materials for Arab adults. CoGrU, 1984. 125 p.   Micro 84-11,461
DAI, v. 45A, Aug. 1984: 477.

1383

Mohammad, Mustafa Abd el-Samie. Egyptian curriculum leaders and social problems: a study of the critical stage of social consciousness. PPiU, 1983. 112 p.   Micro 83-27,703
DAI, v. 44A, Feb. 1984: 2345.

1384

Mohammad, Yousuf Hasan. Recent developments within OPEC: economic perspective. CU-SB, 1983. 209 p.   Micro 84-4098
DAI, v. 45A, Aug. 1984: 580-581.

1385

Mohammadsaid, Ibrahim Abdul-hadi. A plan for improving industrial productivity in Iraq. TU, 1981. 157 p.   Micro 82-3849
DAI, v. 42A, Mar. 1982: 3858.

1386

Mohammed, Abdalla I. The notion of good and evil in the ethics of 'Abd al-Jabbar: a philosophical study, with a translation of "The Determination of justice and injustice" (al-Ta'dīl wa-al-tajwīr). PPT, 1984. 245 p.
Micro 87-16,501
DAI, v. 48A, Oct. 1987: 940.

1387

Mohammed, Elberier Osman. National public policy and natural hazards in developing countries: analysis of absorptive capacity in Kassala, Sudan. NSyU, 1982. 264 p.   Micro 82-29,002
DAI, v. 43B, Mar. 1983: 2843.

1388

Mohammed, Gaafar Bashir. An analysis of smallholder rainfed crop production systems: a case study of the Nuba mountains area, Western Sudan. MiEM, 1982. 280 p.   Micro 83-3829
DAI, v. 43A, Mar. 1983: 3066.

1389

Mohammed, Hassan Yousif. The impact of the transfer of agricultural technology on the Sudan. MBU, 1983. 263 p.   Micro 84-1826
DAI, v. 45A, Sept. 1984: 940.

1390

Mohammed, Hayder Khogali. A descriptive analysis of the Sudanese teachers' emigration to the Arabian Gulf region. PSt, 1986. 172 p.   Micro 86–23,787
DAI, v. 47A, Jan. 1987: 2537.

1391

Mohammed, Mahmoud Gamal. Mass media and development in the Yemen Arab Republic. OU, 1987. 279 p.   Micro 87–17,692
DAI, v. 48A, Nov. 1987: 1047.

1392

Mohammed, Shamil Kamil. Leadership behaviors of youth center superintendents in Iraq as perceived by selected staff members. CoGrU, 1983. 137 p.
Micro 83–28,504
DAI, v. 44A, June 1984: 3639.

1393

al-Mohawes, Nasser Abdullah. Systems modeling and analysis for Saudi Arabian electric power requirements. InLP, 1982. 304 p.   Micro 83–878
DAI, v. 43B, Feb. 1983: 2682.

1394

Mohseni, Masoud. The problems of economic integration in the Middle East. CSdI, 1982. 161 p.   Micro 82–16,926
DAI, v. 43A, Sept. 1982: 907.

1395

Mokbel, Mirella G. Evaluation of nutritionally relevant indicators in villages in Aleppo Province, Syria, and their relation to agricultural development. MU, 1985. 247 p.   Micro 86–2662
DAI, v. 46B, June 1986: 4189.

1396

Momeni, Mahvash Keshmiri. Socio-cultural factors affecting the adaptations of the Dewey Decimal Classification in the Middle East. MdU, 1982. 344 p.
Micro 82–26,491
DAI, v. 43A, Dec. 1982: 1734.

1397

Moneef, Abdullah Ali. The attitude of the Saudi citizens toward the imposition of individual income tax. ScU, 1981. 228 p.   Micro 81–29,470
DAI, v. 42A, Jan. 1982: 3205.

1398

Moon, Chung In. Political economy of the Third World bilateralism: the Saudi Arabian-Korean connection, 1973–1983. MdU, 1984. 412 p.
Micro 85–14,563
DAI, v. 46A, Nov. 1985: 1393.

1399

Moore, Ruth L. Women and warriors: defending Islam in the southern Philip-

pines. CU-S, 1981. 374 p.   Micro 82–5342
   DAI, v. 42A, Mar. 1982: 4061.

1400
Morris, Eric E. Islam and politics in Aceh: a study of center-periphery relations in
   Indonesia. NIC, 1983. 337 p.   Micro 83–28,679
   DAI, v. 44A, Mar. 1984: 2875–2876.

1401
Mortazavi, Seyed-Ali. Islam reaffirmed: the denial of a dream in Iran. PPT, 1987.
   258 p.   Micro 87–11,379
   DAI, v. 48A, Aug. 1987: 427.

1402
Morton, Keith E. Conflict and cooperation in the Mediterranean: implications for
   the U.S. ViU, 1982. 291 p.   Micro 83–1499
   DAI, v. 43A, Apr. 1983: 3412.

1403
Moshaikeh, Mohamed S. H. Patterns of instructional media utilization in preparation of elementary school teachers in Saudi Arabian junior colleges. PPiU,
   1982. 164 p.   Micro 83–3631
   DAI, v. 43A, Mar. 1983: 2863.

1404
el-Moslimany, Ann Paxton. History of climate and vegetation in the eastern
   Mediterranean and the Middle East from the pleniglacial to the mid-holocene.
   WaU, 1983. 241 p.   Micro 83–19,405
   DAI, v. 44B, Oct. 1983: 1041.

1405
al-Mossa, Ibrahim A. A need assessment of Saudi intermediate school teachers of
   science: a basis for inservice and preservice programs. KMK, 1987. 233 p.
                                                             Micro 87–15,193
   DAI, v. 48A, Oct. 1987: 902.

1406
Mostafa, Nidhal Shaban. Cognitive development, spatial ability, and achieve-
   ment in science among Saudi Arabian students. MiU, 1985. 271 p.
                                                             Micro 85–12,475
   DAI, v. 46A, Jan. 1986: 1894.

1407
al-Mottahar, Mohamed Mohamed. Evaluating the consequences of an academic
   innovation: the case of the calendar/curriculum change at Sanaa University in
   the Yemen Arab Republic. MiU, 1986. 327 p.   Micro 87–2672
   DAI, v. 47A, Apr. 1987: 3616.

1408
Mottale, Morris M. The arms build-up in the Persian Gulf. CaOTY, 1982.
   DAI, v. 43A, Apr. 1983: 3413.

1409
Mouakket, Ahmed. Linguistics and translation: some semantic problems in Arabic-English translation. DGU, 1986. 250 p.　　　Micro 86–22,332
DAI, v. 47A, Jan. 1987: 2565.

1410
Moudoud, Ezzeddine. The state, the regional question and regional disparity dilemmas in Africa: a study of Tunisia, 1881–1980. NSyU, 1986. 409 p.
Micro 87–1273
DAI, v. 47A, Mar. 1987: 3589.

1411
Mouhammed, Adil Hasan. Econometric model of development strategies in Iraq, 1951–1980. NbU, 1984. 236 p.　　　Micro 85–21,468
DAI, v. 46A, Feb. 1986: 2380.

1412
al-Mouhandis, Zakiah B. Higher education for women in Saudi Arabia. CSfU, 1986. 198 p.　　　Micro 86–19,509
DAI, v. 47A, Feb. 1987: 2904.

1413
Moukhtari, Fariborz Levaye. Government intervention, price manipulation and agricultural productivity: a comparative analysis of wheat and cotton productivity in Iran and Egypt. DeU, 1983. 242 p.　　　Micro 83–16,560
DAI, v. 44A, Oct. 1983: 1196.

1414
el-Mouloudi, Aziz Bensmaali. Arabic language planning: the case of lexical modernization. DGU, 1986. 341 p.　　　Micro 86–22,323
DAI, v. 47A, Jan. 1987: 2562.

1415
Moursi, Tarek Abdelfattah. Government intervention and the impact on agriculture: the case of Egypt. CU, 1986. 223 p.　　　Micro 86–24,871
DAI, v. 47A, Jan. 1987: 2674.

1416
Mousa, Issam Suleiman. The Arab portrayal: *The New York Times*, 1917–1947. WaU, 1981. 200 p.　　　Micro 81–26,130
DAI, v. 42A, Dec. 1981: 2347.

1417
Moussalli, Ahmed Salah al-Din. Contemporary Islamic political thought: Sayyid Qutb. MdU, 1985. 192 p.　　　Micro 86–8835
DAI, v. 47A, Nov. 1986: 1869.

1418
Moustafa, Ahmed-Elsayed A. A status report of grade 3–5 mathematics instruction in al-Minya city, Egypt, with particular concern for the teaching and

learning of division facts. FTaSU, 1982. 205 p.   Micro 82–14,936
DAI, v. 43A, Aug. 1982: 388.

1419
al-Mozainy, Hamza Qublan. Vowel alterations in a bedouin Hijazi Arabic
dialect: abstractness and stress. TxU, 1981. 292 p.   Micro 81–19,247
DAI, v. 42A, Sept. 1981: 1125–1126.

1420
Mrayyan, Nader Ali. Urban housing for low-income households in Jordan.
NSyU, 1984. 189 p.   Micro 85–764
DAI, v. 45A, May 1985: 3411.

1421
al-Muarik, Sulaiman Ali. Error analysis and English learning strategies among
intermediate and secondary school students in Saudi Arabia. InU, 1982. 149 p.
          Micro 83–1049
DAI, v. 43A, Feb. 1983: 2578.

1422
Mu'aygil, Abdullah Hamed. The political and social views of Mahmud Bayram
al-Tunisi. MiU, 1986. 281 p.   Micro 86–12,587
DAI, v. 47A, Sept. 1986: 925.

1423
Mubarak, Abdulhakeem Mousa. A descriptive study of perceived professional
benefits derived from teachers involvement in the Kent Professional Staff Development Center, with a view toward developing recommendations for in-
service education in Saudi Arabia. MiEM, 1982. 197 p.   Micro 83–8983
DAI, v. 43A, June 1983: 3801.

1424
Mubarak, Ahmad Mohammad Ahmad. A study of Kuwaiti students and their
adjustment problems in the United States. CSdI, 1984. 198 p.
          Micro 84–29,944
DAI, v. 45A, Apr. 1985: 3215.

1425
al-Mubarak, Masoumah Saleh. Internal factors and their impacts on the levels
and trends of interactions between the Arab Gulf states and advanced nations.
CoDU, 1982. 569 p.   Micro 82–29,104
DAI, v. 43A, Jan. 1983: 2443.

1426
al-Mudaiheem, Khalid Nasser. Water resources and provision problems of Riyadh,
Saudi Arabia: an analytical study. OrU, 1985. 277 p.   Micro 86–5825
DAI, v. 47B, July 1986: 117.

1427
Muerdter, David R. Late Quaternary biostratigraphy and paleoceanography of

the Strait of Sicily and the Eastern Mediterranean Sea. RU, 1982. 336 p.
Micro 83–6414
DAI, v. 43B, May 1983: 3511.

1428
Muftah, Hamid Ali. Analysis of the development of a higher-education system in Libya and its impact on the Libyan students. KU, 1982. 178 p.
Micro 83–1700
DAI, v. 43A, Feb. 1983: 2570.

1429
Muftah, Saleh Mustafa. The influences of American-Israeli relations upon American-Egyptian relations—1948 through the Suez War of 1956. CoDU, 1984. 284 p.   Micro 85–216
DAI, v. 45A, May 1985: 3429.

1430
Mufti, Muhammad Ahmed. United States foreign policy toward Egypt under Sadat, 1970–1981. CU-Riv, 1983. 351 p.   Micro 84–5540
DAI, v. 44A, June 1984: 3796.

1431
el-Muhamad, Muhamad Ali. Jordanian multi-purpose agricultural cooperatives as instruments of development: a case in public policy. NSyU, 1984. 295 p.
Micro 85–777
DAI, v. 45A, May 1985: 3446.

1432
Muhammad, Ramona Zakiyyah. Perceptions of the role of teachers and the principal in an Islamic school. NNC-T, 1986. 160 p.   Micro 86–20,392
DAI. v. 47A, Dec. 1986: 1961.

1433
Muhanna, Amin Awwad. Modernization: political stability and instability, the Jordanian case. CLSU, 1986.
DAI, v. 47A, Dec. 1986: 2301–2302.

1434
Mukhtar, Hassan Ali. Attitudes of middle- and secondary-school social studies teachers toward their pre-service preparation program at Umm al-Qura University, Mecca, Saudi Arabia. WMUW, 1984. 241 p.   Micro 85–9264
DAI, v. 46A, Sept. 1985: 682.

1435
al-Mullah, Abdullah Ali. Saudi Arabian industrial development: a study of hydrocarbon-based industry. MMeT-F, 1986. 241 p.
Letter from Wessell Library, Tufts University.

1436
Mullen, Thomas W. Elites, continuity and change in the Baathist regimes of

Syria and Iraq, 1968–1979: a comparative analysis. MdU, 1982. 280 p.

Micro 83–23,567

DAI, v. 44A, Dec. 1983: 1916.

1437
Muludiang, Venansio Tombe. Urbanization, female migration and labor utilization in urban Sudan: the case of the southern region. RPB, 1983. 265 p.

Micro 83–26,015

DAI, v. 44A, Jan. 1984: 2255.

1438
Munson, Henry L. Islam and inequality in northwest Morocco. ICU, 1980.
CDI, 1973–1982, v. 36: 729.

1439
Murad, Hasan Qasim. Ethico-religious ideas of ʿUmar. CaQMM, 1981.
DAI, v. 42A, Apr. 1982: 4483.

1440
Murphy, Christopher P. H. Feasting and fasting: the meaning of Muslim food in Delhi. ViU, 1985. 447 p.

Micro 86–15,559

DAI, v. 47A, Nov. 1986: 1894.

1441
Murshid, Samir Asad. OPEC, its role as residual oil supplier. CCC, 1980. 232 p.

Micro 81–19,946

DAI, v. 42A, Sept. 1981: 1248.

1442
Musa, Mohammed Ali. The subterranean caverns: the East and its progeny in eighteenth-century English and French literature. ArU, 1981. 202 p.

Micro 81–27,259

DAI, v. 42A, Dec. 1981: 2688.

1443
Musallam, Adnan Ayyub. The formative stages of Sayyid Qutb's intellectual career and his emergence as an Islamic dāʿiyah, 1906–1952. MiU, 1983. 305 p.

Micro 83–24,252

DAI, v. 44A, Dec. 1983: 1886.

1444
al-Musallam, Bassama Khalid. Women's education in Kuwait and its effect on future expectations: an ethnography of a girls' sex-segregated secondary school. NBuU, 1984. 325 p.

Micro 84–20,652

DAI, v. 45A, Dec. 1984: 1712.

1445
al-Musfir, Muhammad Salih. The United Arab Emirates: an assessment of federalism in a developing polity. NBiSU, 1985. 243 p.

Micro 85–8851

DAI, v. 46A, Aug. 1985: 508.

1446

Musleh, Khadder Elias. The effects of counselor ethnicity and counseling approach in Arab-Americans perception of counselor credibility and utility. MiDW, 1982. 143 p.   Micro 83–6922
DAI, v. 44A, July 1983: 77.

1447

Musleh, Nagi Elias. Effects of acculturation on the proxemic behavior of Arab-American high school students. MiDW, 1983. 91 p.   Micro 84–5998
DAI, v. 44A, June 1984: 3590.

1448

Muslih, Muhammad Yousef. Urban notables, Ottomanism, Arabism, and the rise of Palestinian nationalism, 1856–1920. NNC, 1985. 393 p.
                                                        Micro 87–10,212
DAI, v. 48A, July 1987: 212.

1449

Musmar, Faisal Taher. A study of the opinions of students, alumni, curriculum planners, and employers about the role of the Jordanian community colleges in preparing people for employment. DGW, 1984. 164 p.   Micro 84–22,003
DAI, v. 45A, Jan. 1985: 1968.

1450

Mustafa, Ali Hajjan. A study of the academic problems encountered by Saudi students at Western Michigan University. MiKW, 1985. 135 p.
                                                        Micro 85–26,121
DAI, v. 46A, Mar. 1986: 2598–2599.

1451

Mustafa, Muhammad Muhammad Hussein. The role of cognitive perceptions: Nasser and Sadat. MBU, 1985. 511 p.   Micro 86–1367
DAI, v. 46A, May 1986: 3476–3477.

1452

Mustajel, Sadaka Yehia. Nuclear capabilities of the Arabs and Israel and their implications for the Arab-Israeli conflict. CCC, 1983. 257 p.
                                                        Micro 83–21,057
DAI, v. 44A, Nov. 1983: 1567.

1453

al-Mutairi, Hezam Mater. An Islamic perspective on public service with reference to the Hajj Research Center (HRC). NAlU, 1987. 310 p.   Micro 87–8638
DAI, v. 48A, July 1987: 217.

1454

Myers, Joseph E. The political economy of ceramic production: a study of the Islamic commonware pottery of medieval Qsar es-Seghir [Morocco]. NBiSU, 1984. 296 p.   Micro 84–16,792
DAI, v. 45A, Oct. 1984: 1153.

1455
Mylroie, Laurie A. Regional security after empire: Saudi Arabia and the Gulf.
MH, 1985. 424 p. Micro 86–2252
DAI, v. 47A, July 1986: 304.

1456
al-Nabeh, Najat Abdullah. Personnel administration of education in the United
Arab Emirates. CCC, 1982. 255 p. Micro 82–28,737
DAI, v. 43A, Jan. 1983: 2166.

1457
al-Nabeh, Najat Abdullah. United Arab Emirates (UAE): regional and global
dimensions. CCC, 1984. 208 p. Micro 84–7445
DAI, v. 44A, June 1984: 3775.

1458
Nabti, Michel G. Coverage of the Arab world in American secondary school world
studies textbooks: a content analysis. CSt, 1981. 340 p. Micro 81–24,113
DAI, v. 42A, Nov. 1981: 2065–2066.

1459
Naccache, Albert Farid. The representation of the long-time-span structures of
human history: the case of the Mashriq. CU, 1985. 277 p. Micro 86–10,157
DAI, v. 47A, Sept. 1986: 1032.

1460
Nachmias, Nitza. The limits of political leverage in a patron-client relationship:
the case of military assistance to Israel, 1967–1984. NNCU-G, 1986. 338 p.
Micro 86–11,369
DAI, v. 47A, Sept. 1986: 1043.

1461
Naddaff, Sandra A. Arabesque: narrative structure and the aesthetics of repetition
in the *1001 Nights* cycle of *The Porter and the Three Ladies of Baghdad*. MH, 1983.
215 p. Micro 84–3028
DAI, v. 44A, June 1984: 3678.

1462
Nader, Anita H. Educational attitudes of Saudi elementary school teachers. IU,
1986. 152 p. Micro 86–23,377
DAI, v. 47A, Jan. 1987: 2404.

1463
Nafil, Mohammed Salih Turki. Investment performance, capital absorptive capacity, oil revenues, and economic development in an oil-based economy: the
case of Iraq, 1951–1978. WaPS, 1984. 153 p. Micro 85–4226
DAI, v. 45A, June 1985: 3700.

1464
Nagadi, Ahmed Hamid. Demand for money in Saudi Arabia: an empirical study.

CCC, 1985. 154 p.   Micro 85–15,196
DAI, v. 46A, Nov. 1985: 1367.

1465
el-Naggar, Zeinab Ali. Performance testing in an in-service training for Egyptian teachers of English. CLU, 1981. 162 p.   Micro 82–1140
DAI, v. 42A, Feb. 1982: 3564.

1466
al-Nahari, Abdulaziz Mohamed. The national library: an analysis of the critical factors in promoting library and information services in developing countries: the case of Saudi Arabia. CLU, 1982. 365 p.   Micro 82–12,860
DAI, v. 43A, July 1982: 6.

1467
Nahas, Maridi. Hegemonic constraints and state autonomy: a comparative analysis of development in 19th century Egypt, Spain and Italy. CLU, 1985. 366 p.
                                                                    Micro 86–3977
DAI, v. 47A, July 1986: 304.

1468
al-Naheet, Mohammed Ali. The Gulf Cooperation Council: progress in achieving integration. CLavC, 1985. 189 p.   Micro 85–11,740
DAI, v. 46A, Dec. 1985: 1691.

1469
Naimi, M. T. Toward a theory of postrevolutionary social change: a six nation comparative study [Algeria and Sudan included]. WaPS, 1985. 470 p.
                                                                    Micro 86–10,374
DAI, v. 47A, Sept. 1986: 1084.

1470
Najafizadeh, Abbas. The structure of the world oil market and the role of OPEC. CU-SB, 1985. 122 p.   Micro 86–5947
DAI, v. 47A, July 1986: 271.

1471
Najai, Ali M. Television and youth in the Kingdom of Saudi Arabia: an empirical analysis of the uses of television among young Saudi Arabian viewers. WU, 1982. 229 p.   Micro 82–25,664
DAI, v. 43A, Feb. 1983: 2483.

1472
al-Najjar, Balkees. The syntax and semantics of verbal aspect in Kuwaiti Arabic. UU, 1984. 231 p.   Micro 84–7310
DAI, v. 44A, June 1984: 3673.

1473
al-Najjar, Majed Flayih. Translation as a correlative of meaning: cultural and

linguistic transfer between Arabic and English. InU, 1984. 320 p.

Micro 84-17,149

DAI, v. 45A, Nov. 1984: 1382.

1474

al-Najjar, Mohammed Aeid. A study of male high school dropouts in the city of Makkah in Saudi Arabia. CLSU, 1984.

DAI, v. 45A, Sept. 1984: 689.

1475

Najm, Mahmoud Abdalla. Agricultural land use in the Benghazi area, Libya: a spatial analysis of cultural factors affecting crop and livestock patterns. MiEM, 1982. 225 p.

Micro 82-16,575

DAI, v. 43A, Aug. 1982: 548.

1476

Nama, Ahmad Mohammed. Human resources development: the case of Qatar. CCC, 1983. 178 p.

Micro 83-8726

DAI, v. 43A, June 1983: 4037.

1477

Namani, Bassam Abdel Kader. Confessionalism in Lebanon, 1920-1976: the interplay of domestic, regional, and international politics. NNC, 1982. 421 p.

Micro 84-27,438

DAI, v. 45A, Apr. 1985: 3207.

1478

Namazi, Kevan H. Assimilation and need assessment among Mexican, Cuban, and Middle Eastern immigrants: a multivariate analysis. OAkU, 1984. 389 p.

Micro 84-14,649

DAI, v. 45A, Sept. 1984: 949.

1479

Namlah, Ali Ibrahim. Infrastructure of information needs and resources in the country of Saudi Arabia: an assessment. OclW, 1984. 293 p.

Micro 84-25,571

DAI, v. 45A, Feb. 1985: 2287-2288.

1480

Naseer, Abdullah Abdulkadir. Managerial attitudes and needs in developing countries: an empirical study of managerial views in the Kingdom of Saudi Arabia. CCC, 1983. 172 p.

Micro 83-9664

DAI, v. 43A, June 1983: 3968.

1481

al-Naser, Fahed. Socio-cultural dimensions of homogamous and heterogamous marriages in Kuwait. MiEM, 1986. 178 p.

Micro 87-431

DAI, v. 47A, Mar. 1987: 3572.

1482

Naser, Kazem Adel. Language problems of Arab students learning English as a

second language in selected universities in America. OkS, 1983. 125 p.
Micro 83–25,830
DAI, v. 44A, Jan. 1984: 2061.

1483
Naser, Sami Anis. The impact of the American culture on male Arab students in the United States. CSfU, 1984. 164 p.   Micro 85–12,113
DAI, v. 46A, Oct. 1985: 914.

1484
Nasr, Faisal Adel. OPEC's and Mexico's petroleum in the context of economic development: competition or cooperation? TxU, 1981. 295 p.
Micro 81–19,349
DAI, v. 42A, Sept. 1981: 1264.

1485
Nasra, Kouider. A cross-cultural study of American and Algerian psychologists and their perceptions of the discipline. CSdI, 1985. 211 p.   Micro 85–12,578
DAI, v. 46B, Oct. 1985: 1326.

1486
al-Nasrullah, Abdulaziz A. An evaluation of internal controls of commercial loans in Saudi Arabian banks. DGW, 1987. 246 p.   Micro 87–7226
DAI, v. 47A, June 1987: 4434.

1487
al-Nassar, Fahd Mohamed. Saudi Arabian Educational Mission to the United States: assessing perceptions of student satisfaction with services rendered. OkU, 1982. 219 p.   Micro 82–15,899
DAI, v. 43A, Oct. 1982: 1056.

1488
el-Nasser, Rachid Abdallah. Morocco, from Kharijism to Wahhabism: the quest for religious purism. MiU, 1983. 686 p.   Micro 83–24,169
DAI, v. 44A, Dec. 1983: 1887.

1489
Nassier, Ahmed Abdulkhader. Perception of Saudi budget officers toward alternative budget systems. CLavC, 1983. 193 p.   Micro 84–5635
DAI, v. 44A, June 1984: 3809–3810.

1490
Nassr, Mohammad Nashaat Gad. Contrasts between quartz grain shapes of the Cambrian and the Carboniferous "Nubia" facies in Gabal Abu-Durba, Sinai, Egypt: Fourier grain shape analysis. ScU, 1985. 394 p.   Micro 85–18,043
DAI, v. 46B, Dec. 1985: 1850.

1491
Nazhat, Saadi Mohammad. Technology diffusion for agricultural development

and desertification control in semi-arid regions. KyU, 1987. 304 p.
Micro 87–15,939
DAI, v. 48A, Nov. 1987: 1319.

1492
Nazzal, Laila Ahmed. The role of shame in societal transformation among Palestinian women on the West Bank. PU, 1986. 428 p.   Micro 86–14,844
DAI, v. 47A, Oct. 1986: 1511–1512.

1493
Nehme, Michel G. Saudi Arabia: political implications of the development plans.
NjR, 1983. 232 p.   Micro 83–8443
DAI, v. 43A, May 1983: 3696.

1494
Nelson, Cherilyn N. S. A methodology for examining ancient textiles and its application to VI–XIX century textiles from Akhmim, Egypt. MnU, 1986.
332 p.   Micro 86–27,032
DAI, v. 47A, Feb. 1987: 3089.

1495
Newhall, Amy W. The patronage of the Mamluk Sultan Qa'it Bay, 872–901/
1468–1496. MH, 1987. 347 p.   Micro 87–11,525
DAI, v. 48A, Aug. 1987: 237.

1496
Newman, Andrew J. The development and political significance of the rationalist (*uṣūlī*) and traditionalist (*akhbārī*) schools in Imāmī Shī'ī history from the third/ninth to the tenth/sixteenth century A.D. CLU, 1986. 955 p.
Micro 87–13,723
DAI, v. 48A, Sept. 1987: 742.

1497
al-Nhar, Taisier. Coeducational vs. single-sex schooling, sex-role orientation and fear of success: results from Jordan. PPiU, 1986. 83 p.   Micro 87–1951
DAI, v. 47A, May 1987: 4018.

1498
al-Nia'ami, Abdul Jabbar Abdul Sattar Abdul Rahman. An investigation of concepts of industry as perceived by Iraqi students and instructors in vocational industrial and general secondary schools. CoGrU, 1985. 238 p.
Micro 85–23,371
DAI, v. 46A, Feb. 1986: 2209–2210.

1499
al-Nifay, Abdullah Musleh. An assessment to redesign in-service training programs for paraprofessionals employed in military hospitals under jurisdiction of the Saudi Arabian Ministry of Defense. PPiU, 1981. 846 p.
Micro 82–18,142
DAI, v. 43A, Sept. 1982: 596.

1500
al-Nima, Sameer Khayri. The mass literacy campaign in Iraq: a critical analysis.
MoU, 1982. 472 p.   Micro 83–26,771
DAI, v. 44A, Jan. 1984: 2011.

1501
Nimer, Ribhi Mustafa Elayyan. An investigation into the use of sources of medical
information by the practicing Jordanian physicians of selected hospitals in
Jordan. PPiU, 1986. 160 p.   Micro 87–2070
DAI, v. 47A, Apr. 1987: 3600–3601.

1502
Nimir, Mutasim Bashir. Wildlife values and management in northern Sudan.
CoFS, 1983. 242 p.   Micro 83–27,984
DAI, v. 44B, Feb. 1984: 2292.

1503
Noda, Phyllis C. Exploratory study of the impact of computer-assisted instruction
on the English language reading achievement of LEP [Limited English Profi-
ciency] Arabic and Chaldean middle school students. MiDW, 1983. 258 p.
                                                             Micro 84–6002
DAI, v. 44A, June 1984: 3590–3591.

1504
al-Noghaimshi, Abdolaziz Mohammed. Students' perception of teachers and
student-teacher personal interaction in Riyadh public high schools. MiU,
1985. 231 p.   Micro 86–398
DAI, v. 46A, May 1986: 3287–3288.

1505
Norman, Barbara A. The Black Muslims: a rhetorical analysis. OkU, 1985.
298 p.   Micro 85–13,838
DAI, v. 46A, Oct. 1985: 841.

1506
Norman, Harry L. Reproductive strategy of Gerbilline rodents in Morocco. AzU,
1983. 139 p.   Micro 84–5506
DAI, v. 44B, June 1984: 3636.

1507
Northrup, Linda S. A history of the reign of the Mamluk Sultan al-Manṣūr
Qalāʾūn, 678–689 A.H./1279–1290 A.D. CaQMN, 1983.
DAI, v. 44A, Nov. 1983: 1540.

1508
Norton, Augustus R. Ḥarakat Amal and the political mobilization of the Shiʿa of
Lebanon. ICU, 1984. 178 p.
Letter from University of Chicago Library.

1509
Nourel-Din, Safwat Ali. The ceramics of Failaka [Kuwait]: a question of the

166

function of tradition in artistic creation. NNU, 1985. 325 p.

Micro 85–21,979

DAI, v. 46A, Feb. 1986: 2111.

1510

Nouri, Mohamed Osman Elamin. Fertility differentials in the Democratic Republic of the Sudan. MsSM, 1983. 264 p.   Micro 84–10,672

DAI, v. 45A, Aug. 1984: 654.

1511

Nowilati, Mohammed Anowar. Managerial in-service training for development: the case of the Public Administration Institute in Saudi Arabia. PBL, 1986. 300 p.   Micro 86–4029

DAI, v. 46A, June 1986: 3858.

1512

al-Nuaim, Mishary Abdalrahman. State building in a non-capitalist social formation: the dialectics of two modes of production and the role of the merchant class, Saudi Arabia, 1902–1932. CLU, 1987. 403 p.   Micro 87–13,719

DAI, v. 48A, Sept. 1987: 735–736.

1513

Nur, Osman el-Hassan Mohamed. On the validity of fertility analysis for Jordan. MiU, 1980. 264 p.   Micro 82–4732

DAI, v. 42A, May 1982: 4941.

1514

Nusair, Naim Ogleh. Regional development and planning in Jordan: Jordan Valley Authority, 1973–1980. NAlU, 1982. 526 p.   Micro 82–16,023

DAI, v. 43A, Sept. 1982: 920.

1515

Nzo-Nguty, Bernard T. The Arab League, United Nations, and Organization of African Unity: contradictions and dilemmas in intra-interorganizational co-operation in conflict management and development. ScU, 1986. 408 p.

Micro 86–15,920

DAI, v. 47A, Dec. 1986: 2306.

1516

Obeidat, Hussein Ali. An investigation of syntactic and semantic errors in the written composition of Arab EFL learners. IU, 1986. 190 p.   Micro 87–1580

DAI, v. 47A, Mar. 1987: 3415.

1517

Obeidat, Marwan Mohammad. The Muslim East in American literature: the formation of an image. InU, 1985. 194 p.   Micro 86–7431

DAI, v. 47A, Aug. 1986: 531.

1518

al-Obeidy, Ibrahim M. The incidence of infant mortality in a sample of house-

holds in Riyadh, Saudi Arabia. MiEM, 1985. 286 p.   Micro 85–20,493
DAI, v. 46A, Jan. 1986: 2082.

1519
Odah, Mohamed Amin. Public enterprise in national development: a study in the
political economy of Egypt. PPiU, 1986. 365 p.   Micro 87–8483
DAI, v. 47A, June 1987: 4444.

1520
al-Odaibi, Abdullah Ibrahim. Analysis of educational competency and training
needs of agricultural extension workers in the Eastern District of Saudi Arabia.
WU, 1983. 221 p.   Micro 83–14,989
DAI, v. 44A, Oct. 1983: 960.

1521
Odhiambo, Mark O. Production risk and decision making: testing alternative
econometric models with evidence from Egyptian cotton production. CU-A,
1983. 236 p.   Micro 84–7113
DAI, v. 44A, June 1984: 3756.

1522
Ogar, Michael O. Urban transportation and public policy in developing
countries: towards improving mobility and accessibility. PU, 1983. 303 p.
                                                      Micro 83–16,066
DAI, v. 44A, Sept. 1983: 890.

1523
el-Okdah, Farouk A. A test of the effects of interactive planning on selected
behavioral variables of Egyptian managers and work environment. PU, 1983.
217 p.   Micro 83–16,012
DAI, v. 44A, Oct. 1983: 1206.

1524
Okoro, Dominic E. The foundation and development of the Organization of
Petroleum Exporting Countries (OPEC). CSdI, 1981. 144 p.
                                                      Micro 81–16,162
DAI, v. 42A, Aug. 1981: 776–777.

1525
Olabode, Olusola O. The feasibility of petroleum as a weapon. CCC, 1981.
529 p.   Micro 82–20,601
DAI, v. 43A, Oct. 1982: 1288.

1526
Olaniyan, Olufemi. Multivariate analyses of sedimentological data at two early
bronze age sites, Bab Edh-Dhra and Numeira, southeast Dead Sea graben,
Jordan. PPiU, 1984. 281 p.   Micro 84–21,314
DAI, v. 45B, Dec. 1984: 1709.

1527
Oluo, Samuel L. O. Conflict management of the Organization of African Unity in

intra-African conflicts, 1963–1980. TxDN, 1982. 226 p.   Micro 82–28,065
DAI, v. 43A, Jan. 1983: 2446.

1528
Omar, Abdulaziz Saud. The effect of using diagnostic-prescriptive teaching on achievement in science of Saudi Arabian high school students. KU, 1984. 109 p.
Micro 85–13,802
DAI, v. 46A, Oct. 1985: 941.

1529
al-Omar, Abdullah Omar A. The reception of Darwinism in the Arab world. MH, 1982. 380 p.   Micro 82–22,584
DAI, v. 43A, Nov. 1982: 1658.

1530
Omar, Emran Hasan. Job satisfaction among hospital middle management in Jordan. CSdI, 1982. 136 p.   Micro 82–16,490
DAI, v. 43A, Aug. 1982: 532.

1531
Omar, Gomaa Ibrahim. Phanerozoic tectono-thermal history of the Nubian Massif, Eastern Desert, Egypt, and its relationship to the opening of the Red Sea as revealed by fission-track studies. PU, 1985. 164 p.   Micro 85–15,431
DAI, v. 46B, Nov. 1985: 1494.

1532
al-Omar, Jasem Ebraheem. A comparison of values and job satisfaction among American and Arab managers. CSdI, 1984. 125 p.   Micro 84–17,502
DAI, v. 45A, Nov. 1984: 1461.

1533
Omar, Mohamed-Maher Mahmoud M. The guidance needs of the secondary school students in the State of Kuwait. MiU, 1983. 438 p.   Micro 83–24,260
DAI, v. 44A, Dec. 1983: 1695–1696.

1534
Omari, Abdalla Mansy. The market society of greater Syrian cities in the later middle ages, 1250–1517. WMUW, 1986. 250 p.   Micro 87–8856
DAI, v. 48A, July 1987: 205.

1535
Omer, Abdel-Hadi Mohamed. Arabic in the Sudanese setting: a sociolinguistic study. InU, 1984. 209 p.   Micro 86–17,825
DAI, v. 47A, Nov. 1986: 1715.

1536
Omer, Abdusalam Hadliyeh. Towards understanding the Somali bureaucracy. TU, 1986. 146 p.   Micro 87–8781
DAI, v. 47A, June 1987: 4509.

1537
Omer, Asha Mohammed. Perceived inservice needs of home economics teachers in Sudan. KMK, 1981. 136 p.   Micro 82–7770
DAI, v. 42A, June 1982: 5044.

1538
Omezzine, Abdallah. Economic analysis of winter vegetable markets in Tunisia. MoU, 1985. 239 p.   Micro 85–29,682
DAI, v. 46A, May 1986: 3441.

1539
Omran, Elsayed M. H. The grammar tradition in Arabic: reform efforts and proposals for reform. DGU, 1983. 222 p.   Micro 84–25,179
DAI, v. 45A, Feb. 1985: 2512.

1540
Opresko, Alan E. Power and influence: analytical concepts in international politics as applied to the Palestine Liberation Organization, 1964–1974. NBiSU, 1984. 580 p.   Micro 84–8388
DAI, v. 45A, July 1984: 297.

1541
Ormsby, Eric L. An Islamic version of theodicy: the dispute over al-Ghazali's "best of all possible worlds." NjP, 1981. 385 p.   Micro 81–18,342
DAI, v. 42A, Sept. 1981: 1205.

1542
Ortiz, Alan T. Towards a theory of ethnic separatism: a case study of Muslims in the Philippines. PU, 1986. 375 p.   Micro 86–14,846
DAI, v. 47A, Jan. 1987: 2729.

1543
al-Osaimi, Muhammad Saʿad M. Jamhoor. The feasibility of modifying the grade-organization of the educational system in Saudi Arabia. InU, 1981. 132 p.
Micro 81–28,055
DAI, v. 42A, Jan. 1982: 3096.

1544
Osborne, Michael A. The Societé zoologique d'acclimatation and the new French Empire: the science and political economy of economic zoology during the Second Empire. WU, 1987. 454 p.   Micro 87–12,432
DAI, v. 48A, Sept. 1987: 734.

1545
Osia, Kunirum. Choice in African international relations: perspectives on Arab and Israeli influences in Africa, 1967 to 1979. DGW, 1981. 740 p.
Micro 81–19,904
DAI, v. 42A, Oct. 1981: 1781.

1546
Osman, Fawzia Mostafa. A proposal for planning an interlending system for the

libraries of Cairo city in Egypt. PPiU, 1981. 233 p.　　　Micro 82-2323
DAI, v. 42A, Feb. 1982: 3334.

1547
Osman, Ibrahim el-Bashir. Islamic perspectives on the question of nationalism
and national integration: the case of the Sudan. CU-Riv, 1984. 348 p.
　　　　　　　　　　　　　　　　　　　　　　　　Micro 84-13,188
DAI, v. 45A, Oct. 1984: 1199.

1548
Osman, Mohamed. Evaluation of the population and development programs's
impact on family planning in rural Egypt. NIC, 1984. 205 p.
　　　　　　　　　　　　　　　　　　　　　　　　Micro 84-15,312
DAI, v. 45A, Nov. 1984: 1530.

1549
el-Osta, Wedad Belghassim. A solar-hydrogen energy system for a Libyan coastal
county (el-Gharabulli). FMU, 1987. 290 p.　　　　　Micro 87-16,153
DAI, v. 48B, Oct. 1987: 1131.

1550
al-Ostad, Ameer Bader. An ethnic geography of Kuwait: a study of eight ethnic
groups. OKentU, 1986. 259 p.　　　　　　　　　　Micro 86-17,072
DAI, v. 47A, Nov. 1986: 1841.

1551
Othman, Jihad Mahmoud. A critique of instructional materials for Near Eastern
studies. WaU, 1981. 160 p.　　　　　　　　　　　Micro 81-21,231
DAI, v. 42A, Oct. 1981: 1655.

1552
Ouaouicha, Driss. Contrastive rhetoric and the structure of learner-produced
argumentative texts in Arabic and English. TxU, 1986. 310 p.
　　　　　　　　　　　　　　　　　　　　　　　　Micro 87-260
DAI, v. 47A, Mar. 1987: 3339.

1553
Overton, Joseph L. Stability and change: inter-Arab politics in the Arabian
Peninsula and Gulf. MdU, 1983. 268 p.　　　　　　Micro 84-19,543
DAI, v. 45A, Nov. 1984: 1515.

1554
Oweidat, Abdulla Ahmed. A study of changes in value orientations of Arab
students in the United States. CLSU, 1981.
DAI, v. 42A, Dec. 1981: 2374-2375.

1555
Ozo-Eson, Peter I. Some implications of oil revenues for the domestic economy in
oil exporting countries: an application to Nigeria. CaOOCC, 1982.
DAI, v. 44A, Jan. 1984: 2200-2201.

171

1556
Oztopcu, Kurtulus. A 14th century Mamluk-Kipchak military treatise: *Munyatu 'l-ghuzat*. CLU, 1986. 503 p.   Micro 87–2657
DAI, v. 47A, Apr. 1987: 3767.

1557
Painter, David S. The politics of oil: multinational oil corporations and United States foreign policy, 1941–1954. NcU, 1982. 599 p.   Micro 83–8342
DAI, v. 43A, May 1983: 3685.

1558
Pannbacker, Alfred R. The Levantine Arabs of Pittsburgh, Pennsylvania. MiU, 1981. 219 p.   Micro 82–15,063
DAI, v. 43A, Oct. 1982: 1290.

1559
Park, Thomas K. Administration and the economy: Morocco 1880 to 1980; the case of Essaouria. WU, 1983. 598 p.   Micro 84–2041
DAI, v. 45A, July 1984: 231.

1560
Parker, Thomas R. U.S. negotiating strategy towards the Arab-Israeli conflict, 1967–1979. NNCU-G, 1985. 261 p.   Micro 86–1683
DAI, v. 46A, May 1986: 3481.

1561
Parkinson, Dilworth B. Terms of address in Egyptian Arabic. MiU, 1982. 460 p.
Micro 82–15,065
DAI, v. 43A, Aug. 1982: 437.

1562
Pasha, Hafiz Ahmed. Seasonal housing markets: a model of pilgrim housing in Makkah. CSt, 1984. 143 p.   Micro 84–20,602
DAI, v. 45A, Dec. 1984: 1820.

1563
Patton, Douglas L. A history of the Atabegs of Mosul and their relations with the *'ulamā'*, A.H. 521–660/A.D. 1127–1262. NNU, 1982. 548 p.
Micro 83–7846
DAI, v. 43A, May 1983: 3675.

1564
Perelman, Leslie S. Something old, something new: the domestic side of Moroccan-Israeli ethnicity. WU, 1983. 269 p.   Micro 83–19,531
DAI, v. 44A, Jan. 1984: 2192.

1565
Perey, Marie-Helene. Essai d'ethno-épistémologie marocaine. CaQMM, 1985.
DAI, v. 46A, May 1986: 3399.

1566
Perry, Stephen K. Structural geometry and tectonic evolution of the southwestern Gulf of Suez, Egypt. ScU, 1986. 605 p.   Micro 87–4643
DAI, v. 47B, May 1987: 4449.

1567
Peteet, Julie M. Women and national politics: the Palestinian case. MiDW, 1985. 404 p.   Micro 86–5028
DAI, v. 47A, July 1986: 226–227.

1568
Pfeifer, Karen A. Agrarian reform and the development of capitalist agriculture in Algeria. DAU, 1981. 428 p.   Micro 82–8063
DAI, v. 42A, May 1982: 4877.

1569
Piesinger, Constance M. Legacy of Dilmun: the roots of ancient maritime trade in Eastern Coastal Arabia in the 4th/3rd millennium B.C. WU, 1983. 1224 p.
Micro 84–508
DAI, v. 44A, June 1984: 3733.

1570
Pinault, David. Stylistic features in selected tales from *The Thousand and One Nights.* PU, 1986. 435 p.   Micro 86–14,849
DAI, v. 47A, Oct. 1986: 1345–1346.

1571
Pirnazar, Saeed. Non-corporate groups and political development in developing areas: the role of non-corporate groups in political development and modernization in the Middle East. KU, 1982. 217 p.   Micro 83–9344
DAI, v. 43A, June 1983: 4026.

1572
Piselli, Kathyanne. A daughter of Palestine: the short fiction of Samirah Azzam. MiU, 1986. 162 p.   Micro 87–2810
DAI, v. 47A, Apr. 1987: 3767.

1573
Pitsuwan, Surin. Islam and Malay nationalism: a case study of the Malay-Muslims of southern Thailand. MH, 1982. 313 p.   Micro 82–22,691
DAI, v. 43A, Nov. 1982: 1671.

1574
Polster, Deborah. The need for oil shapes: the American diplomatic response to the invasion of Suez. OclW, 1985. 292 p.   Micro 85–10,098
DAI, v. 46A, Sept. 1985: 778.

1575
Posner, Nadine F. The Muslim conquest of northern Mesopotamia: an introduc-

tory essay into its historical background and historiography. NNU, 1985. 439 p.
Micro 85–10,523
DAI, v. 46A, Sept. 1985: 726.

1576
Pourghourian-Najafabadi, Mohamad-Sadegh. The Islamic concept of socio-political leadership in Iran. CSdI, 1981. 338 p. Micro 81–20,181
DAI, v. 42A, Oct. 1981: 1775–1776.

1577
Pourtaei, Ali. Toward a synthesis of theories of revolution: the cases of Iran and Egypt. OkU, 1982. 406 p. Micro 82–25,514
DAI, v. 43A, Dec. 1982: 2129.

1578
Pouryoussefi, Hamid. College impact on religiosity of Muslim students studying in the United States. MiKW, 1984. 185 p. Micro 84–14,961
DAI, v. 45A, Sept. 1984: 960.

1579
Powers, William H. A study of those factors influencing teachers working for the Arabian American Oil Company in Saudi Arabia to transfer to non-teaching positions with the Company. CoGrU, 1986. 161 p. Micro 86–21,967
DAI, v. 47A, Dec. 1986: 1932–1933.

1580
Putman, Diana B. A cultural interpretation of development: developers, values, and agricultural change in the Somali context *Isku kalsoonaan baa horumar lagu gaaraa* (Trust leads to success). PBm, 1984. 614 p. Micro 85–5770
DAI, v. 46A, July 1985: 191.

1581
al-Qadi, Wael Amin. Designing instrumentation for assessing the institutional need of higher education in the West Bank universities. PPiU, 1985. 175 p.
Micro 86–1407
DAI, v. 46A, June 1986: 3612–3613.

1582
Qandil, Mahmoud Ahmed. The effect of text structure and signaling devices on recall of freshman Arab students. TxDN, 1986. 83 p. Micro 86–16,052
DAI, v. 47A, Oct. 1986: 1266.

1583
Qaryouti, Yousef Farid. Special education in Jordan: a present status and needs assessment study. MiEM, 1984. 190 p. Micro 84–15,248
DAI, v. 45A, Jan. 1985: 2067–2068.

1584
Qasem, Zaidan Ahmad. The development of an Arabic reading inventory for

Jordanian elementary schools first through fourth grade levels. MiEM, 1986.
187 p.   Micro 86–25,059
DAI, v. 47A, Jan. 1987: 2525.

1585
al Qataee, Abdullah A. The relationship of dogmatism, moral-, ego-development and sex role among college students majoring in different fields in Saudi Arabia. PPiU, 1986. 129 p.   Micro 87–1952
DAI, v. 47A, June 1987: 4320.

1586
Qawasmeh, Rushdi Yousef. A descriptive and explanatory case study of the expansion of the educational system in Jordan, 1950–1980. ICL, 1986. 168 p.
                                                              Micro 86–16,198
DAI, v. 47A, Oct. 1986: 1276.

1587
Qoqandi, Abdulaziz Mohammed Yar. Measuring the level of syntactical growth of Saudi twelfth graders in EFL writing using T-unit analysis. KU, 1984. 279 p.
                                                              Micro 85–13,804
DAI, v. 46A, Oct. 1985: 916–917.

1588
al-Qthami, Hmood Dawi. A study of the use of computers in Arab countries. CoU, 1987. 264 p.   Micro 87–16,232
DAI, v. 48A, Nov. 1987: 1176.

1589
al-Quisi, Issa Hajji. Earning determination and differential in the Kuwait labor market. WaU, 1984. 194 p.   Micro 85–8033
DAI, v. 46A, Aug. 1985: 491.

1590
al-Qunaibet, Mohammad Hamad. An economic analysis of the municipal demand for water in Kuwait. OrCS, 1984. 165 p.   Micro 84–18,145
DAI, v. 45A, Nov. 1984: 1477.

1591
al-Qurashi, Khedir Olayyan Ali. The feasibility of the Arabic language as a medium of instruction in sciences. InU, 1982. 318 p.   Micro 83–1092
DAI, v. 43A, Feb. 1983: 2578.

1592
Qureshi, Regula Burckhardt. Qawwali: sound, context and meaning in Indo-Muslim sufi music. CaAEU, 1981. 513 p.   Micro 82–17,377
DAI, v. 43A, Sept. 1982: 857.

1593
Qutami, Nayfeh Mohamad. Causal attributions for performance in scholastic

achievement of Jordanian sixth and third grade boys and girls. CLU, 1985. 117 p.　　　　　　　　　　　　　　　　　　Micro 85–25,872
DAI, v. 46A, Mar. 1986: 2634.

1594
Qutami, Yusuf Mahmoud. Jordanian children's internality and the validity, reliability indices to the Jordanian achievement responsibility scale. CLU, 1985. 152 p.　　　　　　　　　　　　　　　　Micro 85–25,873
DAI, v. 46A, Mar. 1986: 2634.

1595
al-Rabe, Ahmad Abdulla. Muslim philosophers' classifications of the sciences: al-Kindī, al-Fārābī, al-Ghazālī, Ibn Khaldūn. MH, 1984. 220 p.
　　　　　　　　　　　　　　　　　　　　　　Micro 84–19,296
DAI, v. 45A, Jan. 1985: 2236.

1596
al-Rabghi, Abdulaziz Mohammed. British policy towards Egypt from 1833 to 1882. CCC, 1986. 321 p.　　　　　　　　　　　　Micro 86–6891
DAI, v. 47A, July 1986: 278.

1597
Raccagni, Michelle. Origins of feminism in Egypt and Tunisia. NNU, 1983. 327 p.　　　　　　　　　　　　　　　　　　Micro 83–13,924
DAI, v. 44A, Aug. 1983: 550.

1598
Rached, Mounir Rachid. A money demand and supply model for Egypt. AzU, 1981. 126 p.　　　　　　　　　　　　　　　Micro 82–5286
DAI, v. 42A, Mar. 1982: 4079.

1599
Ragep, Faiz Jamil. Cosmography in the *Tadhkira* [*f ī 'ilm al-hay'ah*] of Nāṣir al-Dīn al-Ṭūsī [13th c. A.D.]. MH, 1982. 653 p.　　　　Micro 82–22,696
DAI, v. 43A, Nov. 1982: 1659.

1600
Rajaee, Farhang. Islam and politics: Ayat-Allah Ruhollah Musavi Khomeyni's fundamental political ideas. ViU, 1983. 271 p.　　　Micro 83–26,988
DAI, v. 44A, May 1984: 3486.

1601
Rajah, Mireille S. The Mauritian Muslim family in transition: structural and ideological changes, a cultural diffusion approach. CU-S, 1987. 344 p.
　　　　　　　　　　　　　　　　　　　　　　Micro 87–20,212
DAI, v. 48A, Dec. 1987: 1548.

1602
Rajehi, Mohammad Owayedh R. The impact of social change on police development in Saudi Arabia: a case study of Riyadh Police Department. MiEM, 1981.

225 p.   Micro 81–17,260
DAI, v. 42A, Aug. 1981: 866.

1603
Raji, Rasheed Ajani. The influence of the *'Ishrīnīyāt* on Arabic and Islamic culture in Nigeria. MiU, 1982. 400 p.   Micro 82–25,023
DAI, v. 43A, Dec. 1982: 1987.

1604
Ramadan, Bassam Ismail. Food security in the Arab world: its significance and means of attainment. NIC, 1986. 245 p.   Micro 86–23,195
DAI, v. 47A, Jan. 1987: 2676.

1605
Ramadan, Jasem Mohammad. Selected physiological, psychological, and anthropometric characteristics of the Kuwaiti World Cup Soccer Team. LU, 1984. 139 p.   Micro 85–11,762
DAI, v. 46A, Oct. 1985: 924.

1606
Ramsey, Virginia O. The relationship of age, sex, experience, religion, and culture to children's concepts of death: a study of American and Palestinian children. TxDW, 1986. 203 p.   Micro 86–26,497
DAI, v. 47A, Feb. 1987: 2881.

1607
al-Rashed, Ali Ahmed S. Content analysis and international comparison of Saudi science curriculum in three grade levels. NBuU, 1986. 175 p.
                                          Micro 86–19,291
DAI, v. 47A, Dec. 1986: 2103.

1608
el-Rashed, Ibraheem Mohammad. Influence of teacher wait-time and question level on eighth grade students' science achievement and attitudes toward science in Saudi Arabia. InU, 1984. 285 p.   Micro 84–17,141
DAI, v. 45A, Nov. 1984: 1358.

1609
Rashedi, Nahid. History of Iranian education: influence of Islam and the West. MiU, 1984. 273 p.   Micro 84–22,318
DAI, v. 45A, Jan. 1985: 2010.

1610
al-Rasheed, Abdullah Ahmad. An investigation of the general affective behavior toward science held by secondary school scientific section students at Riyadh City, Saudi Arabia. CoGrU, 1983. 173 p.   Micro 84–8143
DAI, v. 45A, July 1984: 142.

1611
al-Rasheed, Saud Abdullah M. The construction and validation of achievement

test for students in twelfth grade biology in Saudi Arabia. NBuU, 1987. 187 p.

Micro 87–10,683

DAI, v. 48A, Aug. 1987: 372.

1612

Rashid, Javed. Effect of wheat type and extraction rate on quality of Arabic type leavened flat bread. KMK, 1983. 99 p.　　　　　　　Micro 84–7688

DAI, v. 44B, June 1984: 3709.

1613

al Rashidi, Basheer Saleh. Perceived and preferred goals as a basis for the planning development of an educational system in the State of Kuwait. OU, 1982. 201 p.

Micro 83–198

DAI, v. 43A, Feb. 1983: 2553.

1614

Rasler, Karen A. Conflict and escalation in Lebanon: a dynamic analysis of Civil War and intervention. FTaSU, 1981. 630 p.　　　　　Micro 82–8746

DAI, v. 42A, May 1982: 4925–4926.

1615

Rawabdeh, Musa Agil. Private rates of return to education in Jordan. NSyU, 1984. 220 p.　　　　　　　　　　　　　　　　Micro 85–779

DAI, v. 45A, May 1985: 3399.

1616

Er-Rayyan, Mohammad Rashad Hamd-Allah. Toward the construction of a temporal system for natural language in the light of the data of the Arabic and English languages. PU, 1986. 506 p.　　　　　　Micro 86–16,562

DAI, v. 47A, Nov. 1986: 1714.

1617

Razavi, Mehdi B. Modeling an Islamic economic system: an interaction delivery matrix and Boolean digraph approach. NbU, 1983. 310 p.

Micro 84–12,320

DAI, v. 45A, Aug. 1984: 581.

1618

Razouki, Adnan Ali. Analysis of socio-economic factors on students' academic achievement in the preparatory academic schools in Iraq. PPiU, 1987. 122 p.

Micro 87–19,318

DAI, v. 48A, Dec. 1987: 1372.

1619

Reachard, Danny J. Social and economic integration among countries of the Arab East. DAU, 1987. 260 p.　　　　　　　　　Micro 87–12,618

DAI, v. 48A, Sept. 1987: 759.

1620

Reas, Jane E. An ethnography of economic strategies in modern Cairo. WaU, 1986.

DAI, v. 47A, June 1987: 4431.

1621
Redding, Richard W. Decision making in subsistence herding of sheep and goats in the Middle East. MiU, 1981. 442 p.   Micro 81–16,322
DAI, v. 42A, Aug. 1981: 759.

1622
Redmount, Esther R. A comparison of collective, cooperative, and private sector farm settlements in Jewish Palestine [1929–1936]. ViU, 1985. 216 p.
Micro 86–8548
DAI, v. 47A, Aug. 1986: 599.

1623
Reeves, Edward B. The "*walī* complex" at Tanta, Egypt: an ethnographic approach to popular Islam. KyU, 1981. 458 p.   Micro 81–29,761
DAI, v. 42A, Jan. 1982: 3216.

1624
al-Refaei, Yaqoub S. Y. Administrative leadership in Kuwait's public sector. CCC, 1987. 205 p.   Micro 87–5176
DAI, v. 47A, May 1987: 4184.

1625
Rehemi, Madani Faraj. A survey of the attitudes of Saudi men and women toward Saudi female participation in Saudi Arabian development. CoU, 1983. 184 p.
Micro 83–17,692
DAI, v. 44A, Oct. 1983: 1050.

1626
Reinhart, Arthur K. Before revelation: the boundaries of Muslim moral knowledge. MH, 1986. 362 p.   Micro 86–20,574
DAI, v. 47A, Dec. 1986: 2196.

1627
Reis, Joao J. Slave rebellion in Brazil: the African Mulim uprising in Bahia, 1835. MnU, 1983. 401 p.   Micro 83–14,144
DAI, v. 44A, Aug. 1983: 555.

1628
Reizian, Alice M. Illness behavior and help-seeking behavior among Arab-Americans. CU-Sf, 1984. 241 p.   Micro 85–3739
DAI, v. 45B, June 1985: 3774.

1629
al-Rekaibi, Safaq Abdullah. A descriptive analysis of the development and operation of the Kuwait Stock Exchange. CSdI, 1983. 174 p.   Micro 84–4443
DAI, v. 44A, May 1984: 3254.

1630
Rezig, Aicha. Gender, resources and attitudes toward marital role equality: a

comparison of Algerian and American students. MU, 1985. 209 p.

Micro 86–2680

DAI, v. 46B, June 1986: 4455.

1631

Rice, Karen S. The allocation, dietary intake and productivity in a schistosomiasis-stressed Egyptian village. UU, 1985. 135 p.　　　　Micro 86–2317

DAI, v. 46A, June 1986: 3772.

1632

al-Rifai, Hessa Sayyed Zaid. *al-Nehmah wal-Nahham*: a structural functional, musical and aesthetic study of Kuwaiti sea songs. InU, 1982. 352 p.

Micro 83–7992

DAI, v. 43A, May 1983: 3672.

1633

Rifai, Mukhtar Mahmoud. Interindustry and programming analysis: the case of Libya. NbU, 1981. 130 p.　　　　Micro 81–20,170

DAI, v. 42A, Oct. 1981: 1724.

1634

Rifai, Ziad. The selection and importation of foreign television programs at Jordan television: a case study. FTaSU, 1986. 315 p.　　　Micro 86–19,150

DAI, v. 47A, Dec. 1986: 1915.

1635

Rippin, Andrew L. The Quranic *asbāb al-nuzūl* material: an analysis of its use and development in exegesis. CaQMM, 1981.

DAI, v. 42A, Apr. 1982: 4481.

1636

Rispler, Vardit. Insurance in the world of Islam: origins, problems and current practice. CU, 1985. 203 p.　　　　Micro 86–10,181

DAI, v. 47A, Sept. 1986: 1032.

1637

al-Riyami, Said Amer. An assessment of official development assistance from the OPEC capital-exporting countries, 1974–1979. FMU, 1982. 75 p.

Micro 82–27,766

DAI, v. 43A, Jan. 1983: 2408.

1638

Rizk, Khalil Shukrallah. The poetry of ʿAbd al-Wahhāb al-Bayātī: thematic and stylistic study. InU, 1981. 322 p.　　　　Micro 81–28,039

DAI, v. 42A, Jan. 1982: 3175.

1639

Rizk, Samy Mahmoud Abdallah. Egyptian teachers' knowledge of teaching reading, their perception of pre-service education, and self-assessment. PPiU,

1982. 218 p.   Micro 82–18,182
DAI, v. 43A, Dec. 1982: 1940.

1640
Roberts, Joseph B. Early Islamic historiography: ideology and methodology. OU,
1986. 317 p.   Micro 86–29,425
DAI, v. 47A, Mar. 1987: 3541.

1641
Robinson, Richard D. The process of change in a community organization [Arabs
in Dearborn, Michigan]: an anthropological analysis of an urban system.
MiDW, 1984. 346 p.   Micro 85–4914
DAI, v. 45A, June 1985: 3679.

1642
Robinson, Vaughn D. Organic geochemical characterization of the late
Cretaceous-early tertiary transgressive sequence found in the Duwi and
Dakhla Formations, Egypt. OkU, 1986. 190 p.   Micro 86–17,418
DAI, v. 47B, Nov. 1986: 1903.

1643
Roded, Ruth M. Tradition and change in Syria during the last decades of
Ottoman rule: the urban elite of Damascus, Aleppo, Homs and Hama, 1876–
1918. CoDU, 1984. 428 p.   Micro 85–3369
DAI, v. 45A, June 1985: 3726.

1644
Rogers, Glenn R. The theory of output-income multipliers with consumption
linkages: an application to Mauritania. WU, 1986. 190 p.   Micro 86–15,663
DAI, v. 47A, Jan. 1987: 2677.

1645
Rollman, Wilfrid J. The "New Order" in a pre-colonial Muslim society: military
reform in Morocco, 1844–1904. MiU, 1983. 946 p.   Micro 83–24,273
DAI, v. 44A, Dec. 1983: 1888.

1646
Romeu, Andres A. Biodegradation of Kuwait crude oil in the presence and
absence of the dispersant corexit 9527. TxCM, 1986. 147 p.
                                                             Micro 86–14,994
DAI, v. 47B, Oct. 1986: 1457.

1647
Rose, Richard B. Pluralism in a medieval colonial society: the Frankish impact on
the Melkite community during the first Crusader Kingdom of Jerusalem,
1099–1187. CBGTU, 1981. 560 p.   Micro 82–3207
DAI, v. 42A, Mar. 1982: 4103.

1648
Rosenblatt, Liane S. Building Yamit: relationships between officials and settler

181

representatives in Israel. NRU, 1983. 317 p.   Micro 84–3161
DAI, v. 44A, Apr. 1984: 3107–3108.

1649
Rosenblum, Howard I. A political history of revisionist Zionism, 1925–1938.
NNC, 1986. 440 p.   Micro 86–23,470
DAI, v. 47A, Jan. 1987: 2707.

1650
Rothstein, Daniel H. Consensus *and* conflict: immigrant absorption in Israel,
1948–51. MH, 1985. 358 p.   Micro 86–8652
DAI, v. 47A, Aug. 1986: 634.

1651
Rouhana, Nadim. The Arabs in Israel: psychological, political, and social dimensions of collective identity. MiDW, 1984. 248 p.   Micro 85–4917
DAI, v. 46B, Nov. 1985: 1745.

1652
Roumani, Jacques. The emergence of modern Libya: political traditions and
colonial change. NjP, 1987. 504 p.   Micro 87–14,915
DAI, v. 48A, Oct. 1987: 1008–1009.

1653
Roush, Stephen. An assessment of educational components in foreign aid development projects in Jordan. ViBlbV, 1982. 181 p.   Micro 83–12,321
DAI, v. 44A, July 1983: 46.

1654
Rouzbehani, Fariborz. Internal and external implications of populist-Islamic
revivalism: a survey of evolutionary Islamic development in Iran. CLSU, 1983.
DAI, v. 44A, Nov. 1983: 1567–1568.

1655
al-Rowaithy, Ateiyiah Salem. The effectiveness of the Saudi Arabian government's programs to modernize Saudi society through the development of a non-
oil industrial sector. CCC, 1987. 202 p.   Micro 87–9287
DAI, v. 48A, July 1987: 209.

1656
Rowson, Everett K. [Abū al-Ḥasan] al-ʿĀmirī [d. 992 A.D.] on the afterlife: a
translation with commentary of his *al-Amad ʿalá al-abad*. CtY, 1982. 551 p.
Micro 82–21,746
DAI, v. 43A, Nov. 1982: 1578.

1657
Royal, Anne M. Male/female pharyngealization patterns in Cairo Arabic: a
sociolinguistic study of two neighborhoods. TxU, 1985. 228 p.
Micro 85–27,640
DAI, v. 46A, May 1986: 3338.

1658

Rozi, Abdulghafour Ismail. The social role of scholars (*'ulamā'*) in Islamic Spain: a study of medieval biographical dictionaries (*tarājim*). MBU, 1983. 497 p.

Micro 83–20,011

DAI, v. 44A, Nov. 1983: 1540.

1659

Rubenstein, Sondra M. The Communist movement in Palestine, 1919–1947. NNC, 1983. 439 p.   Micro 85–23,229

DAI, v. 46A, Feb. 1986: 2431.

1660

al-Ruhayli, Saud Dakhil. Old age and lost youth in early Arabic poetry. MiU, 1986. 362 p.   Micro 86–12,461

DAI, v. 47A, Sept. 1986: 924–925.

1661

Runty, Carol J. The political role and status of women in the Muslim world. NbU, 1981. 134 p.   Micro 81–24,521

DAI, v. 42A, Nov. 1981: 2285.

1662

al-Ruwashid, Mohammed Suliman Abdulrahman. The effects of a lecture-only and lecture-laboratory approach on Riyadh Junior College, Saudi Arabia chemistry students' achievement and attitudes. CoGrU, 1984. 232 p.

Micro 84–18,114

DAI, v. 45A, Nov. 1984: 1357.

1663

Ryan, Michael S. Empty bodies on ruined thrones: politics in the thought of Ibn 'Arabī. MH, 1981.

CDI, 1973–1982, v. 37: 514.

1664

Saab, Nouredine. Study of the relationship between acculturation and academic achievement of the Arab students in an elementary school setting. MiDW, 1982. 114 p.   Micro 83–6937

DAI, v. 43A, May 1983: 3502.

1665

Saad, Abubaker M. Iraq and Arab politics: the Nuri as-Said era, 1941–1958. WaU, 1987. 456 p.

Letter from University of Washington Libraries.

1666

al-Saad, Khalid Mohammed. The portfolio behavior of commercial banks in Kuwait. CCC, 1986. 182 p.   Micro 86–16,528

DAI, v. 47A, Nov. 1986: 1803.

1667

Saad Sulayman, Nimir Sulayman. The relationship between teachers' attitudes

toward educational change and their job satisfaction in Sudan. CLU, 1984.
256 p.   Micro 84–28,558
DAI, v. 45A, Mar. 1985: 2842–2843.

1668
al-Saadat, Abdullah Ebrahim. Assessing the inservice training needs of teachers of English as a foreign language in Saudi Arabia. PSt, 1985. 216 p.
                                                          Micro 86–6289
DAI, v. 47A, July 1986: 185.

1669
Saaid-Farahat, Nagia Abdelmogney. Toward successful housing strategies in Egypt. ViBlbV, 1985. 253 p.   Micro 86–5360
DAI, v. 47A, July 1986: 1.

1670
al-Saati, Abdul-Rahim Abdul-Hamid. The Islamic reform in the Saudi Arabian financial system. CoU, 1987. 332 p.   Micro 87–16,233
DAI, v. 48A, Nov. 1987: 1274.

1671
al-Saati, Abdulaziz Jamal. Residents' satisfaction in subsidized housing: an evaluation study of the Real Estate Development Fund program in Saudi Arabia. MiU, 1987. 321 p.   Micro 87–12,053
DAI, v. 48A, Oct. 1987: 765.

1672
Saaty, Abdalelah S. The ecological context of public administration in Saudi Arabia. AU, 1985. 204 p.   Micro 86–774
DAI, v. 46A, May 1986: 3483.

1673
Saaty, Mohammed Amin. The constitutional development in Saudi Arabia. CCC, 1982. 264 p.   Micro 82–28,759
DAI, v. 43A, Jan. 1983: 2440.

1674
Sabah, Saadia. Mediation in a Moroccan setting. InLP, 1984. 311 p.
                                                          Micro 87–988
DAI, v. 47A, Mar. 1987: 3469.

1675
Sabbagh, Hani Raji. Arabic poetry in Israel: the developing expression of the identity and aspirations of the Arabs in Israel. MiU, 1986. 382 p.
                                                          Micro 86–21,368
DAI, v. 47A, Dec. 1986: 2155.

1676
Sabbagh, Suha. Going against the West from within: the emergence of the West as an other in Franz Fanon's work. WU, 1982. 222 p.   Micro 83–4971
DAI, v. 43A, May 1983: 3589.

1677
al-Sabban, Aidros Abdullah Srour. The municipal system in the Kingdom of Saudi Arabia: a case study of Makkah. CCC, 1982. 163 p.

Micro 82–28,738

DAI, v. 43A, Jan. 1983: 2447.

1678
al-Sabban, Mariem Abdullah. Career patterns of girls' elementary school principals in Saudi Arabia: in the cities of Makkah and Jaddah. CoU, 1983. 219 p.

Micro 84–8010

DAI, v. 45A, July 1984: 25.

1679
al-Sabban, Mohammad Salem. Viability of industrial integration within the Gulf Cooperation Council: the case of petrochemical industries. CoU, 1983. 288 p.

Micro 83–17,636

DAI, v. 44A, Oct. 1983: 1152.

1680
Sabella, Epiphan (Bernard) Z. External events and circulation of political elites: cabinet turnover in Jordan, 1946–1980. ViU, 1982. 262 p.

Micro 82–28,631

DAI, v. 43A, Jan. 1983: 2456.

1681
Saber, Mabrouk Mohamed. Land settlement in the Libyan Sahara: The Kufra Settlement Project. KyU, 1983. 191 p. Micro 83–22,986
DAI, v. 44A, Dec. 1983: 1922–1923.

1682
Sabri, Nidal Rashid. Attitudes of Arab businessmen, practitioners, and faculty members towards a school of business program in West bank of Jordan. CoGrU, 1981. 105 p. Micro 81–19,806
DAI, v. 42A, Sept. 1981: 969.

1683
Sachakul, Kanniga. Education as a means for national integration: historical and comparative study of Chinese and Muslim assimilation in Thailand. MiU, 1984. 327 p. Micro 84–22,325
DAI, v. 45A, Jan. 1985: 2010–2011.

1684
Sadiq, Muhammed. Patterns of identity in the Hebrew and Arabic novel. CU, 1981. 331 p. Micro 82–260
DAI, v. 42A, Jan. 1982: 3175.

1685
Sadowski, Yahya M. Political power and economic organization in Syria: the course of state intervention, 1946–1958. CLU, 1984. 331 p.

Micro 84–20,238

DAI, v. 45A, Jan. 1985: 2246.

1686
Saebi, Mohammad. The historical development of public education in the Islamic Republic of Iran: the nature of centralization with a model for decentralization of the personnel function in administration. KU, 1981. 169 p.
Micro 81–28,736
DAI, v. 42A, Jan. 1982: 2958–2959.

1687
Saeed, Abdalbasit. The state and socioeconomic transformation in the Sudan: the case of social conflict in southwest Kurdifan. CtU, 1982. 515 p.
Micro 82–13,913
DAI, v. 43A, July 1982: 206.

1688
Saegh, Abdul-Rahman Ahmed. Higher education and modernization in Saudi Arabia: an inquiry into the societal values of Saudi colleges and universities and their roles in the economic and non-economic development of the Kingdom. CCC, 1983. 398 p.
Micro 83–23,126
DAI, v. 44A, Dec. 1983: 1708.

1689
Safar, Jwad Safar Ali. Employee rewards system, with special emphasis on Kuwait. CCC, 1986. 229 p.
Micro 86–16,536
DAI, v. 47A, Nov. 1986: 1877.

1690
al-Saffar, Abdul-Kareem Abdul-Azeez. Goal programming and game theoretic analyses of some problems of economic policy for Kuwait and the Middle East. TxU, 1985. 265 p.
Micro 86–9451
DAI, v. 47B, Oct. 1986: 1697.

1691
Safizadeh, Fereydoun. Agrarian change, migration and impact of the Islamic Revolution in a village community in Azerbaijan, Iran. MH, 1986. 300 p.
Micro 86–9767
DAI, v. 47A, Sept. 1986: 962.

1692
el-Safy, Hamid el-Tag H. Job satisfaction and job performance among the middle management personnel of the Sudanese public service. CLSU, 1985.
DAI, v. 46A, Mar. 1986: 2497.

1693
Saggaf, Ahmed Abdullah. An investigation of the English program at the Department of English, College of Education, King Abdul-Aziz University, in Mecca, Saudi Arabia. KU, 1981. 202 p.
Micro 82–18,810
DAI, v. 43A, Dec. 1982: 1820.

1694
Saidi, Salama. Patterns and differentials in the urban labor force in Morocco,

1980. PU, 1986. 257 p.   Micro 87-3265
DAI, v. 47A, Apr. 1987: 3881.

1695
al-Saif, Saleh al-Mohammad. Recommended guidelines for the science education
program in the public secondary schools of Saudi Arabia. WyU, 1981. 231 p.
                                                         Micro 82-20,805
DAI, v. 43A, Oct. 1982: 1103.

1696
Saikali, Samir T. A comparison of the achievement in mathematics and science in
the intermediate schools of Lebanon. CLSU, 1987.
DAI, v. 48A, Oct. 1987: 861.

1697
al-Saji, Majid J. Ba'th Socialism and the Iraqi strategy for growth and development: a study of the Iraqi development effort since 1921. UU, 1985. 1038 p.
                                                         Micro 85-9675
DAI, v. 46A, Aug. 1985: 475.

1698
Sakhnini, Hisham M. A. Arabic morophology as described by Ibn Jinnī in *at-
Tafsīr al-mulūkī.* InU, 1984. 121 p.   Micro 84-17,211
DAI, v. 45A, Nov. 1984: 1386.

1699
Salah, Rima Yusuf. The changing roles of Palestinian women in refugee camps in
Jordan. NBiSU, 1986. 354 p.   Micro 86-16,415
DAI, v. 47A, Nov. 1986: 1792.

1700
Salama, Galal Ahmed. Attitudes toward a student-oriented meaningful lecture
method, self-concept, and locus of control of Egyptian science teachers with and
without professional educational training. InU, 1981. 165 p.
                                                         Micro 81-19,077
DAI, v. 42A, Sept. 1981: 1108.

1701
Salama, Mottaz Mahmoud. The city form: a quantitative technique for spatial
arrangement. MiU, 1986. 218 p.   Micro 86-12,619
DAI, v. 47A, Dec. 1986: 2341.

1702
Salama, Tarek Mohammed Said. A cross-cultural study of [Middle Eastern]
family consumer decision-making behavior. CSdI, 1983. 139 p.
                                                         Micro 83-13,145
DAI, v. 44A, July 1983: 271.

1703
Salameh, Kayed M. Administrative reform in the Jordanian ministry of educa-

tion: a field study. CU-Riv, 1986. 336 p.   Micro 87–7002
DAI, v. 48A, Sept. 1987: 533.

1704
al-Salameh, Mohammad Megbel. Factors influencing selection of occupational programs at community colleges in Jordan. OkS, 1984. 121 p.
Micro 85–15,231
DAI, v. 46A, Nov. 1985: 1159.

1705
Salameh, Rashed Mohamad. The stock market and economic stability in a developing surplus economy, case study: Kuwait. CoDU, 1986. 217 p.
Micro 86–19,131
DAI, v. 47A, Dec. 1986: 2259–2260.

1706
Salameh, Tamer Tamer. Strategic posture analysis and financial performance of the banking industry in United Arab Emirates: a strategic management study. CSdI, 1987. 254 p.   Micro 87–19,619
DAI, v. 48A, Dec. 1987: 1498.

1707
Salebi, Mohammed Yusuf. The effects of a teaching method based on contrastive analysis to reduce written errors in English made by Arab students. MsSM, 1986. 92 p.   Micro 86–15,804
DAI, v. 47A, Oct. 1986: 1226.

1708
Saleh, Ali M. M. Impact of agricultural policy on development of Fezzan region, Libya. AzTeS, 1986. 342 p.   Micro 87–4522
DAI, v. 47A, May 1987: 4163.

1709
al-Saleh, Bader Abdullah. Selected factors influencing the use of instructional media by male faculty members at the colleges of education in Saudi Arabian universities. MiEM, 1985. 210 p.   Micro 85–13,880
DAI, v. 46A, Nov. 1985: 1189.

1710
Saleh, Mohammed. A dynamic assimilation model: selected first-generation Arab-Canadians. CaOLU, 1983.
DAI, v. 44A, Apr. 1984: 3160.

1711
Saleh, Osama Abdelkarim. The social studies curriculum in Jordan, with special emphasis on cognitive levels of objectives and questions. ICarbS, 1983. 227 p.
Micro 83–11,023
DAI, v. 44A, July 1983: 62–63.

1712
Salem, Ahmad Abdel-Halim. Basic mathematical skills and attitudes toward

mathematics possessed by tenth graders and their teachers in Jordan. NNC-T, 1984. 144 p.　　　　　　　　　　　　　　　　　　Micro 85-5384
DAI, v. 46A, July 1985: 94.

1713
al-Salem, Ahmed Mohammed. Economic viability of the Saudi Arabian petrochemical industry: methanol as a case study. CU-Riv, 1987. 272 p.
　　　　　　　　　　　　　　　　　　　　Micro 87-14,694
DAI, v. 48A, Oct. 1987: 984.

1714
Salem, Aziza Abdel-Razik Ahmed. A study of determinants of transfer pricing in multinational corporations: the case between U.S. parents and the Egyptian units. MsU, 1986. 226 p.　　　　　　　　　　Micro 87-3479
DAI, v. 47A, Apr. 1987: 3806.

1715
Salem, Mohamed Elmisilhi Mohamed. Lifelong education as perceived by Egyptian university students and faculty. CLSU, 1986.
DAI, v. 47A, Oct. 1986: 1156.

1716
Salem, Mohammed Ahmed. Motivation of national and expatriate construction workers in Jordan. MiU, 1985. 171 p.　　　　　　Micro 85-12,498
DAI, v. 46B, Oct. 1985: 1274.

1717
al-Salem, Mohammed Saad. The interplay of tradition and modernity, a field study of Saudi policy and educational development. CU-SB, 1981. 226 p.
　　　　　　　　　　　　　　　　　　　　Micro 82-6223
DAI, v. 42A, June 1982: 4981.

1718
Salem, Norma. Habib Bourguiba: a study of Islam and legitimacy in the Arab world. CaQMM, 1983.
DAI, v. 44A, Nov. 1983: 1543.

1719
Salem-Murdock, Muneera. Nubian farmers and Arab herders in irrigated agriculture in the Sudan: from domestic to commodity production. NBiSU, 1984. 433 p.　　　　　　　　　　　　　　　Micro 84-13,231
DAI, v. 45A, Oct. 1984: 1156-1157.

1720
Salih, Abdul-Wahid Abod. Problems of beginning elementary teachers in relation to pre-service education in teacher training institutes in Iraq. CoGrU, 1982. 82 p.　　　　　　　　　　　　　　　　Micro 82-6183
DAI, v. 42A, Apr. 1982: 4281.

1721
Salih, Mahmud Husein. Aspects of clause structure in standard Arabic: a study in

relational grammar. NBuU, 1985. 325 p. Micro 85–10,363
DAI, v. 46A, Oct. 1985: 967.

1722
Salih, Siddig Abdelmegeed. The impacts of the government agricultural policies on domestic wheat production in the Sudan. NcD, 1983. 158 p.
Micro 84–10,472
DAI, v. 45A, July 1984: 238.

1723
al-Salih, Sobhi Mahmied. An analysis of the competencies needed for entry level accounting positions in Iraq. PPiU, 1985. 296 p. Micro 85–17,999
DAI, v. 46A, Dec. 1985: 1488.

1724
al-Salim, Maha Hussain. The impact of college on the development and social attitude of undergraduate Arab students. CLSU, 1984.
DAI, v. 45A, Jan. 1985: 1989.

1725
Salma, Nasser Mohammed. The selection, allocation and arrangement of Arabic typography on maps. WaU, 1986. 194 p. Micro 86–26,693
DAI, v. 47A, Mar. 1987: 3529.

1726
Salman, Munir Amin. The Arab League: a critical assessment of the political efficacy of a regional organization. AzFU, 1986. 258 p. Micro 87–5751
DAI, v. 47A, May 1987: 4183–4184.

1727
al-Saloom, Abdul Hussain M. The cognitive process fostered by the Iraqi mathematical textbooks as revealed by content analysis. CoGrU, 1982. 101 p.
Micro 83–1131
DAI, v. 43A, Mar. 1983: 2883.

1728
Samad, Abdus. Dynamics of ascriptive politics: a study of Muslim politicization in East Bengal. NNC, 1983. 178 p. Micro 83–27,288
DAI, v. 44A, Apr. 1984: 3153.

1729
al-Samarrai, Hassan Younis. a process model to assess the educational needs of members in Iraqi agricultural cooperatives. TU, 1981. 143 p.
Micro 82–3813
DAI, v. 42A, Mar. 1982: 3969–3970.

1730
Samatar, Abdi Ismail. The state, peasants and pastoralists: agrarian change and rural development in northern Somalia, 1884–1984. CU, 1985. 307 p.
Micro 86–10,196
DAI, v. 47A, Sept. 1986: 1022.

1731
Samatar, Ahmed Ismail. Self reliance in theory and practice: a critique of Somali praxis, 1969–1980. CoDU, 1984. 409 p.   Micro 85–3796
DAI, v. 46A, July 1985: 257.

1732
al-Samdan, Ahmad Dha'en. Contracts' conflict rules in Arab private international law: a comparative study on principles of Islamic and civil legal systems. NcD, 1981. 255 p.   Micro 81–17,158
DAI, v. 42A, Aug. 1981: 827.

1733
Samhan, Muhammad Hussein. The role of the state in the economic development of Egypt. DAU, 1982. 465 p.   Micro 82–14,860
DAI, v. 43A, Aug. 1982: 502–503.

1734
Samman, Nizar Hasan. Saudi Arabia and the role of the *imarates* [regions] in regional development. CCC, 1982. 801 p.   Micro 82–20,602
DAI, v. 43A, Dec. 1982: 2094.

1735
Sammander, Abdul Raziq. A comparison of spoken with written texts with respect to error and non-error cohesive ties and syntactic structures of adult Arabic-speaking learners of English as a foreign language. InU, 1987. 347 p.
Micro 87–17,836
DAI, v. 48A, Nov. 1987: 1138.

1736
Samore, Gary S. Royal family politics in Saudi Arabia, 1953–1982. MH, 1984. 584 p.   Micro 84–19,403
DAI, v. 45A, Jan. 1985: 2246–2247.

1737
Sanders, Paula A. The court ceremonial of the Fatimid caliphate in Egypt. NjP, 1984. 275 p.   Micro 84–28,194
DAI, v. 45A, Mar. 1985: 2965.

1738
Sanford, Mary K. Diet, disease, and nutritional stress: an elemental analysis of human hair from Kulubnarti, a medieval Sudanese Nubian population [550–1450]. CoU, 1984. 452 p.   Micro 84–28,681
DAI, v. 45A, Mar. 1985: 2915.

1739
Sanousi, Sanousi Salem. A method for assessing the use of small water impoundments for sediment detention and local water supplies on the Wadi Zarat watershed, northwestern Libya. AzU, 1985. 249 p.   Micro 85–22,824
DAI, v. 46B, Feb. 1986: 2603–2604.

1740
Sarayirah, Yasin Khalaf. The centrality of the Customs Office in national development: the case of Jordan. NAlU, 1986. 365 p.   Micro 86–26,727
DAI, v. 47A, Mar. 1987: 3557.

1741
Sarhan, Abdulaziz Ahmed. Assessment of adequacy of elementary school physical facilities in Makkah School District, Saudi Arabia. CoDU, 1986. 182 p.
                                                                                Micro 86–17,669
DAI, v. 47A, Dec. 1986: 1933.

1742
Sari, Saleh Khaled. A critical analysis of Mamluk hoard from Karak [Jordan, 1257–1296]. MiU, 1986. 599 p.   Micro 86–12,621
DAI, v. 47A, Sept. 1986: 955.

1743
Sarsar, Saliba George. The effects of defense and war costs and personal traits on change in foreign policy orientations: a case study of Sadat's Egypt, 1970–1977.
NjR, 1984. 181 p.   Micro 84–24,151
DAI, v. 45A, Jan. 1985: 2250.

1744
Sashegyi, Keith D. A linear dynamic model of the East African jet in a stratified atmosphere [Somalia and Saudi Arabia]. FMU, 1983. 242 p.
                                                                                Micro 84–7486
DAI, v. 44B, June 1984: 3826–3827.

1745
Sattar, Abdus. Relationship between political alignment and scientific communication: a bibliometric study of Egyptian science publications. IU, 1985. 156 p.
                                                                                Micro 85–21,873
DAI, v. 46A, Jan. 1986: 1767.

1746
Saud, Saud Fares. Management and leadership styles of American, Arab, and Southeast Asian managers. CSdI, 1985. 134 p.   Micro 85–20,758
DAI, v. 46A, Jan. 1986: 2010.

1747
Saunders, Harry D. Energy-economy interactions: oil and the world economy.
CSt, 1982. 227 p.   Micro 82–8903
DAI, v. 42A, May 1982: 4878.

1748
el-Sauori, Hassan Ali Mohammed. The process of self-civilianization: the Sudanese experience. DeU, 1984. 279 p.   Micro 85–874
DAI, v. 45A, May 1985: 3439.

1749
Sawa, George D. Music performance practice in the early 'Abbāsid era, 132

A.H./750 A.D.–320 A.H./932 A.D. CaOTU, 1983.
DAI, v. 44A, Mar. 1984: 2619.

1750
el-Sawy, Mohamed Wageeh Zaky. The educational thought of Muhammad
Abduh and Taha Hussein. CtU, 1983. 322 p.   Micro 84–951
DAI, v. 44A, Mar. 1984: 2708.

1751
Sayed, Abdelrahman Ahmed. The phonology of Moroccan Arabic: a generative
phonological approach. TxU, 1981. 178 p.   Micro 81–19,366
DAI, v. 42A, Sept. 1981: 1130.

1752
el-Sayed, Ali Mohamed Mohamed. An investigation into the syntactic errors of
Saudi freshmen's English compositions. PInU, 1982. 234 p.   Micro 83–5222
DAI, v. 43A, Apr. 1983: 3306.

1753
el-Sayed, Said Mohamed. Policymaking in the Egyptian broadcating system: an
historical case-study analysis. WU, 1981. 333 p.   Micro 81–26,629
DAI, v. 42A, Feb. 1982: 3336.

1754
Sbait, Dirgham Hanna. The improvised-sung folk poetry of the Palestinians.
WaU, 1982. 524 p.   Micro 82–18,271
DAI, v. 43A, Sept. 1982: 797–798.

1755
Scek, Aues Abo. Population-health-development policy simulation model for
Somalia. NcU, 1986. 308 p.   Micro 87–11,160
DAI, v. 48B, Oct. 1987: 1018–1019.

1756
Schacknies, Siegbert. The international dimension of national transport decisions
of developing countries: an analysis of the influence of foreign assistance on the
transport sector of Egypt. PPiU, 1986. 391 p.   Micro 87–7580
DAI, v. 47A, June 1987: 4528.

1757
Schaefer, Karl R. Jerusalem in the Ayyubid and Mamluk eras. NNU, 1985.
392 p.   Micro 85–22,065
DAI, v. 46A, Feb. 1986: 2419–2420.

1758
Schulz, David E. Diglossia and variation in formal spoken Arabic in Egypt. WU,
1981. 304 p.   Micro 81–17,533
DAI, v. 42A, Nov. 1981: 2116.

1759
Scott, William A. Egyptian attitudes toward warfare in recent theatre and dra-

matic literature. WaU, 1984. 579 p. Micro 85–1096
DAI, v. 45A, May 1985: 3240.

1760
Scoville, Sheila A. British logistical support to the Hashemites of Hejaz: Ṭā'if to
Ma'ān, 1916–1918. CLU, 1982. 334 p. Micro 82–12,874
DAI, v. 43A, July 1982: 234.

1761
Seale, James L. Fixed effect Cobb-Douglas production functions for floor tile
firms, Fayoum and Kalyubiya, Egypt, 1981–1983. MiEM, 1985. 247 p.
  Micro 86–7128
DAI, v. 47A, Aug. 1986: 600.

1762
Searing, James F. Accomodation and resistance: chiefs, Muslim leaders, and
politicians in colonial Senegal, 1890–1934. NjP, 1985. 616 p.
  Micro 85–23,992
DAI, v. 46A, Mar. 1986: 2782–2783.

1763
Sedighsarvestani, Rahmat. Measuring attitudes of American college students
toward Muslims: a vignette approach. OAkU, 1985. 148 p.
  Micro 84–16,810
DAI, v. 45A, Oct. 1984: 1209.

1764
Sedra, Fayza Iskander. The mathematics assessment of Egyptian students at the
sixth-grade level, 1981. NNU, 1982. 199 p. Micro 82–26,791
DAI, v. 43A, Dec. 1982: 1868.

1765
Seif el Din, Ashraf Emam. Investment climate in Egypt as perceived by Egyptian
and American investors. OU, 1986. 243 p. Micro 87–3614
DAI, v. 48A, July 1987: 187.

1766
Selim, Mohamed Ahmed Mohamed. The effect of discovery and expository
teaching on science achievement and science attitude of male and female fifth
grade students in Egypt. PSt, 1981. 146 p. Micro 81–29,211
DAI, v. 42A, Jan. 1982: 3001.

1767
Sells, Michael A. The metaphor and dialectic of emanation in Plotinus, John the
Scot, Meister Eckhart, and Ibn Arabi. ICU, 1982.
CDI, 1983, v. 5: 385.

1768
Senani, Ahmed H. Underdeveloped in a capital-rich economy [the case of Saudi
Arabia]. IaAS, 1983. 195 p. Micro 84–7123
DAI, v. 44A, June 1984: 3820.

1769

Senani, Mohammed Abdullah. The political impact of His Royal Highness Prince Fahd's Eight-Point Plan for peace in the Middle East. CCC, 1983. 234 p.

Micro 83–21,058

DAI, v. 44A, Nov. 1983: 1568.

1770

Senbel, A. Aziz Abdullah. The goals of women's literacy education in Saudi Arabia as perceived by Saudi Arabian university professors, female literacy teachers and female adult learners. NbU, 1984. 339 p.   Micro 85–9876

DAI, v. 46A, Sept. 1985: 585.

1771

Sepehri, Mohammad. A mathematical analysis of behavioral pattern, behavioral change, and cognitive development of Moslem students in academic organizations. InU, 1982. 268 p.   Micro 83–1121

DAI, v. 43A, Feb. 1983: 2571–2572.

1772

Sesi, Georgette H. Validity of Cloze procedure as an index of readability of Arabic language reading materials. MiDW, 1982. 194 p.   Micro 82–16,169

DAI, v. 43A, Aug. 1982: 411.

1773

Sfeir, Jacqueline Faek. Development and validation of the School Entrance Exam for the West Bank of Jordan. CoGrU, 1984. 166 p.   Micro 84–29,840

DAI, v. 45A, May 1985: 3277.

1774

Sfeir, Leila Antoun. Policymaking in the Egyptian Olympic Committee. IU, 1982. 182 p.   Micro 82–18,558

DAI, v. 43A, Sept. 1982: 721.

1775

Shaaf, Mohammad Bagher. A proposed currency composite approach to pricing OPEC oil: problems and possibilities. TxLT, 1982. 205 p.   Micro 83–2171

DAI, v. 43A, Feb. 1983: 2745.

1776

Shaban, Abdel-Azeem Taha. Social justice and efficiency in Egyptian education: a critical investigation of the bases of the Egyptian educational philosophy, 1952 to the present. PPiU, 1981. 267 p.   Micro 82–13,180

DAI, v. 43A, July 1982: 106.

1777

Shabrami, Ali Sa'ad. The impact of U.S. institutions of higher education on the curricula of Saudi universities: a sociocultural case study of the MBA program at UPM [University of Petroleum and Minerals]. CSt, 1986. 328 p.

Micro 86–19,817

DAI, v. 47A, Dec. 1986: 2051.

1778
Shadukhi, Suliman Mohammed. Application of organization development in Saudi Arabia's public organizations: a feasibility study. FTaSU, 1981. 235 p.
Micro 81–18,510
DAI, v. 42A, Sept. 1981: 1310–1311.

1779
Shaer, Abdulrahman I. A needs assessment survey for the development of a plan for modification and expansion of the Natural History Museum of Saudi Arabia. PPiU, 1983. 195 p.   Micro 84–11,812
DAI, v. 45A, Aug. 1984: 388.

1780
Shafik, Fouad Fahmy. The press and politics of modern Egypt, 1798–1970: a comparative analysis of causal relationships. NNU, 1981. 599 p.
Micro 82–11,020
DAI, v. 43A, Nov. 1982: 1672–1673.

1781
Shafiq, Muhammad Malayam Shah. State Islamicity in the 20th century: a case study of Pakistan—analysis of the constitutional history of Pakistan. PPT, 1982. 302 p.   Micro 82–17,800
DAI, v. 43A, Oct. 1982: 1182.

1782
al-Shagroud, Hamad Mohammad. An examination of in-service training needs of secondary school principals in Saudi Arabia. PPiU, 1987. 143 p.
Micro 87–19,282
DAI, v. 48A, Dec. 1987: 1359.

1783
Shahatit, Kamel Farhan. The contribution of human capital to economic growth and development: the case of Jordan. PPiU, 1983. 235 p.   Micro 84–11,813
DAI, v. 45A, Aug. 1984: 576.

1784
Shahid, Samuel M. Mihyār al-Daylamī: his biography, poetic work, and its characteristics. ICU, 1982.
CDI, 1983, v. 5: 387.

1785
Shahrokhi, Shahrokh. Economic development and dependency: the case of oil-exporting developing countries. FTaSU, 1982. 96 p.   Micro 83–8682
DAI, v. 43A, June 1983: 3980.

1786
al-Shakhis, Mohammed Abdullah. An empirical investigation of the educational leadership styles, attitudes, and needs in Saudi Arabia. TU, 1984. 141 p.
Micro 84–29,577
DAI, v. 45A, Apr. 1985: 3034.

1787

Shakib, Mahmood. The influence of Persian culture during the early 'Abbāsid times: a study of Abu Nuwas' poetry. WaU, 1982. 165 p.   Micro 82–26,598
DAI, v. 43A, Dec. 1982: 1987–1988.

1788

Shalabieh, Mahmoud Ibrahim. A comparison of political persuasion on Radio Cairo in the eras of Nasser and Sadat. OU, 1985. 312 p.   Micro 85–26,247
DAI, v. 46A, Mar. 1986: 2477.

1789

al-Shalal, Khalid Ahmed. The trade union movement in the State of Kuwait: a socio-historical and analytical study. MiEM, 1984. 243 p.   Micro 84–15,201
DAI, v. 45A, Oct. 1984: 1210.

1790

al-Shalan, Abdulaziz Abdulah Rasheed. Word order and passivization in Arabic. WaU, 1983. 269 p.   Micro 84–4878
DAI, v. 44A, May 1984: 3373.

1791

el-Shall, Mohamed Saad el-Alfy. A study of the future cultural foundations of the Egyptian education by the year 2000: an exploratory study using the Ethnographic Delphi technique. MnU, 1982. 225 p.   Micro 82–21,261
DAI, v. 43A, Oct. 1982: 979.

1792

Shaltout, Mohammad Kassem. An investigation of different accounting principles and concepts among accountants in Egypt: a communication approach. MsSM, 1983. 278 p.   Micro 83–17,599
DAI, v. 44A, Sept. 1983: 797.

1793

Shami, Mufeed Mohammad. A model undergraduate business administration program applicable to higher academic institutions in the West Bank of Jordan. TxHU, 1985. 160 p.   Micro 86–7028
DAI, v. 47A, Aug. 1986: 393.

1794

Shami, Seteney Khalid. Ethnicity and leadership: the Circassians in Jordan. CU, 1982. 154 p.   Micro 83–12,967
DAI, v. 44A, July 1983: 213–214.

1795

al-Shamlan, Abdulrahman Rashid. The evolution of national boundaries in the southeastern Arabian Peninsula, 1934–1955. MiU, 1987. 484 p.
Micro 87–12,065
DAI, v. 48A, Aug. 1987: 464.

1796

al-Shammary, Eid Abdullah Salem. A study of motivation in the learning of

English as a foreign language in intermediate and secondary schools in Saudi Arabia. InU, 1984. 177 p. Micro 85–6078
DAI, v. 46A, July 1985: 90.

1797
Shams, Mohamed Mahmod. Oil conservation and economic development in Saudi Arabia. TxU, 1984. 196 p. Micro 85–13,297
DAI, v. 46A, Oct. 1985: 1042.

1798
al-Shamsi, Saeed Mohammad. The al-Buraimi dispute: a case study in inter-Arab politics. DAU, 1986. 268 p. Micro 87–12,452
DAI, v. 48A, Aug. 1987: 474.

1799
al-Shar, Ali Ahmad. An analytical study of the Adonisian poem. MiU, 1982. 299 p. Micro 82–14,855
DAI, v. 43A, Aug. 1982: 442.

1800
Sharafeldin, Ibnomer Mohamed. Human resource management: an Islamic perspective—a study of the Islamic academic institutions in the United States. CCC, 1987. 244 p. Micro 87–5186
DAI, v. 48A, Oct. 1987: 1014.

1801
Shararah, Hussein Hamzah. Evaluation of wall construction techniques based upon economical factors influencing labor and materials [in Saudi Arabia]. OkS, 1981. 194 p. Micro 82–13,068
DAI, v. 43B, July 1982: 198.

1802
Sharif, Hani Ibrahim. A curriculum planning study in mathematics education with an application to the Iraqi mathematics master's degree program. TU, 1984. 341 p. Micro 85–6919
DAI, v. 46A, July 1985: 94.

1803
Sharif, Ibrahim el-Zaroug. Professional occupational adjustment of Libyans educated in United States universities. MdU-P, 1982. 191 p. Micro 82–25,622
DAI, v. 43A, Dec. 1982: 2103–2104.

1804
el-Sharkawy, Samira Ibrahim. The status of educational media and technology in university-level nursing programs in the Arab Republic of Egypt. MBU-E, 1983. 107 p. Micro 83–19,888
DAI, v. 44A, Nov. 1983: 1305.

1805
Sharma, V. Alex. Syntactic errors as indices of developing language proficiency in

Arabic speakers writing English at the intermediate and advanced levels of English as a second language. InU, 1981. 146 p.　　Micro 82–3091
DAI, v. 42A, Mar. 1982: 3986.

1806
Sharvit, Uri. The role of music in the Jewish Yemenite ritual: a study of ethnic persistence. NNC, 1982. 356 p.　　Micro 82–22,485
DAI, v. 43A, Nov. 1982: 1343–1344.

1807
Shawabkeh, Mohammed Ali. The interchange between the Arabs and the West: a thematic study in the modern Arabic novel, 1935–1985. MiU, 1987. 256 p.
Micro 87–20,337
DAI, v. 48A, Dec. 1987: 1465.

1808
al-Shawan, Abdulrahman Mohamad. Social studies goals at the intermediate-school level in Saudi Arabia: present status and future needs. MiEM, 1985. 240 p.　　Micro 85–13,881
DAI, v. 46A, Nov. 1985: 1244.

1809
el-Shawan, Salwa Aziz. al-Mūsīḳá al-ʿArabiyyah: a category of urban music in Cairo, Egypt, 1927–1977. NNC, 1981. 349 p.　　Micro 81–25,281
DAI, v. 42A, Dec. 1981: 2351.

1810
Shawesh, Othman Mohamed. Vegetation types of semi-arid rangelands in northwestern Libya, North Africa. WyU, 1981. 240 p.　　Micro 82–1795
DAI, v. 42B, Feb. 1982: 3060.

1811
Shawish, Bashir Mohammed. Some aspects of the syntax of object complements in literary Arabic. InU, 1984. 282 p.　　Micro 84–22,815
DAI, v. 45A, Jan. 1985: 2085–2086.

1812
Shayegan, Yegane. Avicenna on time. MH, 1986. 282 p.　　Micro 86–20,576
DAI, v. 47A, Dec. 1986: 2186.

1813
Shebabi, Bashir Lamin. Correlates of life satisfaction among older Libyans and Americans. FU, 1984. 183 p.　　Micro 84–29,271
DAI, v. 45A, Mar. 1985: 2812.

1814
al-Shedokhi, Saad Abdul-Karim. An investigation of the problems experienced by Saudi students while enrolled in institutions of higher education in the United States. OrCS, 1986. 212 p.　　Micro 86–29,597
DAI, v. 47A, Mar. 1987: 3337.

1815

Sheehy, Edward J. The United States Navy in the Mediterranean, 1945–1947. DGW, 1983. 334 p. Micro 83–20,054
DAI, v. 44A, Nov. 1983: 1551.

1816

Sheha, Abdelmegeed Abdeltawab. The relationship of faculty perceptions and bases of power to faculty satisfaction and productivity in an Egyptian university. PSt, 1981. 187 p. Micro 81–20,463
DAI, v. 42A, Dec. 1981: 2531.

1817

Shehab, Faysal Issa. Attitudes of graduated students, educators, and employers towards technical education in Bahrain. PPiU, 1987. 135 p.
Micro 87–19,324
DAI, v. 48A, Dec. 1987: 1383–1384.

1818

Shehadeh, Ali Qandil. Determinants of the demand for and supply of money in Jordan, 1967–1980. IU, 1982. 183 p. Micro 82–18,562
DAI, v. 43A, Sept. 1982: 881.

1819

Shehim, Kassim. The influence of Islam on the ʿAfar. WaU, 1982. 240 p.
Micro 82–26,600
DAI, v. 43A, Dec. 1982: 2057.

1820

Shehniyailagh, Manizheh. The relationship between the adaptive behavior of Middle-Eastern children living in the United States and their mothers' child-rearing behaviors and their teachers' classroom behaviors. OkS, 1981. 152 p.
Micro 82–13,069
DAI, v. 43A, July 1982: 104.

1821

al-Sheik, Abdullah Mohammed. Adult basic education teachers in Kuwait. InMuB, 1984. 200 p. Micro 84–10,458
DAI, v. 45A, July 1984: 50.

1822

Sheik-Abdi, Abdi Abdulkadir. Mohammed Abdulle Hassan: African nationalism in Somalia, 1899–1920. MBU, 1985. 741 p. Micro 85–22,967
DAI, v. 46A, Feb. 1986: 2410–2411.

1823

el-Sheikh, Mohamad A. The applicability of Islamic law (*qiṣāṣ* and *dīyah*) in the Sudan. PPT, 1987. 357 p. Micro 87–16,369
DAI, v. 48A, Oct. 1987: 942.

1824

Sheikh Ibrahim, Abdul-Latif M. The interlanguage stress phonology of Arab

learners of English: influence of universals as well as dialect, distance, and task. PInU, 1986. 186 p.   Micro 86–23,645
DAI, v. 47A, Jan. 1987: 2569.

1825
Sheir, Aleya Aly. An analytic study of the errors made in English sentence patterns and their transformations by Egyptian prospective teachers of English as a foreign language (EFL). PSt, 1981. 153 p.   Micro 81–29,212
DAI, v. 42A, Jan. 1982: 3141.

1826
Shelash, Mesad F. Change in the perception of the role of women in Kuwait. OU, 1985. 143 p.   Micro 85–26,248
DAI, v. 46A, Mar. 1986: 2812.

1827
al-Shenaifi, Abdulrahman Abdulaziz. Microcomputer applications to Saudi higher education institutional planning and management. CoU, 1984. 238 p.
Micro 85–8934
DAI, v. 46A, Oct. 1985: 847.

1828
al-Shenaifi, Mohammed Saleh. Crop production activities performed by farmers and agricultural extension workers in Qasim, Saudi Arabia. MoU, 1983. 132 p.
Micro 84–1117
DAI, v. 44A, Apr. 1984: 2957.

1829
Sheng, Tom S. A risk-goal programming approach to whole farm analysis of small-scale farms in developing countries [the case of Abu Raia area in Kafr al-shaykh, Egypt]. CoFS, 1982. 225 p.   Micro 82–27,940
DAI, v. 43B, Jan. 1983: 2309.

1830
Sherif, Khaled Ahmed Fouad. The Egyptian pharmaceutical industry, a sector in transition. MBU, 1986. 242 p.   Micro 86–12,183
DAI, v. 47A, Sept. 1986: 1055.

1831
Sherif-Stanford, Nahla. Modernization by decree: the role of Tunisian women in development. MoU, 1984. 278 p.   Micro 85–12,243
DAI, v. 46A, Oct. 1985: 1109.

1832
Sheshsha, Jamal Abdulaziz. The qualifications of a competent teacher of English in Saudi Arabia as perceived by successful EFL [English as a foreign language] teachers and selected TESOL [Teachers of English to speakers of other languages] specialists. InU, 1982. 166 p.   Micro 82–11,349
DAI, v. 43A, Sept. 1982: 767–768.

1833

al-Shetaiwi, Mahmoud Flayeh Ali Gemei'an. The impact of Western drama upon modern Egyptian drama. IU, 1983. 308 p.   Micro 83–24,502
DAI, v. 44A, Dec. 1983: 1782.

1834

Shibah, Mohammed Mostafa. Analysis of the agricultural competencies need by the farmers in al-Hassa Oasis in Saudi Arabia. OU, 1983. 229 p.
Micro 84–293
DAI, v. 44A, Mar. 1984: 2657.

1835

al-Shiekh, Abdulmalek A. Isaq. Evaluation of arid land food production systems: strategies for Saudi Arabian agriculture. AzU, 1983. 164 p.   Micro 83–22,652
DAI, v. 44B, Dec. 1983: 1649.

1836

Shields, Sarah D. An economic history of nineteenth-century Mosul. ICU, 1986.
DAI, v. 47A, Jan. 1987: 2698.

1837

Shikaki, Khalil Ibrahim. Nuclear deterrence in the Arab-Israeli conflict? A case study in Egyptian-Israeli relations. NNC, 1986. 345 p.   Micro 86–10,812
DAI, v. 47A, Sept. 1986: 1050–1051.

1838

el-Shikhaby, Aly el-Sayed Mohammed. Socioeconomic status and students' placement in public secondary schools in Egypt. PPiU, 1983. 194 p.
Micro 83–27,700
DAI, v. 44A, Feb. 1984: 2593.

1839

Shimshoni, Jonathan. Conventional deterrence: lessons from the Middle East. NjP, 1986. 481 p.   Micro 86–7699
DAI, v. 47A, Aug. 1986: 650.

1840

Shiraishi, Takashi. Islam and Communism: an illumination of the people's movement in Java, 1912–1926. NIC, 1986. 690 p.   Micro 86–23,248
DAI, v. 47A, Jan. 1987: 2702.

1841

Shmuelevitz, Aryeh. Administrative, economic, legal and social relations in the Ottoman Empire in the late 15th and the 16th centuries: the case of the Jewish community as reflected in the responsa. WU, 1981. 377 p.   Micro 81–16,020
DAI, v. 42A, Sept. 1981: 1276.

1842

Shoaib, Mohammed Saleh. Development of social studies education in Saudi

Arabia since 1926. MoU, 1980. 157 p.   Micro 82–2665
DAI, v. 42A, Feb. 1982: 3423.

1843
Shobaki, Jonnie A. In-grade retention of students in Jordanian public schools,
grades 4 through 6. IU, 1986. 196 p.   Micro 86–10,979
DAI, v. 47A, Sept. 1986: 787.

1844
Shojai, Siamack. A macro economic approach to oil production in OPEC coun-
tries. NNF, 1984. 185 p.   Micro 85–6360
DAI, v. 46A, July 1985: 196.

1845
Shokri, Masih. Perspectives on class, gender, and state-profession relations among
prospective architects in Iran: the role of Islam and professionalism as ideologies. TxHU, 1986. 184 p.   Micro 87–9932
DAI, v. 48A, Sept. 1987: 533.

1846
al-Shomrany, Salih Ali. Agricultural land use patters in relation to the physical,
locational, and socioeconomic factors in the Assarah Region of Saudi Arabia.
MiEM, 1984. 342 p.   Micro 84–24,400
DAI, v. 45B, Feb. 1985: 2369.

1847
Shorrab, Ghazi Abed-el-Jabbar. Models of socially significant linguistics varia-
tion: the case of Palestinian Arabic. NBuU, 1981. 254 p.   Micro 82–4117
DAI, v. 42A, June 1982: 5109.

1848
Shrida, Fadel Sultan. A comparative study of physical education program in-
fluences on youth physical fitness levels in public schools in Iraq and the United
States. TNJ-P, 1981. 242 p.   Micro 81–21,593
DAI, v. 42A, Oct. 1981: 1536.

1849
al-Shuaibi, Saleh M. Human resources development in Saudi Arabia. PPiU,
1984. 254 p.   Micro 85–14,971
DAI, v. 46A, Nov. 1985: 1244.

1850
Shuga'a, Ahmed Mohamed Hamoud. Inside the Yemen agricultural camp in
California: characteristics of life and the motivation to migrate. CoGrU, 1984.
177 p.   Micro 84–18,139
DAI, v. 45A, Nov. 1984: 1524.

1851
Shukri, Raghda Khalid. Health needs assessment methodology applied to Albaqa
Refugee Camp, Jordan. TxU-H, 1986. 159 p.   Micro 87–12,606
DAI, v. 48B, Sept. 1987: 721.

1852
Shumaker, Linda C. Word order and case in Middle Arabic. MH, 1980.
CDI, 1973–1982, v. 37: 766.

1853
al-Shuwaikhat, Ahmed M. Language attitudes of Saudi Arabian graduate students in the U.S.: an introduction to the study of differentials of language attitudes of intellectual elites. CSt, 1985. 238 p.   Micro 85–6151
DAI, v. 46A, July 1985: 116.

1854
Shweck, Mohamed Hadi. A comparative study of the Libyan secondary school mathematics program. MoU, 1985. 167 p.   Micro 86–11,762
DAI, v. 47A, Sept. 1986: 820.

1855
Sibai, Mohamed Makki. An historical investigation of mosque libraries in Islamic life and culture. InU, 1984. 447 p.   Micro 84–17,184
DAI, v. 45A, Nov. 1984: 1229–1230.

1856
Sid Ahmed, Abu Bakr Awad. Mass media and development in Sudan. PSt, 1984.
244 p.   Micro 84–19,674
DAI, v. 45A, Feb. 1985: 2304.

1857
Sikainga, Ahmad Alawad Muhammad. British policy in the western Bahr al-Ghazal (Sudan), 1904–1946. CU-SB, 1986. 234 p.   Micro 87–3669
DAI, v. 47A, May 1987: 4165.

1858
Silsby, Susan P. [George] Antonius: Palestine, Zionism, and British imperialism, 1929–1939. DGU, 1986. 317 p.   Micro 86–22,342
DAI, v. 47A, Jan. 1987: 2707.

1859
Silverman, Raymond A. History, art and assimilation: the impact of Islam on Akan material culture. WaU, 1983. 158 p.   Micro 84–4949
DAI, v. 44A, June 1984: 3528.

1860
Simon, Reeva S. Iraq between the wars: the creation and implementation of a nationalist ideology. NNC, 1982. 284 p.   Micro 84–27,474
DAI, v. 45A, Apr. 1985: 3196.

1861
Simpson, Kay C. Settlement patterns on the margins of Mesopotamia: stability and change along the middle Euphrates, Syria. AzU, 1983. 580 p.
          Micro 83–24,462
DAI, v. 44A, Dec. 1983: 1848.
A section on modern communities is included.

1862
Sinbel, Nazek Mostafa. Attitudes of sports leaders toward the professional preparation scheme for sports coaches in Egypt. OrU, 1982. 150 p.
Micro 83–1822
DAI, v. 43A, Mar. 1983: 2929–2930.

1863
Singh, Harbup. The oneness of God in the Qur'an and Guru Granth: a critical study. PPT, 1986. 255 p.
Micro 86–11,932
DAI, v. 47A, Sept. 1986: 949.

1864
Sirles, Craig A. An evaluative procedure for language planning: the case of Morocco. IEN, 1985. 357 p.
Micro 86–914
DAI, v. 46A, May 1986: 3339.

1865
Slavin, David H. Anticolonialism and the French Left: opposition to the Rif War, 1925–1926. ViU, 1982. 506 p.
Micro 83–2572
DAI, v. 43A, Apr. 1983: 3392.

1866
Slomka, Jacquelyn. Medicine and reproduction in urban Morocco. MiU, 1986. 226 p.
Micro 86–21,378
DAI, v. 47A, Dec. 1986: 2216–2217.

1867
Slymovics, Susan E. The merchant of art: an Egyptian Hilali oral epic poet in performance. CU, 1985. 343 p.
Micro 86–10,218
DAI, v. 47A, Sept. 1986: 925.

1868
Smadi, Jamil Mahmoud. A validation study of a Jordanian version of the Autism Behavior Checklist (ABC) of the Autism Screening Instrument for Educational Planning (ASIEP). MiEM, 1985. 89 p.
Micro 85–20,561
DAI, v. 46A, Mar. 1986: 2663.

1869
Smiklo, Charmaine B. The United States and the Palestinian Problem: a case for United States recognition of the Palestine Liberation Organization. CCC, 1982. 230 p.
Micro 82–20,611
DAI, v. 43A, Oct. 1982: 1284–1285.

1870
Smith, Antar ibn Stanford. Significant features of al-Jassās' [917–981] methodology for deriving legal rulings from the Qur'ān. MiU, 1985. 228 p.
Micro 85–20,987
DAI, v. 46A, Feb. 1986: 2321.

1871
Smith, Gary N. From Urmia to the Stanislaus: a cultural-historical geography of

Assyrian Christians in the Middle East and America. CU-A, 1981. 311 p.
Micro 82–11,740
DAI, v. 42A, June 1982: 5247.

1872
Smith, Janet M. Socioeconomic status and other determinants of breastfeeding: the experience of urban Tunisian women. MBU, 1986. 375 p.
Micro 86–16,144
DAI, v. 47A, Oct. 1986: 1493.

1873
Smith, Mitchell W. Improving intergroup relations: the impact of two types of small group encounters between Israeli Arab and Jewish youth. PPT, 1982. 242 p.
Micro 82–11,207
DAI, v. 43B, July 1982: 298.

1874
Smith, Scot E. Application of remote sensing techniques to the study of the impacts of the Aswan High Dam. MiU, 1982. 240 p.
Micro 82–25,047
DAI, v. 43B, Dec. 1982: 1781.

1875
Smyth, William E. Persian and Arabic theories of literature: a comparative study of al-Sakkākī's *Miftāḥ al-'ulūm* and Shams-i Qays' *al-Mu'jam*. NNU, 1986. 363 p.
Micro 87–6785
DAI, v. 47A, June 1987: 4403.

1876
Snaf, Hussein Ahmad. Reform policies and settlements in Transjordan between 1830–1930. OKentU, 1985. 253 p.
Micro 86–4196
DAI, v. 47A, July 1986: 274.

1877
Snavely, Parke D. Depositional and diagenetic history of the Thebes formation (lower Eocene), Egypt, and implications for early Red Sea tectonism. CU-SC, 1984. 750 p.
Micro 84–28,097
DAI, v. 45B, May 1985: 3450.

1878
Sofi, Jamil Yahya. Responses of rural village populations to community development in Saudi Arabia. OclW, 1983. 138 p.
Micro 84–5263
DAI, v. 44A, May 1984: 3497.

1879
al-Solai, Abdallah Hammad. The impact of industrial estates on metropolitan Riyadh City, Saudi Arabia. UU, 1985. 313 p.
Micro 85–15,020
DAI, v. 46A, Nov. 1985: 1371.

1880
al-Soliman, Tarik Mohammed Akeel. School buildings for boys' general educa-

tion in Saudi Arabia: present functioning, future demands and proposed alternatives under conditions of social change. MiU, 1981. 529 p.

Micro 81-25,046

DAI, v. 42A, Dec. 1981: 2333.

1881
Sonbol, Amira el Azhary. The creation of a medical profession in Egypt during the nineteenth century: a study of modernization. DGU, 1981. 304 p.

Micro 82-18,299

DAI, v. 43A, Dec. 1982: 2069.

1882
Sonn, Tamara. Bandalī al-Jawzī's *History of intellectual movements in Islam*, Part one: *The social movements*—a translation and commentary. ICU, 1983.
CDI, 1983, v. 5: 405.

1883
Soraty, Yazid Isa. Ibn Khaldūn's views on man, society, and education. PPiU, 1985. 156 p.

Micro 86-1424

DAI, v. 46A, June 1986: 3629.

1884
Soufi, Adnan Abdulfattah. A conceptual model for managing the portfolio of Saudi Arabia's reserve funds. DGW, 1984. 445 p.   Micro 84-28,948
DAI, v. 45A, Apr. 1985: 3183.

1885
Sowayan, Saad Abdullah. Nabati poetry: the oral poetry of Arabia. CU, 1982. 362 p.   Micro 83-667
DAI, v. 43A, Feb. 1983: 2754.

1886
el-Sowygh, Hamad ibn Zeid. Performance of a Piagetian test by Saudi Arabian students in Colorado colleges and universities in relation to selected sociodemographic and academic data. NmU, 1981. 166 p.   Micro 82-1946
DAI, v. 42A, Feb. 1982: 3532-3533.

1887
Soysal, Orhan. An analysis of the influences of Turkey's alignment with the West and of the Arab-Israeli conflict upon Turkish-Israeli and Turkish-Arab relations, 1947-1977. NjP, 1983. 354 p.   Micro 83-16,815
DAI, v. 44A, Oct. 1983: 1170.

1888
Sproul, Christine. The American College for Girls, Cairo, Egypt: its history and influence on Egyptian women—a study of selected graduates. UU, 1982. 209 p.

Micro 82-21,991

DAI, v. 43A, Oct. 1982: 1064.

1889
Staats, Randolph W. A study of the relationship between vocational aptitude and

classroom performance among Saudi Arabian Navy recruit trainees. CSdI, 1978. 107 p. Micro 85–8418
DAI, v. 46A, Aug. 1985: 410.

1890
Stanislawski, Howard J. Elites, domestic interest groups, and international interests in the Canadian foreign policy decision-making process: the Arab economic boycott of Canadians and Canadian companies doing business with Israel. MWalB, 1981. 530 p. Micro 81–26,896
DAI, v. 42A, Dec. 1981: 2848.

1891
Stassis, Bassel A. The Jordanian student in the ESL classroom: areas of cross-cultural interference. NjR, 1984. 189 p. Micro 84–24,072
DAI, v. 45A, Feb. 1985: 2313.

1892
Staub, Steven D. A folkloristic study of ethnic boundaries: the case of Yemeni Muslims in New York City. PU, 1985. 327 p. Micro 86–3707
DAI, v. 46A, June 1986: 3827.

1893
Stein, Kenneth W. The land question in Mandatory Palestine, 1929–1936. MiU, 1976. 585 p. Micro 81–25,227
DAI, v. 42A, Dec. 1981: 2809.

1894
Stetkevych, Suzanne P. Innovation in a poetic tradition: Abū Tammām, poet and anthologist. ICU, 1981.
CDI, 1973–1982, v. 38: 105.

1895
Stevenson, Thomas B. Kinship, stratification, and mobility: social change in a Yemeni highlands town. MiDW, 1981. 309 p. Micro 82–9372
DAI, v. 42A, May 1982: 4866.

1896
Stino, Laila Elsayed Elmasry. A visual preference study of urban outdoor spaces in Egypt. MiU, 1983. 223 p. Micro 84–2376
DAI, v. 44A, Apr. 1984: 3181.

1897
Stuart, Madeleine F. Developing labor resources in the Arab world: labor activity effects from school attendance and socioeconomic background among women in the east Jordan Valley. CLSU, 1981.
DAI, v. 42A, June 1982: 4980.

1898
Sturchio, Neil C. Geology, petrology, and geochronology of the metamorphic

rocks of Meatiq Dome, central Eastern Desert, Egypt. MoSW, 1983. 236 p.
Micro 84–10,637
DAI, v. 45B, Aug. 1984: 494.

1899
Suaieh, Saadun Ismail. Aspects of Arabic relative clauses: a study of the structure of relative clauses in modern written Arabic. InU, 1980. 401 p.
Micro 81–5973
DAI, v. 41A, Mar. 1981: 4019.

1900
as-Sudais, Abdulaziz Ali Sulaiman. The applicability of the theory of customs unions to the case of the Cooperation Council for the Arab States of the Gulf (the GCC). CoU, 1985. 343 p.
Micro 85–22,640
DAI, v. 46A, Feb. 1986: 2372–2373.

1901
Suhaibani, Abdulrahman Ali. A study of institutional goals in three Saudi universities. OkS, 1984. 110 p.
Micro 85–4386
DAI, v. 45A, June 1985: 3563.

1902
Sulaiman, Khalifa Mohamed. The relationship of selected predictive variables to the academic success of students from the United Arab Emirates at American colleges and universities. DGW, 1987. 118 p.
Micro 87–7551
DAI, v. 47A, June 1987: 4309.

1903
Suleiman, Ibrahim Ahmad-Mosallam. The development of a program for the inservice education of science supervisors in Jordan. NNC-T, 1985. 311 p.
Micro 85–25,524
DAI, v. 46A, Mar. 1986: 2651.

1904
Suleiman, Ibrahim Sharif. Gravity and heat flow studies in the Sirte Basin, Libya. TxEU, 1985. 200 p.
Micro 86–4102
DAI, v. 46B, June 1986: 4163.

1905
Suleiman, Saleh Mahmoud Khalil. Linguistic interference and its impact on Arabic-English bilingualism. NBuU, 1981. 351 p.
Micro 81–22,202
DAI, v. 42A, Oct. 1981: 1620.

1906
al-Suleman, Suleman Saad. A study of earth concept attainment of urban and rural Saudi Arabian social studies students. PPiU, 1987. 165 p.
Micro 87–19,283
DAI, v. 48A, Dec. 1987: 1430.

1907
Sullivan, Denis J. American economic aid to Egypt, 1975–86: political and

bureaucratic struggles over aid disbursement and development choices. MiU, 1987. 272 p. Micro 87–20,349
DAI, v. 48A, Dec. 1987: 1536–1537.

1908
Sullivan, John D. The perceptual basis of British foreign policy: a case study of the Suez Crisis. PPiU, 1983. 537 p. Micro 83–27,619
DAI, v. 44A, Mar. 1984: 2880.

1909
Sullivan, Peggy S. A study of illness and reservoirs associated with *Giardia lamblia* in rural Egypt. TxU-H, 1986. 200 p. Micro 87–12,594
DAI, v. 48B, Sept. 1987: 722.

1910
al-Sultan, Abdullah Abdulmohsen. The Arab-Israeli interaction in the Red Sea: the implications of two contending strategies. NcU, 1980. 408 p.
Micro 81–14,782
DAI, v. 42A, Aug. 1981: 840–841.

1911
Sultan, Mohamed Ibrahim. Geology, petrology, and geochemistry of a Younger Granite pluton, central Eastern Desert of Egypt—importance of mixing. MoSW, 1984. 248 p. Micro 85–9055
DAI, v. 46B, Nov. 1985: 1484.

1912
Sumiyoshi, Andrea F. Orientalismus in der deutschen Literatur: Untersuchungen zu Werken des 19. und 20. Jahrhunderts, von Goethes *West-östlichem Divan* bis Thomas Manns *Joseph*-Tetralogie. CLU, 1983. 450 p. Micro 83–22,034
DAI, v. 44A, Nov. 1983: 1465–1466.

1913
Sumrain, Ibrahim Abed. Academic dishonesty: comparing American and foreign students' attitudes. OrCS, 1987. 174 p. Micro 87–17,046
DAI, v. 48A, Nov. 1987: 1091.

1914
Surur, Radhi Saad. Survey of students' teachers', and administrators' attitudes toward English as a foreign language in the Saudi Arabian public schools. KU, 1981. 160 p. Micro 82–18,811
DAI, v. 43A, Dec. 1982: 1822.

1915
Swagman, Charles F. Social organization and local development in the western central highlands of the Yemen Arab Republic. CLU, 1985. 385 p.
Micro 85–22,345
DAI, v. 46A, Feb. 1986: 2354.

1916
Swails, John W. Austen Henry Layard and the Near East, 1839–1880. GU, 1983.

268 p. Micro 83–14,749
DAI, v. 44A, Aug. 1983: 550.

1917
Swearingen, Will D. In search of the granary of Rome: irrigation and agricultural development in Morocco, 1912–1982. TxU, 1984. 321 p.   Micro 85–13,306
DAI, v. 46A, Oct. 1985: 1059.

1918
Swed, Abdalla Abdalhamid. The historical development of the Arabic verb.
WaU, 1982. 176 p.   Micro 82–26,606
DAI, v. 43A, Dec. 1982: 1960.

1919
al-Sweel, Abdulaziz Ibrahim. Word order in standard Arabic: a lexical approach.
WaU, 1983. 253 p.   Micro 84–4879
DAI, v. 44A, May 1984: 3374.

1920
Swehli, Abubaker Ibrahim. A study of the environmental aspects of schistosomiasis in Libya. MiKW, 1983. 109 p.   Micro 84–5475
DAI, v. 44B, June 1984: 3726.

1921
Swensen, Stephen B. Symbol and sanction: social change and the vitality of Moroccan Islam. ViU, 1983. 118 p.   Micro 84–16,407
DAI, v. 45A, Nov. 1984: 1459–1460.

1922
al-Swilim, Abdul Rahman Fahed. Health manpower in Saudi Arabia: projection of needs for Saudi physicians by the year 2000. NSyU, 1985. 144 p.
Micro 86–3745
DAI, v. 46A, June 1986: 3880.

1923
Syed Hassan, Sharifah Zaleha. From saints to bureaucrats: a study of the development of Islam in the state of Kedah, Malaysia. NIC, 1985. 295 p.
Micro 85–16,985
DAI, v. 46A, Jan. 1986: 1992–1993.

1924
al-Tabba, Yasser Ahmad. The architectural patronage of Nur al-Din, 1146–1174.
NNU, 1982. 610 p.   Micro 83–7807
DAI, v. 43A, May 1983: 3443.

1925
Tabora, Florecita G. Personality profiles of Muslim and Christian Filipinos: implications for Philippine education. INS, 1985. 167 p.   Micro 85–14,785
DAI, v. 46A, Nov. 1985: 1208.

1926
Taboroff, June H. Bistam, Iran: the architecture, setting and patronage of an Islamic shrine. NNU, 1981. 270 p.   Micro 81–27,969
DAI, v. 42A, Jan. 1982: 2914.

1927
Tadayon, Shahrad. An analysis of changes in OPEC's crude oil prices, current account, and surplus investments, with emphasis upon oil revenue purchasing power, 1973 through 1980. CSdI, 1984. 152 p.   Micro 84–20,112
DAI, v. 45A, Dec. 1984: 1814.

1928
Tadros, Kamal I. Effects of grazing intensity by sheep on the production of *Atriplex nummularia* and sheep live weight in Jordan. ULA, 1987. 117 p.
Micro 87–19,448
DAI, v. 48B, Dec. 1987: 1570.

1929
Taha, Hassan Ahmed. The role of the educational system in the economic and social development of a developing country: the case of the Sudan. PPiU, 1985. 282 p.   Micro 85–21,504
DAI, v. 46A, Apr. 1986: 2861.

1930
Taher, Abdulaziz Adeeb H. World oil price shocks and the Saudi Arabian economy: a macro econometric simulation. CoU, 1987. 173 p.
Micro 87–16,307
DAI, v. 48A, Nov. 1987: 1269–1270.

1931
Tahir, Jamil Mohammad. Foreign trade and economic growth: the experience of Jordan, an empirical and econometric investigation. CCC, 1983. 345 p.
Micro 83–2628
DAI, v. 43A, Mar. 1983: 3062.

1932
Takeshita, Masataka. Ibn 'Arabī's theory of the perfect man and its place in the history of Islamic thought. ICU, 1986. 180 p.
Letter from University of Chicago Library.

1933
Taki El Din, Shaker Rizk. The effectiveness of sentence combining practice on Arab students' overall writing quality and syntactic maturity. PInU, 1985. 157 p.   Micro 86–21,576
DAI, v. 47A, Feb. 1987: 3022.

1934
Talaat, Hala Mohamed. The verb phrase in Egyptian Arabic. MiU, 1987. 207 p.
Micro 87–12,220
DAI, v. 48A, Aug. 1987: 382.

1935

Talafha, Hussian Ali. Supply of educated labor in Jordan. NSyU, 1983. 211 p.

Micro 83–26,613

DAI, v. 44A, Jan. 1984: 2212.

1936

Talia, Shawqi Najib. Būlus al-Būshī's Arabic commentary on the Apocalypse of St. John: an English translation and a commentary. DCU, 1987. 426 p.

Micro 87–19,603

DAI, v. 48A, Dec. 1987: 1477–1478.

1937

Tamadonfar, Mehran. The Islamic polity and political leadership: a conceptual and theoretical assessment. CoU, 1986. 428 p.   Micro 86–19,002

DAI, v. 47A, Dec. 1986: 2307.

1938

Taman, Hassan Attiyyeh. MIDS: a modular interactive system for disambiguating Arabic orthography. NBuU, 1986. 301 p.   Micro 86–19,366

DAI, v. 47A, Dec. 1986: 2147.

1939

Tamer, Kemal. A measurement and comparison of selected physical fitness components of American, Middle Eastern, and East and Southeast Asian male students at Oklahoma State University. OkS, 1982. 149 p.   Micro 83–4890

DAI, v. 43B, Apr. 1983: 3154.

1940

al-Tammar, Juman Ahmad. The role of the secondary school principal in the State of Kuwait. DGW, 1983. 165 p.   Micro 84–21,990

DAI, v. 45A, Feb. 1985: 2314–2315.

1941

Tamraz, Ahmad Ali. A study of availability and actual usage of Arabic and English monographs in science and technology in three academic libraries in Saudi Arabia. NjR, 1984. 203 p.   Micro 84–11,583

DAI, v. 45A, Aug. 1984: 332.

1942

Taqi, Ali Abdul-Husain. Perceptions about cooperative education programs in post-secondary education institutes in Kuwait. MiEM, 1983. 180 p.

Micro 84–636

DAI, v. 44A, Mar. 1984: 2648.

1943

Tarabzouni, Mohamed Ahmed. Computer-enhanced Landsat images for ground water exploration in the northern Arabian Shield: Ha'il test site. TU, 1981. 298 p.   Micro 82–9002

DAI, v. 42B, May 1982: 4513–4514.

1944
Tarabzune, Muhiadin Rashad. The development of human resources through the application of the concept of the public Comprehensive Community College to Saudi Arabia. ArU, 1983. 353 p.   Micro 83–22,915
DAI, v. 44A, Dec. 1983: 1657–1658.

1945
Taras, David. Canada and the Arab-Israeli conflict: a study of the Yom Kippur War and the domestic political environment. CaOTU, 1983.
DAI, v. 45A, Aug. 1984: 630.

1946
Tarhouni, Ali Abdussalam. A production approach to regional economic integration [Egypt and Libya]. MiEM, 1984. 222 p.   Micro 84–24,481
DAI, v. 45A, Feb. 1985: 2578.

1947
Tarish, Laila Habib. Kuwaiti students' English language acquisition as related to the native and the nonnative teacher. DGU, 1982. 299 p.   Micro 84–9429
DAI, v. 45A, July 1984: 174.

1948
al-Tarrah, Ali Ahmad. Economic development and the structure of the Kuwaiti labor force. MiEM, 1983. 216 p.   Micro 84–527
DAI, v. 44A, Mar. 1984: 2891.

1949
Tarzi, Shah Mohmood. The political economy of American foreign oil policy and the Middle East: the influence of the multinational oil corporations, 1969–1979. CU-Riv, 1982. 354 p.   Micro 83–3936
DAI, v. 43A, Apr. 1983: 3410.

1950
Tash, Abdulkader T. M. A profile of professional journalists working in the Saudi Arabian daily press. ICarbS, 1983. 224 p.   Micro 83–26,572
DAI, v. 44A, Jan. 1984: 1961.

1951
Tashkandi, Mohammad Omar. Effects of instruction and personal traits of Saudi pre-service science teachers on the use of higher cognitive questions. InU, 1981. 214 p.   Micro 81–19,037
DAI, v. 42A, Sept. 1981: 1088–1089.

1952
al-Tassan, Abdulrahman Musa. An analytic and evaluation study of government employee housing programs in Saudi Arabia: using the analytic hierarchy process. MiU, 1986. 584 p.   Micro 87–2661
DAI, v. 47A, Apr. 1987: 3591.

1953
Tata, Giovanni. The development of the Egyptian textile industry. UU, 1986.

274 p.
Letter from Marriott Library, University of Utah.

1954
Tavakoliyazdi, Mohammad. Assimilation and status attainment of Middle Eastern immigrants in the United States. MnU, 1981. 312 p.　　Micro 82–11,554
DAI, v. 42A, June 1982: 5263.

1955
Tawil, Othman Abdullah. Efficacy of the Mini-Mult as a differentiating measure of mental disorders in Saudi Arabia. CoGrU, 1982. 191 p.　　Micro 83–1181
DAI, v. 43B, May 1983: 3745.

1956
Tayaa, M'hammed. Modeling storm induced erosion and sedimentation in northern Morocco. MnU, 1985. 290 p.　　　　　　　　　　　　Micro 86–8910
DAI, v. 47B, Aug. 1986: 550.

1957
Taylor, Richard C. The *Liber de causis (Kalām fī mahd al-khair)*: a study in medieval neoplatonism. CaOTU, 1982.
DAI, v. 43A, Sept. 1982: 827.

1958
al-Tayyeb, Muhammad Ali. Information technology transfer to Saudi Arabia. PPiU, 1982. 302 p.　　　　　　　　　　　　　　　　Micro 82–24,617
DAI, v. 43A, Nov. 1982: 1330.

1959
Tchaitchian, Mohammad Ali. Uneven capitalist development, peripheral urbanization, and petty commodity production in Iran and Egypt: a comparative study with a focus on Tehran and Cairo, 1800–1970. MiEM, 1986. 412 p.
　　　　　　　　　　　　　　　　　　　　　　　　　　Micro 87–7199
DAI, v. 47A, June 1987: 4527.

1960
Tel, Shadia Ahmad. An examination of cognitive representation in [Arabic-English and English-Arabic] bilinguals. InU, 1984. 175 p.　　Micro 85–6138
DAI, v. 46A, July 1985: 108.

1961
Telhami, Shibley Zeki. International bargaining and the level of analysis problem: The case of Camp David. CU, 1986. 488 p.　　　Micro 87–18,180
DAI, v. 48A, Nov. 1987: 1311.

1962
el-Tell, Khalaf. An analytic approach to primary health care planning in developing countries with an application to Jordan. NTR, 1983. 154 p.
　　　　　　　　　　　　　　　　　　　　　　　　　　Micro 83–29,617
DAI, v. 44B, Mar. 1984: 2874–2875.

1963
Terrill, Wallace A. Jordan and the crisis in the Arab system. CCC, 1983. 279 p.
Micro 83–9649
DAI, v. 43A, June 1983: 4032.

1964
Thabet, Jamal Saeed. Work goals and job satisfaction: a cross-cultural study of Italian-American, Polish-American and expatriate Yemeni nationals, CSdI, 1985. 159 p.   Micro 85–14,843
DAI, v. 46A, Nov. 1985: 1349.

1965
al-Thakafi, Yousif Ali. The diplomatic relationship between the Ottoman Empire and the mamluk Empire in the first quarter of the sixteenth century. MiEM, 1981. 264 p.   Micro 81–17,206
DAI, v. 42A, Aug. 1981: 813–814.

1966
Thani, Hassan M. Ali. Level of integration into academic and social system of college and the rate of Saudi student attrition in American universities. CLSU, 1987.
DAI, v. 48A, Aug. 1987: 349.

1967
Thayer, James S. Religion and social organization among a West African Muslim people: the Susu of Sierra Leone. MiU, 1981. 387 p.   Micro 81–25,212
DAI, v. 42A, Dec. 1981: 2749–2750.

1968
Thiab, Sadik Farag. The relationship between student academic achievement and student professional performance during the practicum in the College of Education, University of Baghdad. CoGrU, 1983. 90 p.   Micro 83–24,361
DAI, v. 44A, Dec. 1983: 1683.

1969
al-Thomaley, Mohammad Mosleh. Meeting labor shortage with expatriate workers: the effects of immigration on domestic wage and employment levels in the private non-agricultural sector in Saudi Arabia. PU, 1986. 188 p.
Micro 86–23,967
DAI, v. 47A, Jan. 1987: 2687.

1970
Thomas, Charles D. United States arms transfer policy toward the Arab-Israeli Zone, 1945–1980. DGW, 1985. 401 p.   Micro 85–8995
DAI, v. 46A, Aug. 1985: 514.

1971
Thoumy, Aimee Salim. University publishing in Lebanon: a historical and comparative study of the publishing programs of the five universities in Lebanon. InU, 1981. 175 p.   Micro 82–11,189
DAI, v. 42A, June 1982: 4964.

1972

al-Thubaiti, Abdullah Ayed. The impact of the school as a social system, and of family background, on student achievement in selected schools in the western part of Saudi Arabia. MiEM, 1983. 268 p. Micro 83–24,684
DAI, v. 44A, Jan. 1984: 2255.

1973

al-Thubaity, Awad Mastour. Department chairpersons' perception of their position regarding the requirements and process of selection, the major responsibilities and the requirements for job satisfaction in Saudi Arabian universities. MiEM, 1981. 197 p. Micro 82–2385
DAI, v. 42A, Feb. 1982: 3452–3453.

1974

al-Thubaity, Khudhran Khadhir. Rural migrants in Taif: their migration and residential mobility. MiEM, 1981. 297 p. Micro 82–2386
DAI, v. 42A, Feb. 1982: 3755.

1975

al-Thumali, Said A. Family, peer, and school influence on Saudi Arabian high school seniors' undergraduate college plans and academic majors. TxHU, 1984. 322 p. Micro 85–9000
DAI, v. 46A, Nov. 1985: 1132–1133.

1976

al-Thuwaini, Saud Ibrahim. Attitudes of supervisors and teachers toward the social studies curriculum in Saudi Arabian elementary schools. CoDU, 1986. 205 p. Micro 86–26,340
DAI, v. 47A, Feb. 1987: 2989.

1977

el-Tikaina, Ibrahim S. Hamid. A lexical approach to the Arabic verb conjugations. WaU, 1982. 284 p. Micro 82–26,534
DAI, v. 43A, Dec. 1982: 1957.

1978

al-Tikriti, Sabah Adama Hishan. Toward a conceptual framework for developing Iraqi school curricula. CoU, 1984. 208 p. Micro 84–22,585
DAI, v. 45A, Jan. 1985: 1969.

1979

Tildon, Ralph B. Prelude to war: the Egyptian decisions of 1967 and 1973. NNC, 1982. 296 p. Micro 82–22,498
DAI, v. 43A, Nov. 1982: 1678.

1980

Tippit, Phyllis R. The biostratigraphy and taxonomy of Mesozoic Radiolaria from the Samail Ophiolite and Hawasina Complex, Oman. TxU-Da, 1981. 403 p. Micro 81–26,594
DAI, v. 42B, Dec. 1981: 2282.

1981
Titgen, Richard H. The systematics and ecology of the decapods of Dubai, and their zoogeographic relationships to the Arabian Gulf and the Western Indian Ocean. TxCM, 1982. 304 p.　　　　　　　　　　Micro 83–6823
DAI, v. 43B, May 1983: 3449.

1982
Tlemcani, Rachid. State and revolution in Algeria: an approach to the study of state-formation in post-colonial society. MBU, 1984. 365 p.　　Micro 84–6761
DAI, v. 44A, June 1984: 3812.

1983
Toaima, Afaf Ahmad. A critique of the home economics education program materials in the Arab Republic of Egypt. MnU, 1981. 146 p.
　　　　　　　　　　　　　　　　　　　　　　　Micro 82–6431
DAI, v. 42A, Apr. 1982: 4335.

1984
Todd, Daniel R. An annotated, enumerative bibliography of the criticism of Lawrence Durrell's *Alexandria Quartet* and his travel works. LNT, 1984. 483 p.
　　　　　　　　　　　　　　　　　　　　　　　Micro 85–4839
DAI, v. 45A, June 1985: 3636.

1985
Toga, Hussein Omar. The National Security Administration of the Hashemite Kingdom of Jordan. CLSU, 1983.
DAI, v. 44A, Nov. 1983: 1571–1572.

1986
al-Tokhais, Ibrahim Abdullah I. Alternative future of junior colleges in Saudi Arabia. NBuU, 1986. 269 p.　　　　　　　　　　Micro 86–9087
DAI, v. 47A, Aug. 1986: 353.

1987
Tokhais, Ibrahim Abdulrahman. Social justice in Islamic law. CCC, 1982. 265 p.
　　　　　　　　　　　　　　　　　　　　　　　Micro 82–15,213
DAI, v. 43A, Aug. 1982: 530.

1988
Toledano, Ehud R. The suppression of the slave trade in the Ottoman Empire in the nineteenth century. NjP, 1979. 395 p.　　　　　Micro 80–3796
DAI, v. 40A, Feb. 1980: 4705.

1989
Tolefat, Salem Abdulaziz. Toward an integrative-responsive model for educational evaluation in Qatar. NBuU, 1983. 327 p.　　　Micro 83–20,300
DAI, v. 44A, Dec. 1983: 1683.

1990
Tombe, Wani Luan J. Decentralization and development: the regional experi-

ment in Sudan. TxU, 1985. 242 p.　　　　　　　　Micro 86-9434
DAI, v. 47A, Aug. 1986: 601.

1991
Tomich, Thomas P. Private land reclamation in Egypt: studies of feasibility and adaptive behavior. CSt, 1984. 534 p.　　　　　　　　Micro 84-29,561
DAI, v. 45A, Apr. 1985: 3180.

1992
Tongun, Lako L. The political economy of national planning in the Sudan: determinants of choices and priorities. CU-A, 1983. 470 p.　　　Micro 84-7931
DAI, v. 45A, Sept. 1984: 943.

1993
Topping, John T. Chinese Muslim militarist: Ma Hongkui in Ningxia, 1933–1949. MiU, 1983. 313 p.　　　　　　　　Micro 84-2390
DAI, v. 44A, Apr. 1984: 3137.

1994
Toth, James F. Migrant workers in the Egyptian Delta. NBiSU, 1987. 640 p.
　　　　　　　　Micro 87-20,674
DAI, v. 48A, Dec. 1987: 1489.

1995
Touchie, Hanna Yousef. Transfer and related strategies in the acquisition of English relative clauses by adult Arab learners. TxU, 1983. 247 p.
　　　　　　　　Micro 83-19,693
DAI, v. 44A, Oct. 1983: 1075.

1996
Toufik, Suliman Ibrahim. The emergence of a national identity in Saudi Arabia. IdU, 1985. 335 p.　　　　　　　　Micro 85-18,198
DAI, v. 46A, Dec. 1985: 1729.

1997
Tucker, Judith E. Women and the family in Egypt, 1800–1860: a study in changing roles and status. MH, 1981.
CDI, 1973–1982, v. 38: 369.

1998
Tully, Dennis. Culture and context: the process of market incorporation in Dar Masalit, Sudan. WaU, 1984. 394 p.　　　　　　　　Micro 84-4962
DAI, v. 44A, May 1984: 3428.

1999
Tunnicliff, Kim H. The United Nations and the mediation of international conflict [the Arab-Israeli case]. IaU, 1984. 357 p.　　　Micro 84-28,305
DAI, v. 45A, Mar. 1985: 2988.

2000
Turaki, Yusufu. The institutionalization of the inferior status and socio-political

role of the non-Muslim groups in the colonial hierarchical structure of the northern region of Nigeria: a social-ethical analysis of the colonial legacy. MBU, 1982. 512 p.　　　　　　　　　　　　　　　　　　Micro 82–21,039
DAI, v. 43A, Oct. 1982: 1197.

2001
Turki, Hedi. A study of management's budget-oriented behavior in Tunisian business enterprises. IU, 1981. 218 p.　　　　　　　Micro 81–14,491
DAI, v. 42A, Aug. 1981: 755.

2002
al-Turki, Ibrahim Abdulaziz. Modeling the Saudi Arabian agricultural sector for planning and policy analysis. WaPS, 1986. 507 p.　　　Micro 87–2527
DAI, v. 47A, Apr. 1987: 3826.

2003
Turner, Richard B. Islam in the United States in the 1920's: the quest for a new vision in Afro-American religion. NjP, 1986. 234 p.　　Micro 86–27,947
DAI, v. 47A, Feb. 1987: 3079.

2004
Turner, William O. U.S. arms sales to Saudi Arabia: implications for American foreign policy. DGW, 1982. 342 p.　　　　　　　Micro 82–17,596
DAI, v. 43A. Nov. 1982: 1678.

2005
Turpin, Ruth E. Classroom climate, general ability, and anxiety in a basic skills program for Saudi Arabian naval trainees. CSt, 1982. 266 p.
　　　　　　　　　　　　　　　　　　　　　　　Micro 82–8916
DAI, v. 42A, May 1982: 4710.

2006
Turri, Alan L. Computer training and development for non-data processing specialists in Egypt. MH, 1986. 246 p.　　　　　　Micro 86–20,726
DAI, v. 47A, Dec. 1986: 2134.

2007
Tutwiler, Richard N. Tribe, tribute, and trade: social class formation in highland Yemen. NBiSU, 1987. 600 p.　　　　　　　　　Micro 87–10,921
DAI, v. 48A, Aug. 1987: 429.

2008
al-Tuwaijri, Abdulrahman. Exploration of optimal strategies for the development of an oil-based economy: the case of Saudi Arabia. IaAS, 1985. 185 p.
　　　　　　　　　　　　　　　　　　　　　　　Micro 86–4441
DAI, v. 46A, June 1986: 3798.

2009
al-Tuwaijri, Saleh Hamad. The relationship between ideal and actual supervisory

practice as perceived by supervisors in Saudi Arabia. OrU, 1985. 231 p.
Micro 85–29,492
DAI, v. 46A, May 1986: 3323.

2010
Tyson, Carolyn A. Making foreign policy: the Eisenhower Doctrine. DGW, 1984.
345 p.   Micro 84–16,751
DAI, v. 45A, Oct. 1984: 1188–1189.

2011
Udeke, Onwuatuegwu Obediah. A comparative analysis of Nigerian international oil marketing model and the models of four selected OPEC members, and a proposed new model for Nigeria. OCUCE, 1986. 413 p.   Micro 87–14,240
DAI, v. 48A, Oct. 1987: 984.

2012
Ul-Haq, Zia. Negation in Arabic: a morpho-syntactic and semantic description.
InU, 1984. 340 p.   Micro 84–17,220
DAI, v. 45A, Dec. 1984: 1770.

2013
Urice, Stephen K. Qasr Kharma: an early Islamic monument in the Transjordan.
MH, 1981.
CDI, 1973–1982, v. 38: 404.

2014
al-Usmani, Abdulrazak S. An analytical comparative study of television systems and decision-making processes in four Arabian Gulf States (Saudi Arabia, Kuwait, Bahrain and Qatar). WU, 1984. 282 p.   Micro 84–28,862
DAI, v. 45A, May 1985: 3232.

2015
Uthaimeen, Yousef A. The welfare state in Saudi Arabia: structure, dynamics, and function. DAU, 1986. 391 p.   Micro 87–12
DAI, v. 47A, June 1987: 4523–4524.

2016
van de Bilt, Eduardus F. Proximity and distance: American travellers to the Middle East, 1819–1918. NIC, 1985. 274 p.   Micro 85–25,688
DAI, v. 46A, Mar. 1986: 2791.

2017
Van Dyken, Julia R. What literacy teachers should know about language: an assessment of in-service training needs of reading acquisition teachers in southern Sudan using the Gudschinsky literacy method. InU, 1984. 365 p.
Micro 84–17,185
DAI, v. 45A, Nov. 1984: 1372.

2018
Varisco, Daniel M. The adaptive dynamics of water allocation in al-Ahjur,

Yemen Arab Republic. PU, 1982. 727 p. Micro 83–7372
DAI, v. 43A, June 1983: 3962.

2019
Venzke, Margaret L. The sixteenth-century Ottoman *Sanjaq* of Aleppo: a study
of provincial taxation. NNC, 1981. 618 p. Micro 82–4551
DAI, v. 42A, Mar. 1982: 4105.

2020
Vernon-Carter, Richard. The value of children and the costs of contraception:
predictors of reproductive ideals and contraceptive practice in Egypt. ICU,
1982.
DAI, v. 43A, Sept. 1982: 938.

2021
Viscio, Albert J. The oil market and macroeconomic activity in the industrialized
countries. NNU, 1981. 254 p. Micro 81–27,973
DAI, v. 42A, Jan. 1982: 3236.

2022
Vogel, Lester I. Zion as place and past: an American myth—Ottoman Palestine
in the American mind perceived through Protestant consciousness and experience. DGW, 1984. 513 p. Micro 84–10,496
DAI, v. 45A, Sept. 1984: 875.

2023
Voss, Don L. Ibn al-Haytham's *Doubts concerning Ptolemy*: a translation and com-
mentary. ICU, 1985.
DAI, v. 46A, June 1986: 3832.

2024
Vuich, Sharon H. A comparative study of elementary teachers in the Omani
school system. MiU, 1987. 116 p. Micro 87–20,357
DAI, v. 48A, Dec. 1987: 1408.

2025
al-Wabli, Sulaiman Mohammed. An evaluation of selected aspects of the second-
ary teacher preparation program at the Umm al-Qura University, Makkah,
Saudi Arabia, based on a follow-up of 1978–79 graduates. MiEM, 1982. 256 p.
Micro 82–16,516
DAI, v. 43A, Aug. 1982: 423.

2026
al-Waer, Mazen. Toward a modern and realistic sentential theory of basic structures in standard Arabic. DGU, 1983. 213 p. Micro 84–1490
DAI, v. 44A, Apr. 1984: 3046.

2027
Wafai, Mohamed Amin. Political behavior, legitimation, and social control: U.S.
senators, the Mideast and TV news. MnU, 1983. 237 p. Micro 83–29,599
DAI, v. 44A, Mar. 1984: 2615–2616.

2028

Wahba, Wafaa Abdel-Faheem Batran. *Wh*-constructions in Egyptian Arabic. IU, 1984. 190 p.   Micro 84–22,170
DAI, v. 45A, Jan. 1985: 2086.

2029

el Wakeel, Ahmed Suliman. Seedling establishment, nodulation, and acetylene reduction of *Leucaena leucocephala* under drought stress [in western Sudan]. ULA, 1986. 263 p.   Micro 87–4948
DAI, v. 48B, July 1987: 24.

2030

Walbridge, John T. The philosophy of Quṭb al-Dīn Shīrāzī: a study in the integration of Islamic philosophy. MH, 1983. 402 p.   Micro 83–22,462
DAI, v. 44A, Dec. 1983: 1818.

2031

Walker, Robert L. Inflation in Saudi Arabia. MH, 1979.
CDI, 1973–1982, v. 38: 502.

2032

Walt, Stephen M. The origins of alliances: superpower and regional diplomacy in the Middle East, 1955–1979. CU, 1983. 569 p.   Micro 84–15,508
DAI, v. 45A, Oct. 1984: 1203.

2033

Walton, David J. A. A comparative study of computer-assisted instruction, programmed instruction, and lecture in the teaching of English conditional sentences to native speakers of Arabic. NBuU, 1986. 314 p.   Micro 86–19,371
DAI, v. 47A, Dec. 1986: 2012.

2034

Waltz, Susan E. Value conflict and alienation: the case of rural Tunisia. CoDU, 1980. 324 p.   Micro 81–21,424
DAI, v. 42A, Nov. 1981: 2286.

2035

Wani, Jukeria. The African refugees: a case study of the refugees in the Sudan as a regional problem and an international concern. IdU, 1983. 284 p.
     Micro 83–28,341
DAI, v. 44A, Feb. 1984: 2574–2575.

2036

Ward, Seth. Construction and repair of churches and synagogues in Islamic law: a treatise by Taqī al-Dīn ʿAlī b. ʿAbd al-Kāfī al-Subkī. CtY, 1984. 366 p.
     Micro 86–22,020
DAI, v. 47A, Feb. 1987: 3058.

2037

Warner, Chester J. A study of the relationships between TOEFL scores and

selected performance characteristics of Arabic students in an individualized competency based training program. TU, 1981. 119 p.   Micro 82–9009
DAI, v. 42A, May 1982: 4810.

2038
Wasserstrom, Steven M. Species of misbelief: a history of Muslim heresiography of the Jews. CaOTU, 1986.
DAI, v. 47A, Dec. 1986: 2195.

2039
Watts, Thelma L. Perceptions of present and future programming in selected centers for disabled persons in Morocco. NbU, 1986. 214 p.   Micro 86–9813
DAI, v. 47A, Sept. 1986: 870.

2040
Watyan, Mohammad S. A cross-cultural comparison of perspectives on investment decision making between Americans and Kuwaities. CSdI, 1985. 124 p.
Micro 85–14,844
DAI, v. 46A, Nov. 1985: 1368.

2041
Webber, Sabra J. Local history narratives in a Mediterranean Tunisian town. TxU, 1981. 205 p.   Micro 81–19,394
DAI, v. 42A, Sept. 1981: 1267–1268.

2042
Webster, Sheila K. The shadow of a noble man: honor and shame in Arabic proverbs. InU, 1984. 237 p.   Micro 85–6143
DAI, v. 46A, July 1985: 231.

2043
Weeks, Alvin E. The Dhahran Academy: a case study. UU, 1982. 396 p.
Micro 82–20,066
DAI, v. 43A, Oct. 1982: 1007.

2044
Weidner-Read, Barbara L. Water, women, health, and housing: a case study of rural reconstruction in Egypt. UU, 1983. 206 p.   Micro 83–19,370
DAI, v. 44A, Oct. 1983: 1143.

2045
Weinberger, James W. The rise of Muslim cities in Sogdia, 700–1220. CU, 1984. 224 p.   Micro 84–27,128
DAI, v. 45A, Mar. 1985: 2967.

2046
Weisburd, David L. Deviance as social reaction: a study of the Gush Emunim settlements in Israel. CtY, 1985. 352 p.   Micro 86–999
DAI, v. 46A, May 1986: 3498.

2047

Wenk, Karen L. A description and analysis of the process of educational planning in Egypt. CLSU, 1982.
DAI, v. 43A, Oct. 1982: 981.

2048

Westrate, Bruce C. Imperialists all: the Arab Bureau and the evolution of British policy in the Middle East, 1916–1920. MiU, 1982. 316 p.   Micro 82–15,104
DAI, v. 43A, Aug. 1982: 521.

2049

Wezermes, Ibrahim Issa. A comparison of physical education teachers job satisfaction with other academic teachers in Jordan. CLSU, 1984.
DAI, v. 45A, Jan. 1985: 2033.

2050

Whiting, Steven H. Essays on the structure of the Egyptian financial system, 1961–1981. MiU, 1983. 293 p.   Micro 84–2404
DAI, v. 44A, Apr. 1984: 3121–3122.

2051

Whittaker, Alan G. Theoretical and operational biases in deterrence: an experimental assessment in a simulated political decision-making context. ScU, 1983. 222 p.   Micro 84–9336
DAI, v. 45A, July 1984: 298.

2052

Whittington, Dale. Water management in Egypt: a case study of the Aswan High Dam. TxU, 1980.
DAI, v. 42B, May 1982: 4554.

2053

Widatalla, Elnour Khalifa. Sudan's health services: relevance and evaluation. CCC, 1985. 137 p.   Micro 85–12,016
DAI, v. 46A, Oct. 1985: 1087.

2054

Wilcox, Judith C. The transmission and influence of Qusṭā ibn Lūqā's "On the difference between spirit and the soul." NNCU-G, 1985. 355 p.
Micro 85–8747
DAI, v. 46A, Aug. 1985: 498–499.

2055

Williams, Naomi J. Intervention by Syria in the Lebanese Civil War of 1975–1976. NNC, 1981. 489 p.   Micro 83–27,322
DAI, v. 44A, Mar. 1984: 2880.

2056

Wishart, David M. The political economy of conflict over water rights in the Jordan Valley from 1890 to present. IU, 1985. 180 p.   Micro 85–21,905
DAI, v. 46A, Jan. 1986: 2034–2035.

2057
Witter, Scott G. Information value using variable precision data to delineate wheat expansion areas in Syria. MiEM, 1982. 128 p.   Micro 83–9026
DAI, v. 43A, June 1983: 4042.

2058
Witty, Cathie J. The struggle for progress: the socio-political realities of legal pluralism [in Lebanon]. CU, 1975. 269 p.
CDI, 1973–1982, v. 38: 719.

2059
al-Wohaibi, Fahed Abdulrahman. Survey of Umm an-Namel Island, State of Kuwait. InU, 1987. 378 p.   Micro 87–17,781
DAI, v. 48A, Nov. 1987: 1241–1242.

2060
al-Wohaibi, Saleh Sulaiman. Qur'ānic variants (*'ilm al-qirā'āt*): an historical-phonological study. InU, 1982. 249 p.   Micro 83–8841
DAI, v. 43A, June 1983: 3893–3894.

2061
Wolf, Judith L. Selected aspects in the development of public education in Palestine, 1920–1946. MChB, 1981. 319 p.   Micro 82–3957
DAI, v. 42A, Mar. 1982: 3891.

2062
Wolf, Kenneth B. Christian martyrs in Muslim Spain: Eulogius of Cordoba and the making of a martyrs' movement. CSt, 1985. 267 p.   Micro 85–6269
DAI, v. 46A, July 1985: 237.

2063
Wolfe, Ronald G. Ibn Maḍā' al-Qurṭubī and the *Book in Refutation of the Grammarians*. InU, 1984. 329 p.   Micro 85–6145
DAI, v. 46A, July 1985: 143.

2064
Wolle, Amde. Regional, provincial, rural-urban and city size differentials in labor force participation: the case of Sudan. PU, 1984. 314 p.   Micro 85–5147
DAI, v. 46A, July 1985: 272.

2065
Wong, Simin Saedi. Planning for a relevant medical education in the Kingdom of Saudi Arabia. PPiU, 1981. 265 p.   Micro 82–13,187
DAI, v. 43A, July 1982: 93.

2066
Woodman, Nancy C. The need for mining education programs in the Gulf States region. MsU, 1981. 181 p.   Micro 81–28,124
DAI, v. 42A, Jan. 1982: 3096.

2067

Works, Nancy M. A study of the use of English sentence stress for the comprehension of meaning by adult second language learners. IU, 1985. 167 p.

Micro 86–349

DAI, v. 46A, May 1986: 3340.

2068

Wright, Charles E. Feasibility of correlating incidence of diarrhea with characteristics of rural Egyptian households by means of an environmental survey. TxU-H, 1985. 253 p. Micro 86–1804

DAI, v. 46B, May 1986: 3809.

2069

Ya'coub, Riad Moh'd Amin. Life satisfaction among Jordanian university students. CLU, 1984. 197 p. Micro 85–5688

DAI, v. 46A, July 1985: 109.

2070

Yacoub, Suheil A. The eight formal organizational variables in Hage's axiomatic theory applied to teacher training institutes in Iraq. OAkU, 1981. 177 p.

Micro 81–17,735

DAI, v. 42A, Sept. 1981: 958.

2071

el-Yacoubi, Jane B. M. A comparative analysis of Islamic and Western democratic political thought. CoU, 1983. 522 p. Micro 84–8027

DAI, v. 45A, July 1984: 296.

2072

Yafi, Adnan Abdulbadie. Management of some large-scale logistical problems of *ḥajj* (the Muslim pilgrimage to Makkah and the Holy Areas). TxU, 1983. 207 p. Micro 84–14,472

DAI, v. 45A, Sept. 1984: 929.

2073

Yaghmour, Farouk Abdul-Khaleg. The relationship between historical growth and planned development growth of the Balqa-Amman region of Jordan. NBuU, 1981. 158 p. Micro 82–4138

DAI, v. 42B, Mar. 1982: 3773–3774.

2074

Yaghmour, Mohamed-Ahmed Kazem. An empirical study and statistical analysis of manufacturing variables which influence overall strategic performance [in Saudi industries]. PSt, 1985. 184 p. Micro 85–16,120

DAI, v. 46A, Feb. 1986: 2366.

2075

Yahya, Hasan Ayel Ahmed. Development of a programmed instruction text for Saudi Arabian intermediate school geography. CoDU, 1986. 294 p.

Micro 86–12,850

DAI, v. 47A, Sept. 1986: 782.

2076
Yahya, Khawla Ahmad. A cross-cultural study of an instrument for measuring the problem behavior of children in regular classes in the public schools of Jordan. MiEM, 1982. 99 p.   Micro 82–24,495
DAI, v. 43A, Feb. 1983: 2637.

2077
Yahya, Mahmud Mohamed. Management education and training in Somalia: the case of the Somali Institute of Development Administration and Management (SIDAM). CLU, 1984. 464 p.   Micro 85–5689
DAI, v. 46A, July 1985: 55.

2078
Yakovee, Rehavia U. Arms for oil–oil for arms: an analysis of President Carter's 1978 planes "package deal" sale to Egypt, Israel and Saudi Arabia. CCC, 1983. 406 p.   Micro 83–21,062
DAI, v. 44A, Nov. 1983: 1568.

2079
Yarrison, James L. Force as an instrument of policy: European military incursions and trade in the Maghreb, 1000–1355. NjP, 1982. 474 p.   Micro 82–23,288
DAI, v. 43A, Nov. 1982: 1640.

2080
Yaseen, Juma Abdullah. Alienation and authoritarianism between traditionalist and modernist male adults in Kuwait. CSdI, 1983. 129 p.   Micro 83–18,603
DAI, v. 44B, Oct. 1983: 1224–1225.

2081
Yaseen, Nawal Hamed. A study of the factors relating to admission and academic achievement of female students in the College of Education, Mecca, Saudi Arabia. CoGrU, 1983. 126 p.   Micro 83–13,983
DAI, v. 44A, Aug. 1983: 378–379.

2082
Yasin, Mahmoud Mohm'd. Assessing managerial, technical and academic motivation in the Arab culture: the relationships of needs for achievement, affiliation and power with effectiveness. ScCleU, 1986. 175 p.   Micro 86–27,217
DAI, v. 47A, Feb. 1987: 3111.

2083
el-Yasin, Mohammed K. Voice phenomena in Jordanian Arabic. NIC, 1982. 140 p.   Micro 82–10,849
DAI, v. 42A, June 1982: 5106.

2084
al-Yasin, Yasin T. Mustafa. A critical analysis of modernization in Kuwait as reflected by selective print media, 1960–1982. MiDW, 1985. 302 p.
Micro 86–4970
DAI, v. 47A, July 1986: 18.

2085

al-Yasiri, Hussein Noori. An investigation of the relationship between selected environmental factors and the presence of mild mental retardation among children in elementary schools in Iraq. CoGrU, 1982. 161 p.

Micro 83–1132

DAI, v. 43A, Mar. 1983: 2956.

2086

al-Yassini, Ayman. The relationship between religion and state in the Kingdom of Saudi Arabia. CaQMM, 1983.
DAI, v. 44A, Nov. 1983: 1561.

2087

Yoder, Lawrence M. The introduction and expression of Islam and Christiantiy in the cultural context of north central Java. CPFT, 1987. 563 p.

Micro 87–12,933

DAI, v. 48A, Sept. 1987: 673–674.

2088

Yotvat, Shlomo. British and American attitudes and disputes concerning the Palestine Question, 1942–1947. WU, 1983. 531 p.   Micro 83–13,937
DAI, v. 44A, Sept. 1983: 842.

2089

Youldash, Mohammed Zaid. Analysis and recommended model for staff development in King Abdulaziz University, Saudi Arabia. NBuU, 1987. 371 p.

Micro 87–10,769

DAI, v. 48A, Aug. 1987: 368.

2090

Younes, Munther Abdullatif. Problems in the segmental phonology of Palestinian Arabic. TxU, 1982. 186 p.   Micro 82–27,746
DAI, v. 43A, Jan. 1983: 2338.

2091

Young, Jerome E. Municipal government and politics in the West Bank. OCU, 1984. 214 p.   Micro 84–20,923
DAI, v. 45A, Dec. 1984: 1861.

2092

Younis, Abdi Ibrahim. Factors related to the decisions of secondary school teachers in Somalia to continue in or leave the teaching profession. IU, 1987. 129 p.   Micro 87–11,907
DAI, v. 48A, Aug. 1987: 357.

2093

Younis, Abdul Razeq Mustafa. Components of a proposed resource sharing and information network for academic and special libraries in Jordan. PPiU, 1983. 355 p.   Micro 84–11,679
DAI, v. 45A, Aug. 1984: 333.

2094
Yousef, Abdelhadi Abdallah. An optimum currency peg for developing countries: the case of fifteen Arab countries. ScU, 1981. 128 p.   Micro 81–29,508
DAI, v. 42A, Jan. 1982: 3247.

2095
Yousif, Hassan Musa. An integrated economic-demographic theoretical framework for the analysis of the factors related to the rural labor force in the Gezira Scheme: a micro household level analysis. PU, 1985. 303 p.
Micro 85–23,469
DAI, v. 46A, Feb. 1986: 2452.

2096
Youssef, Michael A. al-Jihad: an Islamic social movement. GEU, 1984. 458 p.
Micro 84–20,303
DAI, v. 45A, Dec. 1984: 1886.

2097
Youssef, Mohsen A. M. Factors affecting career choice and labor market success for Egyptian university graduates. OU, 1984. 217 p.   Micro 85–4101
DAI, v. 46A, Oct. 1985: 1054.

2098
Yousuf, Hilmi Shadi. African-Arab relations: political and economic aspects. DHU, 1982. 403 p.   Micro 84–4054
DAI, v. 44A, Apr. 1984: 3159.

2099
Yungher, Israel. United States-Israeli relations, 1953–1956. PU, 1985. 435 p.
Micro 85–15,472
DAI, v. 46A, Nov. 1985: 1394.

2100
Yusuf, Mamun Abdel-Gadir. The Sudanese Civil War: a study of conflict resolution. DGW, 1983. 295 p.
Thesis and dissertation card catalog, Gelman Library, George Washington University.

2101
Yusuf, Muhsin Dhia. The economic history of Syria during the 4/10–5/11th centuries. NjP, 1982. 436 p.   Micro 82–15,647
DAI, v. 43A, Aug. 1982: 521–522.

2102
Zabara, Zaid Ali. The impact of external financial resources on the economic growth in North Yemen during the period 1963–1983. DHU, 1986. 282 p.
Micro 87–1904
DAI, v. 47A, Apr. 1987: 3836.

2103
Zafar, Abdulwahab Ahmad. An evaluation of the mathematics curriculum given

at the College of Education, Mecca, from the perspective of the teachers who graduated from the College in the years 1976–1980. MiEM, 1982. 256 p.

Micro 82–16,602

DAI, v. 43A, Nov. 1982: 1415–1416.

2104
Zafarian, Hossein. Analytical approach to correlation between Marxism and Iran's Islamic Revolution. CCC, 1984. 195 p.   Micro 84–16,470
DAI, v. 45A, Oct. 1984: 1203.

2105
Zagalai, Bascer Mabruk. A systems approach to OPEC oil pricing strategies. CLSU, 1982.
DAI, v. 43B, Dec. 1982: 1945–1946.

2106
Zagallai, Faisal Abdulazez. Environmental conduciveness for building rural co-operative institutions: the case of KSP [Kufra Settlement Project], Kufra, Libya. CoFS, 1982. 213 p.   Micro 82–18,413
DAI, v. 43A, Sept. 1982: 947.

2107
el Zaghl, Mostafa Mohamed. Model for implementing an international educational cooperative program in hotel administration between Egypt and the U.S.A. TU, 1982. 195 p.   Micro 83–3734
DAI, v. 43A, Apr. 1983: 3242.

2108
Zaher, Aida Abdel Maksoud Hassan. Cognitive training of Egyptians for reading English science textbooks. CLU, 1981. 162 p.   Micro 82–1171
DAI, v. 42A, Feb. 1982: 3530–3531.

2109
Zaher, Ghazi Ghaleb. Factors associated with choice of school and major area of study by Arab graduate students. TxDN, 1984. 158 p.   Micro 85–1524
DAI, v. 45A, May 1985: 3292.

2110
Zahrai, Mehdi Masoud. The origins and the causes of the Iranian Iraqi War. IdU, 1983. 382 p.   Micro 84–18,385
DAI, v. 45A, Feb. 1985: 2645–2646.

2111
al-Zahrani, Abdul-Razzag Homoud. Saudi Arabian development: a sociological study of its relation to Islam and its impacts on society. WaPS, 1986. 260 p.

Micro 86–21,975

DAI, v. 47A, Dec. 1986: 2338.

2112
al-Zahrani, Khodran Hamdan. Competencies needed by poultry producers in the

231

Eastern Province of Saudi Arabia. OU, 1983. 234 p. Micro 84–153
DAI, v. 44A, Mar. 1984: 2655.

2113
al-Zahrani, Saad Abdallah. Institutional goals in Saudi universities: current and preferred status of goals. MiEM, 1985. 229 p. Micro 86–3370
DAI, v. 46A, June 1986: 3613.

2114
Zahrani, Saeed A. The education of allied health personnel in Saudi Arabia. PPiU, 1983. 233 p. Micro 84–11,818
DAI, v. 45A, Aug. 1984: 434.

2115
Zahrani, Said Aeid. A study of the effectiveness of returning Saudi Arabian graduates from American universities in the national development of Saudi Arabia. CLSU, 1986.
DAI, v. 47A, Dec. 1986: 1933.

2116
Zahrany, Saleh Faris. Political representation in Islam. DCU, 1983. 475 p.
Micro 83–6546
DAI, v. 44A, Aug. 1983: 567–568.

2117
al-Zaidi, Abdullah Aoudh. Adequacies of curriculum and training in agriculture provided at three Saudi institutions as assessed by administrators, instructors, senior students, and regional directors. OkS, 1982. 159 p. Micro 83–4838
DAI, v. 43A, Apr. 1983: 3187.

2118
Zakari, Omar Mohammad Madani. A comparison between the effects of specific behavioral objectives versus study questions on learning of undergraduate Saudi Arabian biology students. FTaSU, 1982. 125 p. Micro 83–14,417
DAI, v. 44A, Aug. 1983: 452.

2119
Zalatimo, Yasira Najati. Curriculum design for a developing society: a vocational business and office education program for women in Saudi Arabia. ICarbS, 1981. 192 p. Micro 82–6511
DAI, v. 42A, Apr. 1982: 4246.

2120
Zamel, Yousef Abdulla. On the role of international trade in development: the case of the Gulf countries. CoU, 1986. 304 p. Micro 87–6464
DAI, v. 47A, May 1987: 4150.

2121
al-Zameli, Ali Abed Jassim. The relationship between teachers' evaluation and students' academic achievement in the sixth grade of Iraqi elementary schools.

PPiU, 1985. 104 p.   Micro 86–17,216
DAI, v. 47A, Nov. 1986: 1704.

2122
Zandi, Farrokh Reza. The effects of an oil price rise on inflation, output and the exchange rate in the case of subsidization policy. CaOOCC, 1982.
DAI, v. 44A, Oct. 1983: 1158.

2123
Zaroug, Hassabelrasoul Hussein Ahmed. Citizen participation: the experience of Sudanese local government. CLSU, 1983.
DAI, v. 45A, Sept. 1984: 954.

2124
Zarrugh, Omar Salem. Developing a training program for civil service employees: a model training program for the Socialist People's Libyan Arab Jamahiriya.
InMuB, 1981. 166 p.   Micro 82–1897
DAI, v. 42A, Feb. 1982: 3542.

2125
al-Zayani, Mona Rashid. An analysis of English reading curriculum and instruction in Bahrain elementary schools. CLSU, 1985.
DAI, v. 46A, Feb. 1986: 2173.

2126
al-Zayer, Jamal Ahmed. On some mathematical planning models for the management of the oil, gas, and petrochemical industry in Saudi Arabia. TxU, 1986.
229 p.   Micro 87–160
DAI, v. 47B, Mar. 1987: 3936.

2127
Zayid, Jamal E. The foreign sector and economic development: analysis and simulations of an econometric model of the Sudan. InU, 1986. 183 p.
                                                      Micro 86–17,798
DAI, v. 47A, Nov. 1986: 1823.

2128
Zeguan, Bashir Hosni. The development of mathematical understanding and its application to Libyan secondary school methamatics. NcGU, 1982. 259 p.
                                                      Micro 82–18,683
DAI, v. 43A, Sept. 1982: 712.

2129
Zeidan, Joseph Tufeek. Women novelists in modern Arabic literature. CU, 1982.
544 p.   Micro 83–13,039
DAI, v. 44A, July 1983: 182.

2130
Zentani, Omar Mohamed. Impact of educational experience in the United States on Muslim students. MoU, 1986. 90 p.   Micro 86–25,981
DAI, v. 47A, Feb. 1987: 2925.

2131
Zerkine, Habiba Mounira. The Federation of Elected Muslims of the Department of Constantine. DGU, 1984.
DAI, v. 46A, Apr. 1986: 3129.

2132
Zidan, Atta Taha. The effects of immediate presentation versus delayed presentation of the written form in the teaching of English as a foreign language to beginning students in Egypt. PPiU, 1982. 181 p.   Micro 83–3654
DAI, v. 43A, Mar. 1983: 2913–2914.

2133
Zierenberg, Robert A. Recent seafloor metallogeneses: examples from the Atlantis II Deep, Red Sea and 21 N East Pacific Rise. WU, 1983. 231 p.
Micro 83–21,781
DAI, v. 44B, Feb. 1984: 2361.

2134
el-Ziltini, Abdussalam Mukhtar. Mass media for literacy in Libya: a feasibility study. OU, 1981. 376 p.   Micro 81–28,995
DAI, v. 42A, Jan. 1982: 2918.

2135
Zimbrolt, Carole F. Ideology, policy and identity: family planning in a Yemenite community in Israel. MnU, 1984. 211 p.   Micro 84–13,839
DAI, v. 45A, Sept. 1984: 883–884.

2136
Zohny, Ahmed Younis. The contribution of national service to social and economic development: a case study of Egypt's experience. PPiU, 1984. 430 p.
Micro 85–284
DAI, v. 45A, May 1985: 3414.

2137
Zreg, Mohamed Mohamed B. Identification of specific Arabic language interference problems and their effect on the learning of English structure. KU, 1983. 344 p.   Micro 83–17,956
DAI, v. 44A, Oct. 1983: 1076.

2138
al-Zubi, Ahmed Muhammad. Death in the contemporary Arabic novel. MiU, 1982. 195 p.   Micro 83–4435
DAI, v. 43A, Apr. 1983: 3330.

2139
Zughaibi, Abdulwahab Mohamed. Construction productivity in Saudi Arabia: the influence of multi-national labor force. TxU, 1987. 248 p.
Micro 87–17,577
DAI, v. 48B, Nov. 1987: 1458.

2140

Zurub, Abdel Rahman Amin. An assessment of need among secondary level Jordanian science teachers. ICarbS, 1982. 182 p.   Micro 83–11,039
DAI, v. 44A, July 1983: 130–131.

2141

Zussman, Mira F. The fellahin of Tebourba: rural development and farmer strategies in Northern Tunisia. CU, 1982. 288 p.   Micro 83–13,041
DAI, v. 44A, July 1983: 215.

2142

Zysow, Aron. The economy of certainty: an introduction to the typology of Islamic legal theory. MH, 1984. 552 p.   Micro 84–19,463
DAI, v. 45A, Dec. 1984: 1840.

INDEX

Note: *Italicized* numbers refer to dates, not entries.

236

Arms transfer
  Soviet, 400
  United States, 1211
  1945–1980, 1970
Art
  and politics, Fatimids, 409
  Islamic, in Ghana, 1859
Art education
  Libya, 244
  Saudi Arabia, 158
Asbāb al-nuzūl, 1635
al-Ash'arī, 'Alī ibn Ismā'īl, 1096
Ashraf Sayf al-Dīn Qā'it Bay, *1468–1496*, 1495
'Āshūr, Nu'mān, 1228
Assyrians in United States, 1871
  1910–1985, 994
Astrology, 13th c., 1307
Aswan High Dam, 1874, 2052
Atabegs, *1127–1262*, 1563
Audiovisual aids; *see* Instructional media
Auditing, Egypt, 323, 938
Authorial disavowal in literature, 1359
Authoritarianism, Kuwait, 2080
Autism Behavior Checklist for Jordan, 1868
Averroës, 392, 422, 874
Avicenna, 1196, 1812
Awlād 'Alī, Egypt, 77, 570
Ayyubids, *1168–1250*, 1239
'Azzām, 'Abd al-Raḥmān and nationalism, 501
'Azzām, Samīrah, 1572

Bahaism, 364, 1095
Balance of payments
  and OPEC countries, 834
  Sudan, 599
  United States, and OPEC, 201
Balḥārith ibn Ka'b, 825
Banks
  Central Bank of Kuwait, 616
  commercial
    Kuwait, 582, 1666
    Saudi Arabia, 1486
  Faisal Islamic Bank of Egypt, 164
  international, and Egypt, 909
  Islamic, 164, 416, 813
  Libya, 398
  Saudi Arabia, 1039
  United Arab Emirates, 1706
Banū Hilāl, 1214, 1867
Barbary States and United States, 296, 466
Barlow, Joel, United States consul, Algiers, 466

Basic needs in Sudan, 129
Ba'th Party, Iraq and Syria, *1968–1979*, 1436
al-Bayyātī, 'Abd al-Wahhāb, 1638
Beckett, Samuel, 685
Bedouins
  1790–1977, 627
  Egypt, 77, 936
  Israel, 429, 1002
  Jordan, 927, 991
  Saudi Arabia, 267, 591, 820
  see also Nomadic settlements
Berber language
  Kabyl, 1362
  phonology, 319
Bilharziasis, Sudan, 43
Bilinguals, 1905, 1960
Biographical dictionaries; *see Tarājim*
Biology curriculum, Saudi Arabia, 1611, 2118
Biology teachers, Kuwait, 893
Biomedical technology and Islam, 587
Birth control and Islam, 587
  see also Contraceptives; Family planning
al-Bīrūnī, 452
Black Muslims, 1505
Bone remodeling, Nubia, 1295
Book in Refutation of the Grammarians, 2063
Boundaries
  Arabian Peninsula, *1934–1955*, 1795
  Middle East, 376
  Saudi Arabia, 64
  Syria, 376
Bourguiba, Habib, 1718
Bowles, Paul, and North Africa, 512
Boycott of Canadian business, 1890
Brazil
  immigration to, 52
  Muslim rebellion in, *1835*, 1627
Bread
  Arabic, 1612
  Egyptian, 803
Breastfeeding
  Egypt, 1072
  Tunisia, 1872
  Yemen, 798
Broadcasting, 647
  Egypt, 1753
  Saudi Arabia, 307, 810
Budget
  Egypt, 603
  Jordan, 1206
  Libya, 320
  Saudi Arabia, 162, 266, 1351, 1489
al-Buraimi dispute, 1798

239

240

Foreign assets, Saudi Arabia, *1963–1983*,
1142
Foreign borrowing
Algeria, 771
Jordan, 200
Foreign capital in Egypt, 60
Foreign exchange market, Lebanon, 410
Foreign investment
Egypt, 233, 432, 722, 1765
Kuwait, 754
Middle East, 407
Saudi Arabia, 754
United Arab Emirates, 754
Foreign labor
Bahrain, 710
Libya, 405
Middle East, 946
Saudi Arabia, 258, 281, 363, 748, 1969,
2139
United Arab Emirates, 1257
Foreign policy
Egypt
1945–1981, 669
1970–1972, 304
1970–1977, 1743
Iraq, *1968–1982*, 27
Jordan, 643, 1130
Kuwait, *1974–1978*, 1083
Saudi Arabia, *1970–1980*, 1187
Union of Soviet Socialist Republics,
and Arab press, 769
United States
1933–1945, 1279
1973–1974, 1075
and Arab press, 769
Foreign relations
Saudi Arabia, *1965–1984*, 1323
Sudan, *1969–1982*, 377
Foreign sector, Sudan, 2127
Foreign service, Saudi Arabia, 590
Foreign trade
Gulf, 2120
Jordan, 1931
Libya, *1750–1830*, 583
Morocco, 19th c., 781
Saudi Arabia, 829
Forests, national, Morocco, 972
France
and Algeria, *1830–1848*, 58
and Egypt
1798–1801, 782
1882, 497
and Morocco
1911–1912, 497
1912–1932, 1274

1925–1926, 1865
and Tunisia, *1881*, 497
Freight transportation, Saudi Arabia,
1371
Fromentin, Eugène, 1194
Front de libération nationale; *see* Algeria

Gaam society, Sudan, 1204
Gas industry, Saudi Arabia, 2126
Gas liquefaction, Algeria, 478
Gaza Strip
1967–, 255
GCC; *see* Gulf Cooperation Council
Genealogy, Yemen, 504
Geochemistry
Hierakonpolis, Egypt, 870
Red Sea, 673, 2133
Geographic education
Libya, 334
Saudi Arabia, 1000, 1133, 2075
Geography, 1725
physical
Egypt, 1531
Red Sea, 1531
Saudi Arabia, 84, 151
Geology
Abu Dhabi, 219
Arabian Sea, 1336
Egypt, 510, 1642, 1877
Eastern Desert, 1898, 1911
Red Sea Hills, 100
Sinai, 1490
Jordan, 1526
Kuwait, 435
Lebanon, 1113
Libya, 1069, 1171, 1285
Sirte Basin, 804
Mediterranean, 644, 1076, 1427
Oman, 797, 1980
Red Sea, 1877
Sudan, 101
Suez, Gulf of, 734, 1566
Geophysics
Kuwait, 435
Somali Basin, 488
Gerbilline rodents, Morocco, 1506
Germany and OPEC, 1220
Gezira Scheme, Sudan, 11, 626, 800, 1375,
2095
Ghalib, 1120
al-Ghazzālī, 540, 1541
and epistemology, 401
and Islamic law, 392
juristic doctrine of, 864
al-Ghīṭānī, Jamāl, 1322

Kinship
  in Arab culture, 687
  resources in, Libya, 730
  Yemen, 1895
Kitāb al-amānāt wa-al-iʿtiqādāt, 1151
Kitāb al-dalālah al-lāmiʿah, 837
Kitāb al-lumaʿ, 1096
Kitāb sullam al-najāh, 175
Koran
  Christians in, 1231
  exegesis, 1635
  God in, 1863
  structural coherence in, 1352
  thematic coherence in, 1352
  variants in, 2060
Korea and Saudi Arabia, 1973–1983, 1398
Kūmidyā Ūdīb, 1228
Kurdish language, 123, 716
Kurds, 1144
Kuwait
  Failaka Island, 1509
  National Assembly, 1106
Kuwait Finance House, 1298
Kuwait Institute for Scientific Research,
  223

Labor
  Egypt, 1936–1954, 387
  Morocco, 1980, 1694
  Sudan, 1437, 2095
  see also Foreign labor
Labor force
  female
    Egypt, 476
    Morocco, 476
  Iraq, 1960–1984, 929
  Kuwait, 1948
  participation of, Sudan, 2064
  see also Manpower; Workers
Labor-management disputes, Jordan,
  1263
Labor market
  Egypt, 2097
  Kuwait, 1589
Labor migration, 189
  international, Middle East, 1970s, 946
  Jordan, 1283
  Sudan, 23
Labor movement, Egypt, 1930–1954, 786
Labor policy, Egypt, 604
Labor resources, Jordan Valley, 1897
Labor supply, Jordan, 1935
Land reclamation, Egypt, 1991
Land settlement, Libya, 1681
Land use

Jordan, 354
Saudi Arabia, 1846
Landholding, Egypt, 1740–1850, 506
Language
  and al-Farabi, 46
  attitudes of Saudis toward, 1853
Language laboratories, Saudi Arabia, 141
Law, 1368
  Druse, 1057
  international, 1732
  of the sea, 260
    and Algeria, 558
  Sudan, 612
  see also Islamic law; Legal change, etc.
Lawrence [of Arabia], T. E., 188
Layard, Austen H., 1916
Leadership
  Egypt, 638
  Islamic
    Iran, 1576
    Senegal, 1762
    Saudi Arabia, 1165
League of Arab States, 1726
  and regional security, 108
  and United Nations, 1515
Lebanese in United States, 1163
Lebanon
  19th–20th c., 52
  and Palestinians, 1967–1976, 1127
  and Syria, 1975–1976, 2055
  civil war, 620, 873, 1614, 2055
  see also Arab-Israeli conflict; Identity
    conflicts
Legal change, Sudan, 1238
Legal system, 1550–1258, 1107
Legal theory, Islamic, 2142
Liber de causis, 1957
Librarians, Jordan, 871
Libraries
  academic, Saudi Arabia, 135
  Arabian Peninsula, 29
  Egypt, 1546
  Jordan, 2093
  mosque, 1855
  national, Saudi Arabia, 1466
  public, Saudi Arabia, 5
  Saudi Arabia, 291, 554
  school
    Saudi Arabia, 1289
    Sudan, 17
  university, Saudi Arabia, 992
Library science, Morocco, 1358
Libya
  1835–1911, 974
  1911–1912, 482

Quṣṭā ibn Lūqā, 2054
Quṭb, Sayyid, 1417, 1443
Quṭb al-Dīn Shīrāzī, 2030

Radio
  Egypt, 611
  Jordan, 928
Radio Cairo
  and Nasser, 1788
  and Sadat, 1788
Range management, Sudan, 2029
Reading, 1360, 1582
Reading miscues of bilingual students,
  1344
Reason in Islam, 1246
Refugees
  1939–1956, 303
  African, in Sudan, 2035
  in Jordan, 904, 1699, 1851
Regional security
  and League of Arab States, 108
  in Gulf, 1092
  see also National security
Rehabilitation services, Kuwait, 732
Religion
  and mental health, 1003
  in Sudan, *1899–1983*, 1188
  see also Politics, and religion
Religious orders, 430
Remote sensing
  Egypt, 1001
  techniques, 1874
Rent control, Egypt, 1273
Reserve funds, Saudi Arabia, 1884
Resource allocations, Sudan, *1971–1980*,
  1376
Responsa, 1841
Response to the Grammarians, 20
Revelation in Islam, 1246
Rewards system, Kuwait, 1689
Ribā, 793
Rice, demand for, 212
Rijāl fī al-shams, 1208
Roads
  Saudi Arabia, 44
  Sudan, 631
Robinson Crusoe, 328
Rodents, Morocco, 1506
Ruckert, Friedrich, 1912
Rural areas
  Egypt, 257, 1548, 1909
    1740–1850, 506
  Iraq, 420
  Libya, 183
  Morocco, 19th c., 781

Saudi Arabia, 1132
Somalia, *1884–1984*, 1730
Syria, 1109
Tunisia, 2034

Saadia Gaon, 1151
Sadat, Anwar, 297, 531, 789, 1451
  and Radio Cairo, 1788
Safawis, 384
Safety, industrial, Saudi Arabia, 1020
Saʿīd, ʿAlī Aḥmad (Adūnīs), 1136, 1799
al-Saʿīd, Nūrī and Iraq, *1941–1958*, 1665
Saints, Muslim, 28, 1623
al-Sakkākī, 1875
Salafī movement, Syria, *1885–1914*, 495
Salespersons, Iraq, 593
Ṣalīḥ, Ṭayyib, 875
Sālim, ʿAlī, 1228
Sanctity (*wilāyah*), 1036
Sand invasion, Saudi Arabia, 55, 1105
Satellite communications, Saudi Arabia,
  978
Saudi Arabia
  al-Kharj District, 374
  American influence in, 378
  and Egypt, *1962–1970*, 317
  and Gulf, 1455
  and Korea, *1973–1983*, 1398
  and Middle East peace, 1769
  and Turkey, 554
  and United States, 154
    1933–1945, 470
    1933–1953, 785
    1973–1979, 516
    1978, 2078
  and Yemen, *1962–1970*, 317
  Council of Ministers, 971
  Dhahran Academy, 2043
  non-oil sectors, 853
  private sector, 703
  royal family
    politics, *1953–1982*, 1736
    succession to the throne, 426
Saudis, American-educated, 378
Savings behavior, 1054
Schistosomiasis
  Egypt, 1631
  Libya, 1920
  Sudan, 43
Schizophrenic patients, Egypt, 1377
Scholarships and Saudi graduate students,
  726
School buildings, Saudi Arabia, 1880
School climate, Saudi Arabia, 676
School discipline and Bahraini youths, 228

258

and Arab-Israeli conflict
  1945–1980, 1970
  1956, 1159, 1574, 2099
  1967–1979, 1560
  1969–1975, 1276
  1973, 231
  1977–1981, 1310
and Barbary States, 296, 466
and Egypt
  1948–1956, 1429
  1967–1978, 324
  1970–1981, 1430
  1978, 2078
and Gulf, 1162
  1968–1976, 404
  1980–1985, 712
and Gulf states, *1968–1978*, 285
and Israel, *1967–1984*, 1460
and Jerusalem, *1947–1967*, 688
and Libya, *1969–1982*, 633
and Mediterranean, 296, 1402, 1815
and Middle East, 359, 2027
  1919–1953, 1221
  1943, 571
and Morocco, *1880–1906*, 1199
and North Africa, *1940–1942*, 1222
and Palestine, *1942–1947*, 2088
and Palestine Liberation Organization,
  1869
and Saudi Arabia, 154
  1933–1945, 470
  1933–1953, 785
  1973–1979, 516
  1978, 2078
and Somalia, *1953–1986*, 1211
and Syria, *1941–1949*, 1193
Arabs in, 134, 186, 778, 966, 1088,
  1093, 1163, 1558, 1850, 1871, 1892,
  1964
in Egyptian history textbooks, 535
Libyans educated in, 1803
Middle East history programs in, 832
Middle Easterners in, 1216, 1478, 1954
Saudis educated in, 378
Voice of America, Arabic Service, 302
Yemeni Jews in, 1353
Universities
faculty of
  Egypt, 1816
  Kuwait, 850
  Saudi Arabia, 190, 692, 885, 1006,
  1973
goals of, Saudi Arabia, 1901, 2113
Gulf, 956
Iraq, 261, 1158

Jordan, 1252
Kuwait, 499, 850
promotion at, 677
Saudi, 202, 662, 1009, 1070, 1134
  administration of, 314, 1301
  impact of American universities on,
  1777
secular, Saudi Arabia, 378
staff of, 2089
United Arab Emirates, 6
West Bank, 1581
Yemen, 1407
Urayq al-Buldan, Saudi Arabia, 1105
Urbanization
  Egypt, 147, 1701, 1896, 1959
  Libya, 1357
  Morocco, *1912–1956*, 940
  Saudi Arabia, 248, 720, 975
  Sudan, 1437
al-ʿUrḍī, Abū al-Wafā ibn ʿUmar, 765
U.S. News and World Report and Arabs,
  1980–1983, 894
USAID; *see* United States, Agency for
  International Development
ʿUshr, 485
Usury, 793, 1123

Values and Saudi students, 741
Vatican and Arab-Israeli conflict, *1962–*
  1982, 990
Vegetable markets, Tunisia, 1538
Vegetation
  Libya, 1810
  Morocco, 972
Vernet, Horace, 347
Videotex, Saudi Arabia, 521
VOA; *see* United States, Voice of America
Vocational education
  Egypt, 316, 321
  Jordan, 1131
  Kuwait, 1942
  Saudi Arabia, 1160, 1272, 2119
  see also Technical education
Voice of America; *see* United States, Voice
  of America
Voilquin, Suzanne, and Egypt, 178
Volney, C. F.
  and Egypt, 1210
  and Syria, 1210
von Hofmannstahl, Hugo, 1912
Le Voyage en Égypte et en Syrie, 1210

Wadi Darnah/al-Fatayah Scheme, Libya,
  399
Wahbah, Saʿd al-Dīn, 1228